CAPITAL AND POLITICS

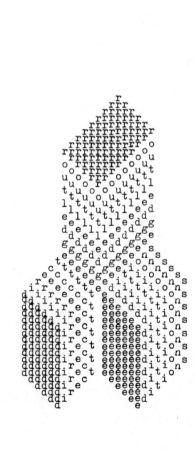

CAPITAL AND POLITICS

Edited by
ROGER KING
Department of Behavioural Sciences,
Huddersfield Polytechnic

ROUTLEDGE DIRECT EDITIONS

ROUTLEDGE & KEGAN PAUL
London, Boston, Melbourne and Henley

First published in 1983
by Routledge & Kegan Paul plc
39 Store Street, London WC1E 7DD,
9 Park Street, Boston, Mass. 02108, USA,
296 Beaconsfield Parade, Middle Park,
Melbourne, 3206, Australia, and
Broadway House, Newtown Road,
Henley-on-Thames, Oxon RG9 1EN
Printed in Great Britain by
Hartnoll Print, Bodmin, Cornwall.

Library of Congress Cataloging in Publication Data

Main entry under title:
Capital and politics.
   (Routledge direct editions)
   Bibliography p.
   Includes index.
   1. Social classes - Great Britain - Addresses, essays,
lectures. 2. Capitalism - Addresses, essays, lectures.
3. Trade and professional associations - Great Britain -
Addresses, essays, lectures. I. King, Roger.
HN400.S6C36 1983   305.5'0941   83-4424
ISBN 0-7100-9445-0

CONTENTS

v

CONTRIBUTORS

ALAN CAWSON Lecturer in Politics, School of Social Sciences, University of Sussex.

PETER SAUNDERS Lecturer in Sociology, School of Cultural and Community Studies, University of Sussex.

JOHN URRY Senior Lecturer in Sociology, Department of Sociology, University of Lancaster.

MICHAEL MORAN Lecturer in Government, Victoria University, Manchester.

WYN GRANT Senior Lecturer in the Department of Politics, University of Warwick.

ROB FLYNN Lecturer in Sociology, Department of Sociological and Anthropological Sciences, University of Salford.

ROGER KING Principal Lecturer in Sociology, Huddersfield Polytechnic.

NEIL KILLINGBACK Research Fellow, University of Sussex.

BRIAN ELLIOTT Senior Lecturer, Department of Sociology, University of Edinburgh.

FRANK BECHHOFER Reader, Department of Sociology, University of Edinburgh.

DAVID McCRONE Lecturer in Sociology, Department of Sociology, University of Edinburgh.

STEWART BLACK Research Associate, Department of Social Administration, University of Edinburgh.

INTRODUCTION
Roger King

This book contains, in revised form, eight of the papers presented
at the annual political sociology conference held at the University
of Sheffield in January 1981 and 1982. These conferences were
organised by the Political Sociology Study Group which receives
support from both the British Sociological Association and the
Political Studies Association of the UK. Six of the papers were
presented at the 1981 conference on 'Capital, Ideology and Politics'
and two have been taken from the 1982 conference on 'Urban and
Regional Studies'. A theme running through both conferences was the
mode by which capital and its constituent elements or sectors
organises its interests and mediates with government, although in
the second conference there was a much more explicit concern with
both the spatial reorganisation of capital in 'de-industrialising'
societies and local political processes.

Several people at the conferences expressed surprise that political
sociologists should be concerned with such matters as the political
organisation of capital or urban social movements. They evinced
puzzlement about political sociology's domain and surfaced hazy
notions that it was to do with electoral behaviour, political
socialisation or the search for the stabilising conditions of liberal
democracy. This vagueness is understandable. These days political
sociology lacks the orthodoxy that characterised the 1950s and 1960s
when it had a central purpose in a sociology of democracy and which
rested on the assumed acceptability of existing liberal democracies
and a search for their stabilisation. An overarching concern was to
explain how a viable system of political decision-making is achieved
in the face of the fissures and divisions of interest produced by
industrialisation and particularly how the cleavages and supports of
wider stratification systems get translated into political forms.

Two related themes emerge in this period. First, an examination
of the creation of national political communities through an extension
of citizenship rights to the lower classes in exchange for their
acceptance of the liberal democratic state. This, as Urry notes in
Chapter 2, dramatically weakens the effectivity of class struggle
and marks a decline in the dominance of the sphere of circulation in
civil society. However, rather than necessarily resulting in the
stabilisation of democracies, Urry sees the extension of the state

1

into the sphere of the reproduction of labour power and its provision
of education, welfare and other benefits, as reflecting the growing
demands on the state from a wider variety of social groupings within
civil society (e.g., women, professional groups, class fractions).
The more general formal equality is achieved, the greater the bases
on which groupings will seek to establish a degree of substantive
equality, especially when they undergo similar experiences in relation
to the labour market and their organisation by capital. However,
political sociology in the 1950s and 1960s lacked a political economy,
and the incorporation of the masses was viewed only as positive, as
providing order for political regimes, while the constraints on
political action that were also entailed were largely ignored. The
result was that the implications of this work for theories of state
power were never really pursued, and during this period political
sociology generally turned away from a concern with the state. In so
doing it ignored increasing state intervention in modern society,
particularly the economy, and was unprepared for those social
movements in the late 1960s and 1970s that challenged state regulation
and existing political arrangements (and which, as Elliott et al.
note in Chapter 8, came from the right as well as the left).

Second, it was assumed that the stability of liberal democracies
depends on the ability of individuals who feel strongly about a
matter to get together and press their claims on government. In
particular, interest groups were regarded as crucially mediating
between society and responsive political elites. Theories of
pluralism were central to this approach and sought to demonstrate
why no single interest, not even capitalist interests, always
dominates. Rather, as Berger (1981a, p.5) remarks in characterising
this view, 'crosscutting cleavages in society, the overlapping
memberships of groups, social mobility - all work to maintain a
fluidity in the relations among various organised interests and to
undermine the bases on which a situation of permanent domination
could be constructed'. However, this model of the origins and
practice of interest groups has appeared increasingly inadequate in
the changed circumstances of the 1970s and 1980s. As the two
chapters on business association by Grant (Chapter 4) and King
(Chapter 6) particularly illustrate, interests are not simply
'provided' by the socio-economic system but are often created and
shaped by governmental and organisational processes. Governments
see in the incorporation of major economic associations, for example,
ways of ameliorating potential conflict and the development of
corporatist patterns of representation may thus be explained as a
means for insulating key policy decisions from the popular demands
and rising expectations that characterise electoral politics.
Corporatism may thus be a response to the instabilities of pluralism
and a way of ensuring the pre-eminence of capitalist interests.

Thus, the dominant orthodoxy of the sociology of democracy that
characterised political sociology until the late 1960s has gradually
disintegrated. The limitations of the approach have been exposed
by the eruption in the West of more conflictful political events
than assumed by the model and by the theoretical assaults on it by
radical, often Marxist, critiques that have become more influential
in the social sciences.

The chapters in this book offer some of the theoretical advances

and empirical applications to be found in the 'new political
sociology' while also recognising continuities with the older
orthodoxy. A striking feature of contemporary political sociology
is the extent to which Marxists and non-Marxists frequently share
an interest in similar problems, such as a concern with theorising
the state, particularly its relationships with socio-economic forces.
Occasionally they come to similar conclusions, in part the result of
an increasing recognition that Marxist political sociology has
encountered many of the problems experienced earlier in mainstream
social science. This is exemplified by the functionalism, circularity
and economism of some recent Marxist theories of the state, problems
taken up in the chapters by Cawson and Saunders, and Urry.

Both suggest that a basic problem in some contemporary Marxist
schemes concerns the articulation of 'action' and 'struggle' with
notions of structural determination. In other words, why, and how,
does class struggle result in the state functioning in the long-term
interests of capital, as is claimed? Cawson and Saunders note that
this raises familiar problems of teleology and tautology in functional
analysis which are not solved by simply describing the state as
'relatively autonomous'. This explains everything and nothing:
state intervention on behalf of non-capitalist interests can be
explained in terms of the state's autonomy, while state policies
favouring capital are explained by the relative delimitation of this
autonomy. Consequently there is no way of empirically testing the
theory. Cawson and Saunders claim that the two theoretical approaches
of instrumentalism and pluralism, often regarded as exclusive or
incommensurable, are complementary, and that each can provide the
counterfactual conditions of the other. A unitary theory of the
state is therefore rejected in favour of an ideal-typical model in
which different functions serving different interests tend to be
discharged in different ways through different levels of the state
apparatus. While capitalist interests operate successfully at
national level, in which policy-making is centred upon production
activity, and where corporatist forms of interest representation are
more generally developed, local policy-making is subject to different
determinations. Here occur non-class, consumption/reproduction
struggles (over education, housing, health-care provision, etc.), and
policy-making is characterised by an imperfect pluralism, in which
other than capitalist interests are likely to prevail.

A number of problems may still remain with Cawson and Saunders's
formulations – the ideal-typical approach leaves unclear the amount
of expected divergence between the ideal-typical representation and
reality, whilst substantively they may underestimate the development
of local corporatist tendencies (see the chapters by Flynn and King) –
but they valuably point to the importance of avoiding simple
replications of national state processes at the local level. Urry,
too, notes a decline in the importance of class struggle in 'de-
industrialising' countries and the emergence of relatively novel
political forms and varying social structures in localities. However,
in contrast to Cawson and Saunders, he suggests that while the
decomposition of classes heightens the importance of non-class
social movements seeking to protect local social structures against
capital and the state, these are focused on production and aim at
the recapitalisation of local economies.

The renewed interest in the state within political sociology,
which revives themes largely overlooked in the 1950s and 1960s, none
the less displays continuities with the sociology of democracy of
the post-war years in the concern to understand the modes in which
the conflicts and supports of the wider social and economic systems
are both translated into and are created by political forms. This
coincides with the persisting recognition of the importance of
analysing relationships between organised groups and the polity for
understanding the operation and transformations of advanced societies.
However, recognition that pluralism is an unstable system of interest
representation and is associated with major problems of inflation
and regime 'ungovernability', has led to developing awareness of the
part played by more direct forms of interest representation to
government as a means of securing social order, legitimacy and
capital accumulation. Theories of corporatist intermediation, for
example, point to the significance of less visible patterns of
representation, often at officials level, in which the leaders of
non-competitive, hierarchically ordered and functionally differentiated
groups are granted representational monopoly and participation in
policy-making by the state in return for securing support (or absence
of opposition) from members for state policies. This is regarded as
a particularly appropriate description of relationships between major
economic organisations and the state in many advanced industrial
societies, including Britain, in recent years. Grant's chapter on
the first fifteen years of the CBI (Chapter 4) certainly indicates
the close relationships established by its leaders with government,
particularly officials, although Grant notes the continuing presence
and recent pre-eminence of an alternative, 'anti-corporatist' school
of opinion in the CBI, relying more on market forces and penal law
than state-supported partnership with the trade unions to instil
labour discipline. However, participation in the formulation and
often the implementation of public policy has become an 'authoritative'
or 'governmental' characteristic of large producer interest groups
such as the CBI in the 1970s.
    Yet Grant, and other authors in the book, raise doubts about the
development of corporatist intermediation as somehow 'inevitable',
the characteristic representational face of advanced capitalism,
rather than as cyclical and unstable. Corporatist forms of interest
intermediation still lack democratic 'legitimacy' and often encounter
public and membership resistance. Thus groups like the CBI cannot
ignore parliamentary politics, and the inception of annual conferences
and support for proportional representation in recent years testifies
to a sharpened awareness of the relationship between governmental
partisanship and interests. This, too, has been reinforced by recent
strains in the representational links between organised business and
the Conservative party. Both Grant and King illustrate the difficulties posed for business associations by Conservative administrations at national and local level. Not only do they apparently feel
more disposed than Labour administrations to dispense with business
advice, claiming, as the 'businessman's party', to know business
sentiment just as well, if not better, than business groups, but they
are also more likely to favour market and legal methods for securing
discipline and capital accumulation, which may pose considerable
risks to at least some sections of business. Grant and King also

note membership resistance to 'governmental' tendencies in business
organisations and the absence in them of the compelling requirement
for collective control found in trade unions.

The chapters by Moran and Grant indicate that organised interests
are not simply 'given' by social and economic differentiation, and
then find expression in political practice, but are also created by
the state through the attribution of status or resources, or through
the content and sequence of its policies which may trigger organised
responses. Grant points to the state's role in facilitating and
resourcing the CBI in its early years, while Moran suggests that
increasing state control and intervention in the economy is one
explanation for the recent spread of the 'pressure group habit' in
the world of finance capital. Moran makes two further points that
are often overlooked in corporatist literature. First, increased
contact and access to government decision-makers can indicate
declining power: the City's developing immersion into the bureaucratic, committee-dominated world of Whitehall politics in the 1960s
and 1970s marks a recognition of the City's tightening exclusion
from key areas of policy-making as a consequence of its preferred
reliance on social and personal networks. Second, it is still
important when describing increases in bureaucratised, organised
forms of interest representation not to ignore the persistence of
more informal means of co-ordination for capital. Moran notes that
public and private policy-makers inhabit the same social world and
that public incorporation can become a natural extension of private
intercourse. Among the reasons why the City arrived late in the
organised world of interest group politics was the long-standing
effectiveness of its reliance on family links. King, too, in
discussing the Leeds Chamber of Commerce and Industry, indicates
the continuing importance of social and civic networks in linking
business leaders and local public decision-makers, despite an
increase in more formal, organisational relationships. Elliott
et al., in discussing the Freedom Association, also note that the
ways in which it advances its views reflects the similarities of
educational and social experience of its leaders, and that it
possesses a network of social contacts that can be utilised to
spread the message to those well placed in the structures of wealth
and power. Furthermore, even formal meetings can gain considerable
efficacy from the informal contacts they generate.

These multiplex, private-public relationships may also provide
part of an explanation for the 'taken-for-granted' consensus on
economic and planning objectives between industrialists and the local
authority revealed by Flynn in Chapter 5. Flynn, like several of
the authors, also recognises the part played by economic decline in
encouraging closer ties between government and the private sector.
A growing interest by planners in directly involving industrialists
in discussions of policy options, which accompanies a more 'bullish'
conception of their own role in encouraging economic growth, and an
emphasis on expanding commercial development rather than limiting
it, springs in large measure from a concern to protect even
previously prosperous areas from recession and unemployment.

A further theme that emerges throughout the following chapters is
the questioning of assumptions about 'common capitalist interests'
and a willingness to consider the differing strata or fractions

within capital. This is not to suggest that it is clear where the
line should be drawn between sectors or sizes of business. Moran,
for example, found great difficulty in seeing where industrial capital
ended and finance capital began, not least because of the close
personal and corporate ties between them. However, the small business
sector in particular periodically finds itself at odds with large
capital and the state, and this disaffection quickened appreciably
in the 1970s according to Elliott et al. Their charting of the
National Federation of the Self-Employed valuably indicates how the
economic and political processes described elsewhere in the book,
such as the increased centralisation and concentration of capitalist
and state power, and the development of corporatist forms of interest
intermediation, invokes a response from those entrepreneurs feeling
excluded or squeezed in the middle between organised labour and large
capital. Moreover, their protest chimes with a more general or
popular disenchantment with bureaucratic regulation in contemporary
societies.

   Again we see in Elliott et al.'s chapter how the trajectory or
'career' of business and other groups is in part crucially determined
by political structures, or, in their description, how 'the pathways
of protest' are shaped by the structures of power and are not simply
generated by the system of social stratification or the individual
characteristics of a group or stratum. Small business leaders, for
example, are encouraged by officials and political parties laying
electoral claim to a small business constituency to model themselves
on conventional lobbies, which means routinising their behaviour,
accepting compromise, and abstaining from flamboyant public gestures.
Thus groups such as the National Federation for the Self-Employed,
originally seeking to advance their interests by public demonstrations
or eye-catching, disruptive 'events', become more conventional
business associations, lobbying for the specific interests of
members, rather than espousing more general, oppositional philosophies.
A willingness by at least part of the small-business stratum to
accept, even embrace, collective and organised forms of political
representation and regulation is not new. Killingback (Chapter 7),
for example, casts a critical eye on the idea that small businessmen
are too individualistic and competitive to combine effectively. His
study of taxi-drivers in London in the 1930s shows them as positively
viewing protectionism and rejecting economic liberalism. They were
only too aware that government regulation protected small enterprises
and that trade association was a necessity for both the provision of
services and effective consultation with the state.

   The concluding chapter by Elliott et al. well illustrates several
important points made in preceding chapters. One is the suspicion
and often fractiousness that characterises relations between capital
and the Conservative party. An explanation for both the development
of corporatist structures and new party and non-party organisations
seeking to represent capital, or parts of capital, may lie in the
ambivalence with which sections of the business world views the
Conservatives. Second, although many of the chapters point to
increasingly organised forms of capitalist representation, informal
and family ties remain significant for connecting businessmen and
public policy-makers. Finally, there is acknowledgment of the
importance of local social processes in understanding developments

in contemporary British politics, but which have slipped from the
sociological agenda since the work of Lockwood and others in the
1960s.   The localist orientations of businessmen in organisations
like Chambers of Commerce or the National Federation of the Self-
Employed, for example, may reflect not only the increased significance
of reorganised local political institutions but also important changes
in local class and non-class structures, involving both consumption-
and production-based movements, and efforts to defend or expand local
economies in competitive struggle with other, recession-hit localities
for capital investment.

Chapter 1

CORPORATISM, COMPETITIVE POLITICS AND CLASS STRUGGLE
Alan Cawson and Peter Saunders

> It is time that we gave up the struggle to fit the state into
> the Procrustean bed of a single theory but recognized ... the
> need for a typology of kinds of power and forms of social
> control (Ray Pahl, 1977b, p.12).

FIVE RELATED QUESTIONS

Compared with only ten years ago, the level of theoretical argument
and debate on questions of political domination and ideological
hegemony is today quite sophisticated. No longer can it be simply
asserted that the capitalist class controls and manipulates the
state apparatus in its own interests, nor that it manipulates a
'false consciousness' among the working class by virtue of its
cunning and conscious direction of the schools and the media. Things,
it seems, are more complicated than that; capitalist societies are
not generally run by huddled cliques of conspiring business leaders;
capitalist interests sometimes lose as a result of state policies
while working-class interests sometimes win; dominant ideologies
may contain and express elements of working-class life experience
and working-class values; and so on.

Much of the credit for recent theoretical advances lies with two
traditions of Marxist thought - the French 'structuralism' of
Poulantzas and his disciples such as Castells, and the German
'critical theory' of Habermas and Offe. However, although the
problems have been posed within Marxist theory, it is clear that
they have not been resolved there. As Poulantzas himself recognises,
the problem of establishing the relation between the economic, the
political and the ideological still remains.

In this chapter, we seek to re-examine this problem in the context
of our recent concerns with questions of corporatism, social policy
and the local state (see Cawson, 1978, 1982; Saunders, 1979, 1980).
More precisely, we shall consider the problem in terms of five
related questions:

8

(i) How does the state operate 'relatively autonomously'?

As a description of what the state does, the Poulantzian 'relative
autonomy' concept seems to us entirely appropriate. Thus, while the
capitalist state does and must function in the long-term interests
of large capital (since any state must secure the conditions of
existence of continued productive activity which, in the context of
a capitalist society, means the maintenance of levels of profitability
which are adequate to attract new investment), it is also clearly the
case that it may and often does respond to the political demands and
grievances of other interests in society, and that this may involve
short-term erosion rather than support of private-sector profitability.
    As an analysis of how this 'relative autonomy' comes about,
however, the Poulantzian schema is woefully inadequate. As Clarke
(1977) and others have shown, the basic problem concerns the relation
between structural determination and class struggle. Put simply, if
(in Poulantzas's well known formulation) the state is to be understood as the 'political condensation of class struggle', then how
does the cause (class struggle) necessarily result in the function
the state has to perform in the overall structure (i.e., regulation
of class struggle and maintenance of the long-term interests of the
capitalist class)? Not only does this point to the familiar problem
of teleology which arises in other functionalist theories, but it
also suggests a strong tautological element in Poulantzas's reasoning
in that the concept of relative autonomy turns out to be an infinitely
malleable explanatory device. Armed with this theory, it becomes
possible to 'explain' any given intervention by the state, for
policies which favour non-capitalist interests can be accounted for
by the state's autonomy from capital, while those which favour
capital are just as easily explained in terms of the fact that this
autonomy is only relative! The concept thus explains everything and
nothing. As a description it is undoubtedly valid, but as a causal
explanation it is fatuous and empty.

(ii) Is a unitary theory of 'the' state appropriate?

Later in the chapter we shall propose a solution to this question of
how the state comes to act relatively autonomously by suggesting that
different functions serving different interests tend to be discharged
in different ways and often through different levels of the state
apparatus. What this argument amounts to is that we should not
expect to be able to develop a single general theory of 'the' state
if different processes requiring different modes of theoretical
explanation are at work at different points in the state apparatus.
What is particularly significant from our point of view is the
relation between central and local state organs.
    Although we began by pointing to the increased sophistication of
recent (mainly Marxist) work on the state and ideology, it is
nevertheless the case that Marxist writing on the so-called 'local
state', is 'relatively undeveloped and based on fairly crude notions
of central-local government relations, emphasising broad structure
much more than detail and variety' (Boddy and Fudge, 1980, p.11).
Since Cockburn first coined the term, the assumption seems to have

been that the 'local state' can be analysed and explained simply by
applying general theories of the state to local political processes.
Although the specificity of the local state in terms of its function
(i.e., consumption provisions aiding the reproduction of labour-
power) has often been noted, there has been a conspicuous failure
in the Marxist literature to take account of its specificity in
terms of its mode of operation.

If our argument that different agencies of the state are subject
to different political determinations is accepted, then our argument
against a unitary theory of 'the' state follows logically. It is
in this way that we shall propose a tentative solution to the
problem of explaining the relative autonomy of the state 'as a
whole', for the overall picture of what the state does can only be
explained through an appreciation that capitalist interests may
operate successfully in relation to certain areas of policy generated
at particular levels of government, but that other interests may
prevail in other areas and at other levels.

(iii)   What is the relation of political struggles to class struggles?

In Poulantzas's work, the concept of 'relative autonomy' performs a
dual role. On the one hand, it applies to the relation between
structures and practices (i.e., in the argument that, although class
practices correspond to each level or 'instance' of the structure,
class struggles cannot simply be read off from structural contradictions). On the other, it refers to the relation between
different instances of the structure and different levels of class
practice (i.e., the argument that the state has a certain autonomy
vis-à-vis the economy, or that political struggles cannot simply be
reduced to economic class categories).

We shall not be concerned with the first sense of relative
autonomy, except merely to note that the recognition by Poulantzas
that the intensification of contradictions within the capitalist
system may provoke a range of different responses (and non-responses?)
on the part of non-capitalist interests effectively re-poses the
familiar problem of how a class-in-itself becomes a class-for-
itself - a problem which Poulantzas himself claims to have transcended
and which necessitates analysis of human agency and human consciousness which his work is intent on ignoring. Quite simply, if contradictions give rise to, but do not determine the pattern of, class
struggles, then we need to know what affects people's responses to
system crises.

More interesting from our present perspective, however, is the
application of the relative autonomy concept to the relation between
political struggles and economic class categories. As Hirst (1977)
has competently demonstrated, Poulantzas fudges the issue by
introducing the notion of 'representation' of classes in political
struggles (i.e., the argument that political groupings somehow
represent classes but cannot be reduced to the class categories of
capital and labour). Posed starkly, the question which this
formulation fails to address is whether and under what conditions
political issues can be analysed in class terms. In other words,
we need to be able to identify those situations in which the

functional interests of capital and labour are directly represented in political struggle, and to distinguish these from those cases where political mobilisation takes place on other than a class base.

The contemporary significance of this question is obvious (e.g., witness the debates over the relation between the women's movement and the labour movement). Its significance for our own concerns with the politics of public service provision is also apparent, for we have seriously to examine the question of whether campaigns and struggles waged around issues of collective consumption and the social wage bear any 'necessary correspondence' to the fundamental class categories of Marxist political economy.

(iv)   What is the relation of consumption struggles to class struggles?

We argue that the realm of class politics, where representatives of capital and labour mobilise politically, relates to the production activities of the state (i.e., those policies and interventions bearing on the capital-labour relation - incomes policies, investment grants, trade-union legislation, provision of physical infrastructure, etc.) which are generally organised at national and regional levels of government, displaying what Middlemas (1979) has termed a 'corporate bias'.

Those struggles which arise around other aspects of the state's role (e.g., its consumption function as expressed in housing provisions, education, health care and so on) cannot be analysed in class terms even though they may draw upon an homogenous class base for their support (e.g., fights against council-house rent rises are likely to draw almost exclusively on a working-class constituency) and may have significant implications for the capital-labour relation (e.g., in terms of the cost of reproducing labour-power). In arguing thus, we follow Poulantzas to the extent that we agree that classes are constituted in and through struggle (they do not first 'exist' and then 'act'). The classes grounded in the capital-labour relation thus exist in struggles constituted around that relation, whether they be economic (e.g., wage bargaining), political (e.g., social contracts) or ideological (e.g., anti-nationalisation propaganda). It follows that other struggles which are constituted around other relations (e.g., relations of domination based on gender categories, distribution relations based on consumer categories, etc.) cannot be seen as class struggles but have their own specificity. The fact that it is mainly working-class people who mobilise over council-house rents does not therefore make rent issues class issues. This argument obviously has important implications for local anti-cuts movements, and we consider these later.

(v)   How do we explain the relative autonomy of ideology?

The Poulantzian concept of relative autonomy applies not only to the political level, but also to the level of ideology. In other words, just as the state is seen as relatively autonomous from any

one class, so too is the dominant ideology; in the same way as the
state is a condensation of political class struggles, so the dominant
ideology is a condensation of the ideologies and life experiences of
all the classes in the social formation. As Poulantzas points out,
it could hardly be otherwise since the working class is unlikely to
endorse a system of values and beliefs which fails to correspond at
all to their direct experience of the world.

Again, however, we find that Poulantzas's concept of relative
autonomy provides a fruitful description but falls short in its
explanatory power. Just as we suggest that the explanation for the
relative autonomy of the state must be located in an analysis of
the different ways in which different functions come to be discharged
through different levels of government, so too we suggest in this
chapter that it is possible to identify different ideological
traditions grounded in different sets of core values which have
today become insulated from each other through their association with
different aspects of state provision. Ideologies of need and social
rights thus exist side by side with ideologies of profit and rights
of private property, and the subordination of the former to the
latter is a function of the subordination of consumption (use values)
to production (exchange values), democratic politics to corporate
politics, local government to central government.

A NOTE ON METHODOLOGY

Before proceeding, it is necessary to preface our analysis with
three methodological points which may serve as a guide through what
is to follow.

(i)   Testability and the need for counterfactuals

We noted that Poulantzas's proposed explanation for the relative
autonomy of the capitalist state is tautologous in that it can be
used retrospectively to cover *any* state intervention. To say that
the state is relatively autonomous is simply to say that the
capitalist class may win or the working class may win - i.e., it
says nothing.

To achieve explanatory power it is necessary to specify those
situations in which different class interests may be expected to
prevail and thus to stipulate counterfactual conditions which enable
empirical investigation. As it stands, the concept of relative
autonomy is inherently immune from empirical evaluation of any sort
because it combines two opposing theoretical traditions - instrumentalism (according to which the state is simply a tool of capitalist
interests) and pluralism (according to which the state responds to
different interests on different issues according to the strength
and intensity of political mobilisation). On their own, each of
these traditions is *in principle* open to some form of empirical
evaluation - if capitalists lose out, we may come to doubt the
instrumentalist case, whereas if they come to prevail in many
different issues we may come to doubt the pluralist position. In
other words, these two theoretical traditions provide the counter-

factual conditions of each other (if not instrumentalism, then
pluralism, and vice versa - hence the long and bitter community
power debate in America during the 1950s and 1960s). When they are
effectively fused, as they are in Poulantzas's work, this mutual
counterfactuality is cancelled out and the possibility of empirical
evaluation disappears.

We believe that one of the strengths of the framework to be
developed below is that by breaking with a unitary theory of the
state it is possible to identify specific areas of policy, levels of
government and so on where we would expect to find capitalist
interests prevailing, and other areas/levels where other interests
may achieve success. In this way it is possible to re-establish
the conditions of counterfactuality, and thus the possibility of
empirical evaluation, while still recognising that neither the
instrumentalist nor the pluralist positions on their own provide
an adequate explanation of the political process.

We are, of course, aware of the fact that counterfactuality in
principle does not guarantee empirical testability in practice,
and we would certainly wish to distance ourselves from a naive
Popperian position of falsifiability. The fact that the community
power debate dragged on for so long in the USA should itself be
enough to alert us to the fact that evidence does not speak for
itself in adjudicating between different theories. Nevertheless,
we do believe that testability is an important condition of
theoretical adequacy and that a theory, such as that of Poulantzas,
which is inherently immune from empirical evaluation should be
rejected on that ground alone. Our position, in other words, is
that any theory should be expected to identify the sort of evidence
(and the criteria for recognising such evidence) which would be
inconsistent with its key postulates.

(ii) The compatibility of paradigms

While recognising that observation will always be theory-dependent,
and hence that criteria of empirical testability and of empirical
adequacy must therefore be embedded within particular perspectives
(i.e., there is no independent and universal criterion of empirical
adequacy), we would nevertheless wish to point to the degree of
commensurability which undoubtedly exists between different
traditions or 'paradigms' within the social sciences. As Sayer
(1979) has shown, theory-dependency does not imply theory-determinacy
of observation, and different perspectives may well see much of the
world in much the same way. For example, while one theorist may
'look' at the growth of the welfare state in Britain and 'see'
working-class incorporation while another 'sees' working-class
advance and the progressive erosion of a capitalist order, both
are likely to agree on a range of 'facts' concerning the level of
services, patterns of expenditure and so on. Very rarely in the
social sciences do disputes approximate the famous gestalt metaphor
in which the protagonists literally cannot see what the other sees.

The particular significance of this for our chapter is that we
seek to bring together different theories to explain different
aspects of the state's activities, and that we see these theories as

complementary rather than as mutually exclusive. In particular, we
do not believe that Marxist analysis is incompatible with so-called
'bourgeois' theories, and we would suggest that it is precisely such
a belief which has prevented recent Marxist work from confronting
and possibly resolving some of the key problems which now beset it.
Put explicitly, our suggestion is that insights gleaned from the
Marxist tradition may prove valuable in analysing some aspects of
state activity and some types of political struggles, but that they
must be complemented by other work from other traditions which have
hitherto often been seen as incompatible.

(iii)   The use of an ideal type framework

The core of the analysis which follows consists of the development
of an ideal-type framework, on the basis of which we attempt to
construct a theoretical approach to the analysis of the state,
political struggle and ideology. To avoid subsequent confusion, it
is necessary to emphasise here that our ideal type is not an
empirical statement and makes no claim to empirical validity
(although it is, of course, grounded in prior empirical observation).
Nor is it a model which attempts to replicate empirical reality on
a more manageable scale, nor a theoretical statement, nor an
hypothesis (although it can be used to generate theories and
hypotheses). Like all ideal types, it is a tool of analysis whose
function is to simplify the complexity of the real world to
facilitate our understanding of it. It is the product of a
selection of certain aspects of social reality according to what
Weber termed the criterion of 'value relevance' (i.e., we are
focussing on those aspects which we consider interesting and
important), and of a deliberate exaggeration and logical purification
of those aspects. The world is not like our ideal type, but we will
only begin to understand that world through the conceptual clarity
which such an ideal type provides. Like Weber, therefore, we see
such a conceptual exercise as an essential precondition to the
development of knowledge although the exercise itself cannot add to
that knowledge.

An example is in order. In what follows, we draw upon the work
of O'Connor (1973), and in particular on his three-fold classification
of state expenditures. Although he does not admit or recognise it,
this classification is, of course, ideal typical. Thus O'Connor
(and many subsequent commentators and critics) accepts that any
given example of state expenditure is likely to fall across all
three categories, but he nevertheless maintains, quite justifiably,
that the conceptual distinctions remain fruitful in helping us to
understand the patterns and dynamics of state spending. Of course
in the real world, everything is related to everything else and
different aspects of reality are not neatly compartmentalised, but
it is for precisely this reason that conceptual clarification is a
necessary preliminary to empirical analysis and theoretical
development:

> Sociological analysis both abstracts from reality and at the same
> time helps us to understand it, in that it shows with what degree
> of approximation a concrete historical phenomenon can be subsumed

under one or more of these concepts.... The more sharply and precisely the ideal type has been constructed, thus the more abstract and unrealistic in this sense it is, the better it is able to perform its functions in formulating terminology, classifications and hypotheses (Weber, 1978, pp.20-1).

RESOURCE ALLOCATION, FUNCTIONS AND LEVELS OF THE STATE

We can distinguish in ideal-typical terms three basic processes of resource allocation, each of which implies a different pattern of state intervention (see Table 1.1).

(i)   The market mode

There are clearly a number of different concepts by which market processes can be defined, but both Adam Smith's 'invisible hand' and Marx's 'law of value' are based upon the identification of an impersonal or objective law or mechanism which allows resources to be allocated independently of the exercise of political authority. In modern economics the price mechanism is argued to play this role and represents the foundation upon which the edifice of neo-classical economics has been constructed. There now seems to be an emergent consensus among certain Marxist and non-Marxist economists alike that in the advanced capitalist economy there is a dual structure, part of which comprises firms subordinate to a market, but the larger part of which consists of large corporations which have developed a significant degree of market power (Galbraith, 1972, 1974; Holland, 1975; Mandel, 1975; O'Connor, 1973).

In a system of market allocation power is diffused because no single producer has control over his competitors: each producer is subordinate to the market. But market processes cannot operate wholly independently of state involvement, for its guarantee of private property and the enforcement of contracts at law are necessary prerequisites for market processes to operate (Macpherson, 1966; Holloway and Picciotto, 1978). The state thus facilitates the accumulation of capital (Winkler, 1976). The extent of the state's role is minimal, and its legislation is concerned primarily with the regulation of the private market economy. There is no attempt to plan the allocation of investment or other economic resources; capital flows to where the rate of return can be maximised. The dominant ideology associated with the market is competitive individualism based on the institution of private property (Macpherson, 1962). The mode of interest articulation is pluralist, based on the protection of private property rights through the voluntary association of individuals.

(ii)   The bureaucratic mode

By contrast with the market mode, in a bureaucratic system resources are allocated politically by state institutions separated from civil

society. The allocation process is governed by explicit rules,
devised and applied within the state apparatus. Power is concentrated
and centralised in the state which plays a directive role with respect
to economic processes, determining levels of investment, prices and
incomes. Economic planning is accomplished by state imperatives
through the formulation of detailed legislation defining the sphere
of responsibility of each actor at every level of the system.
Command structures of this type are associated with certain kinds of
state socialist ideologies, which lay stress on objective equality as
a fundamental principle of distribution.   Interest articulation is
concerned with inputs into the authoritative structures, and is
monist in form - usually the monopoly of a single political party
(Schmitter, 1974, p.97).

The structures of bureaucratic resource allocation conform to
the ideal type of bureaucracy identified by Weber, in which activities
are ordered by rules, there is a firm hierarchy of roles with a clear
chain of command, business is conducted through written records,
management is a specialised and expert activity, and officials are
career bureaucrats with specialised knowledge of administrative
processes. Thus the bureaucratic mode of resource allocation
requires a separate and distinctive form of organisation, in contrast
to the market mode which operates by structural determination rather
than by rational action, and also in contrast to our third mode of
resource allocation, corporatism.

(iii)   The corporatist mode

Late capitalism has developed from the competitive phase of capitalism
through the differentiation of a dual economic structure, comprising
a competitive sector of small firms and a corporate sector of large-
scale and often multinational enterprises. A working class
represented by powerful trade unions succeeded, at least for a time,
in obtaining through the agency of the state a guarantee of full
employment. The trade unions enjoy a monopoly in the representation
of working-class interests on economic and political questions. This
is not, of course, to imply that labour and capital are equally
powerful partners in corporatist structures, but it does imply that
unions exercise some independent power. The principal form of
decision-making in the corporate sector of the economy is bargaining.
By defining in ideal-typical terms corporatism as a mode of resource
allocation, we can start to examine the identity of the parties to
the bargaining process, and the major structural influences upon it.

Corporatist decisions are neither imposed by objective laws nor
by a determinate political authority. They reflect the outcome of
a bargaining process between corporate interests, which implies the
assumption that each party is able independently to exercise some
form of sanction. Power is thus neither pluralistically dispersed,
nor concentrated, but polycentric within an overall hierarchy. The
private economy cannot operate independently of the state, but the
state does not control private capital. (1) The state intervenes to
safeguard and protect capital accumulation (Offe, 1975), but it must
legitimate its intervention to both capital and labour (Macpherson,
1977). Such intervention is not pursued by means of bureaucratic

structures, but by the establishment of ad hoc agencies on which the
interests of labour and capital are directly represented. (2) The
characteristic pattern of legislation is discretionary and enabling:
the agency is given powers to intervene in a manner which discriminates
between capitals or between sectors, rather than as in the bureaucratic mode via a universally applicable code of rules. Economic
planning in a corporatist system is essentially indicative, whether
in the form of specifically negotiated planning agreements, or via
the co-ordination of information to feed into the economic
calculation of individual corporations (Schonfield, 1965).

The ideology associated with corporatism is both holistic and
reformist: Jessop has argued corporatism to be the 'highest stage
of social democracy' (1979, p.207). The emphasis, as Winkler (1976
and 1977) has argued, is on efficiency and productivity via social
order at the level of the nation state. The corporatist system is
a non-egalitarian one in which privilege is accorded by virtue of
contribution to the national product. Interest articulation is
according to economic function, with interest groups involved in the
implementation as well as the determination of policy (Schmitter,
1974; Cawson, 1978).

These three ideal types of modes of resource allocation have of
necessity been constructed in skeletal terms for the purpose of
suggesting hypothetical relationships between them and the different
levels and functions of the capitalist state in order to give more
analytical precision to the concept of relative autonomy outlined
in the first section of this chapter. For convenience their essential
features are summarised in Table 1.1. In the remainder of this

TABLE 1.1 Market, bureaucratic and corporatist modes of resource
allocation

	A MARKET MODE	B BUREAUCRATIC MODE	C CORPORATIST MODE
1 Basis of legit- imate decisions	law-governed	rule-governed	bargain-governed
2 Distribution of power	diffuse/ pluralistic	centralised/ concentrated	polycentric/ hierarchical
3 Role of the state	facilitative	directive	interventionist
4 Form of legislation	regulatory	detailed	enabling
5 Form of planning	non-planning	imperative	indicative
6 Associated ideology	competitive individualist; private property	state socialist; egalitarian	social democra- tic/reformist; security/efficien- cy/abundance
7 Form of interest group politics	individual/ protective; pluralist/ competitive	holistic/input; monist	producer/input- output; hierarchical

section we will attempt to establish the hypothetical links between
these three processes of resource allocation and the different
functions and levels of the state.

PRODUCTION, CONSUMPTION AND LEGITIMATION

Following O'Connor's (1973) classification of state expenditure as
social investment, social consumption and social expenses, we can
identify the three basic functions of the capitalist state as
maintaining production, ensuring reproduction through the provision
of either privatised or collective/public consumption, and maintaining social order. In late capitalism the state intervenes directly
in production to safeguard capital accumulation, but cannot use
bureaucratic means for this, since bureaucracies are inflexible and
ill-suited to innovatory policy-making (Offe, 1975). The productive
function of the state is discharged through bargains struck with
those interests whose participation is essential for the implementation of policies. Thus for production, state intervention is
associated with the corporatist mode of resource allocation.
Consumption, by contrast, is a process where in addition to the
private commodity form, the state provides use-values directly,
whether in the form of physical commodities (e.g., council housing)
or services (e.g., education). Here the state can allocate according
to impersonal criteria through bureaucratic structures, with
eligibility for benefit laid down according to detailed rules
applied to individuals.
    In addition to its function with respect to capital accumulation,
the state attempts to maintain a social consensus which helps to
reproduce capitalist relations of production. This legitimation
function includes national defence, the police and courts, as well
as more general ideological support accorded to institutions, such
as electoral arrangements, which are important in consensus
formation. The capitalist state under competitive market conditions
gained its legitimacy from the operation of the market itself, through
the ideology of fair exchange. But with market failure and the
necessity for state intervention to maintain the economic function
of accumulation, this ideology collapses (Habermas, 1976). The
integration at the level of the state of what were once autonomous
spheres - the economic and the political - not only transforms
economic decisions into political ones, but creates an increased
need for legitimation. Thus, for example, a decision to give state
support to major industries threatened with bankruptcy violates the
traditional separation of the economic and the political, and runs
counter to the principle that the state is neutral with respect to
specific capitals. The decision is legitimated as a 'special case'
which requires 'temporary intervention' (e.g., British Leyland) in
an effort to deny any suggestion that the failure is a product of
structural features integral to late capitalist accumulation.
    State intervention based on these different resource allocation
modes will be legitimated in different ways. So far, in Britain
at least, no political party has made corporatist themes the cornerstone of its ideological appeal, so that corporatist intervention
does not consciously follow corporatist legitimation. But in

response to the fiscal crisis of state expenditure, many Western governments, including Mrs Thatcher's, have deliberately adopted the market mode as a strategy of state intervention in accordance with a neo-liberal ideology. When corporatist intervention has taken place, especially in industrial restructuring and in incomes policy, it has been justified by circumstance, as a pragmatic response to pressing policy questions. In this sense there is a representational crisis in late capitalism because liberal democratic ideology cannot affirm that its institutions are inadequate to resolve the economic problems of accumulation (Cawson, 1979).

LEVELS OF THE STATE

It is our view that the assumption that the state possesses an essential unity, which has dominated much recent Marxist work, needs to be abandoned, not only with respect to the functions of the state, but also for its level of operation. In essence this means taking as a starting point the position that there is a systematic variation in how the state functions, its forms of intervention, and the pattern of interest representation, according to the level of the state under analysis. For example, while we can distinguish between national, regional and local levels, it is clear that legitimation through the electoral validation of political authority takes place only at national and local levels, although regional assemblies in Britain have been canvassed from time to time. Thus the basis for the legitimation of the state at regional level is fundamentally different, depending upon the appeal to expertise (technocracy) and the co-option of functional interests. Those areas of state activity which have been organised on a regional basis - water and health, for example - have been kept separate from local government and administered by co-opted experts. As we shall see, the characteristic mode of resource allocation in these areas is corporatist, the dominant concern of policy is with production, and the prevailing pattern of interest representation is corporatist.

At the national or central level of the state the hitherto dominant form of interest representation through political parties and parliament is being transformed as power has shifted to the executive, and has become increasingly exercised through collaboration with functionally organised interest groups. The development of this corporatist pattern of politics is most marked where state intervention has been concerned with reorganising the relations of production in furtherance of capital accumulation. Thus incomes policy centred on the need to restrain wages and enhance profitability in the private sector has required the collaboration of trade unions, and industrial policy concerned with reorganising the structure of production has been implemented through para-statal agencies run by co-opted representatives of labour and capital. In both of these areas the model of competitive politics implicit in the liberal-democratic paradigm does not explain the simultaneous formation and implementation of policy by a process of bargaining between functional groups: in effect the fragmentation of state power. It is for this reason that we have used the term 'corporatist'

to describe both the pattern of interest representation and the mode
of state intervention, for in this mode representation and intervention are fused within corporatist structures (Jessop, 1979). By
contrast market and bureaucratic modes are separated from the means
of representation; in the former state power is focused on maintaining
capitalist economic criteria as the ground rules for both public and
private enterprise, subject of course to ad hoc exceptions. In the
bureaucratic form, resource allocation is accomplished within the
structure of the state itself, with interest representation the
preserve of a single institution.

Local government is pre-eminently in the sphere of competitive
politics and there are as yet few examples of corporatist policy-
making. In part this is because corporatism is a response to the
problems of capitalist production, the dynamic of which has shifted,
through increasing concentration and scale, to the regional and
central levels of the system. The local level is mainly where
provision for collective consumption is made - where services such
as education, health and housing are delivered to the consumer.
Without wishing to argue that policy in these services is made at
this level - for clearly the relationship between production and
consumption provides a set of constraints which shapes some of the
contours of policy - there is a good deal of scope at the local
level for competitive politics, in which classes do not appear as
classes, to influence important aspects of the provision of these
services. Thus within national guidelines and standards there are
important variations in the level of provision of services at the
local level, and in part these can be explained by the differential
impact of competitive politics in different areas.

THE APPLICATION OF THE ANALYTICAL FRAMEWORK

We noted that ideal types are to be judged on their usefulness in
organising our knowledge of the world, and in enabling the development of hypotheses. In this section we shall demonstrate the
fruitfulness of our framework in aiding our understanding of
historical and comparative variations in patterns of state policy-
making. In the final section we shall go on to show how it can
also help to resolve the relative autonomy question.

(i)   Shifts in state policy in post-war Britain

Using the framework outlined above we can describe some of the ways
in which state policy has shifted in Britain since 1945. The way
in which the constituent elements have been combined in concrete
cases will suggest some potentially fruitful explanatory hypotheses.
This section is necessarily selective and schematic, and is intended
to show how the analysis might be done, not to do it.

The method is to establish the empirical 'mix' between patterns
of resource allocation, and the levels and functions of the state
at different intervals. Particularly important is our specification
of the relationship between economic management and social policy,
between the production and consumption functions of the state. There

are three distinct ways in which this relationship has been portrayed in the literature. One is the position held on the 'right' by Bacon and Eltis (1978) and Milton Friedman (1962), and on the 'left' by Bullock and Yaffe (1975) and Fine and Harris (1976). In this view social welfare spending is seen as a 'burden' on the productive sector of the economy; all taxation is seen as a deduction from profit or surplus value. Thus the expansion of state expenditure on social welfare programmes poses problems for capital accumulation, and there are definite limits, asserted but not always specified, beyond which the welfare state cannot advance.

The second view, dominant in the literature on social administration, specifies no particular relationship between social policy and economic policy, tracing the growth of social spending in terms of the identification and meeting of social needs through the liberal-democratic process, and as essentially pragmatic responses to changing circumstances (Titmuss, 1963; Fraser, 1973).

The third view, closest to the analysis presented here, is best expressed by Gough (1979) who sees the welfare state as a contradictory phenomenon in two ways: on the one hand there is the contradiction rooted in the conflict between social classes, and on the other that between capital accumulation and legitimation. Not all welfare spending is a burden on capital, since part can help to lower the cost of reproducing labour-power, and constitutes a 'return flow' of benefits back to the capitalist sector (p.108 and Appendix C). Only that part solely concerned with keeping the social peace, that is, the social expenses of legitimation, is a net drain on the productive sector. Thus for Gough it is an empirical question whether particular patterns of social spending fetter the accumulation process (p.117).

Our approach differs from Gough's, however, in that it seeks to restrict the applicability of class conflict as an explanatory factor in determining the overall shape of state policy. There are two strands to this argument. First, the development of the corporate sector of interest representation according to the functional division of labour, but within the context of class differentiation, suggests that it is not simply the 'balance of class forces' which determines the form and content of state policies. Second, much state spending, particularly with respect to the provision of collective consumption, occurs at the local level. Local government itself has a degree of autonomy from the central level (Dearlove, 1979, p.242) which renders problematic the simple insertion of the 'local state' into an hierarchical and unified model of the state apparatus (Cockburn, 1977; Gough, 1979, p.63).

In reviewing developments in British social and economic policy since 1945, we would want to examine their productive, reproductive and legitimating aspects (as Gough has indeed done), but in addition draw inferences from the structural location of policy at different levels of the state, according to our broad correlation between corporatist politics at the central and regional levels, and competitive politics at the local or urban level (Cawson, 1978; Saunders, 1979, chapter 4). This is particularly important if we wish to speculate in a theoretically informed way on the political consequence of cuts in public expenditure.

   As an example of the way in which this analysis might be applied,
we can examine the location of different aspects of state policy at
different levels of the state over time. We can then, using the
framework, hypothesise the causes and consequences of shifts in
location and form of intervention. As an illustration we will take
the case of land-use planning. Planning can be broken down into
its production aspects (e.g., the location of industry in relation
to its labour force and transport systems), its consumption aspects
(e.g., the provision of recreational facilities, parks and so on),
and its legitimation aspects (social balance, co-ordination and so
on). In 1947 the Town and Country Planning Act nationalised the
right to develop land, taxed at 100 per cent the value added to land
through development, and established planning machinery at central,
regional (shortly afterwards scrapped as an 'economy measure'),
and local (county and county borough) level. The instrument of
planning was the statutory development plan, which was drawn up by
the local authority and used to control the granting of planning
permissions for development. This mode of planning intervention
was quintessentially bureaucratic, in the strict sense as defined
above, and its location at the local level made planning decisions
open to the competitive political process.
   In 1968 the planning system was reorganised, and a new concept -
the structure plan - was introduced. Structure plans were to be
statements of strategy; local plans were to show how it was
proposed that structure plan strategy be implemented at the local
level. Following local government reorganisation in 1972, structure
plans are produced by counties and metropolitan counties, local
plans by districts and metropolitan districts. Although the
bureaucratic mode was partly preserved, as development control would
operate as before, important corporatist elements entered the
process, in that structure plans were to be prepared and legitimated
by examination-in-public based upon corporate participation, rather
than by public inquiry at which any individual would have the right
to object (Cawson, 1977; Flynn, 1979). At the same time that
planning became more local (in that districts became planning
authorities for the first time in 1974) its strategic (essentially
productive) aspects were removed to a higher level of government.
It is worth noting that trunk roads (essentially productive) are
planned and built directly by central government.
   Although one can point to a correlation between the development
of the corporate sector of the economy (the share of the top 100
firms in industrial output increased from a fifth in 1950 to a half
in 1970) and the development of planning structures sensitive to
corporate sector influences, it would be dangerous to assert a priori
that planning conflicts between county and district, between
structure plan and local plan, will inevitably be resolved in favour
of the former. Indeed the greater penetrability of lower-tier
local authorities to competitive sector influences, and the location
of the development control function at the lower tier, suggest that
local government and local planning will continue to be a problem
for corporate capital. It is precisely empirical questions such
as these which can be fruitfully posed using this framework. In
such a way the argument between those who see the planning system
as having hindered capital accumulation (Hall et al., 1973) and

those who see it as essentially the legitimation of capitalist
urban development processes (Ambrose, 1976) might be capable of
resolution.

INTERNATIONAL COMPARISONS

A more developed version of the framework outlined here would provide
a systematic basis for a comparative analysis between different
capitalist societies, and between capitalist and state socialist
societies. Pahl (1977b) has criticised the tendency of Marxist state
theories to label as specifically 'capitalist' tensions which exist
in any industrial society. But to go further than Pahl does, we
need to know how to frame the appropriate questions for empirical
research. The issue of central-local relations in different
countries is one that is a central concern of current research
(SSRC, 1979). The typology outlined in this paper is capable of
suggesting hypotheses which relate levels of the state to distinct
processes of political mediation, and to the discharge of state
functions through different modes of resource allocation. The
Anglo-American comparison of urban politics highlights the importance
of explaining why specific policies are located in one system at the
local level, and in another at regional or central levels of
government. Such work would build on approaches developed in a
single country (such as those of Friedland, Piven and Alford, 1977;
Esping-Andersen, Friedland and Wright, 1976) and would concentrate
upon devising theoretically informed questions for empirical research
in different countries, rather than the cataloguing of institutional
variation at the empirical level.

MODES, LEVELS, FUNCTIONS AND THE RELATIVE AUTONOMY PROBLEM

Although it can facilitate analysis of comparative and historical
variations in patterns of state policy-making, perhaps the most
interesting application of our ideal-type framework is in its
potential as a basis for theorising the relative autonomy of the
state and ideology vis-à-vis the interests of capital. Basically,
our argument is that there is no single theory appropriate to the
analysis of 'the' capitalist state (or 'the' dominant ideology)
since different aspects of the political process have to be explained
by means of different theoretical positions.
   We begin with the distinction between production and consumption
policies (social investment and social consumption in O'Connor's
terms). This is not a clear-cut empirical distinction but a
conceptual one, for we are aware that consumption and production
processes entail and relate to each other (cf. Marx, 1973 edn,
pp.90-4), but we nevertheless argue that it is crucially important
to distinguish those areas of state intervention which directly
benefit capital by socialising or subsidising constant capital
investment costs from those which directly benefit non-capitalist
interests by providing resources such as housing, health care and
education which the market might otherwise fail to provide or
provide only at prohibitive cost. The production activities of the

state (together with its more traditional role in fiscal management)
are thus oriented directly to the problem of maintaining capital
accumulation while its consumption activities are oriented to the
problem of maintaining a certain quality of life among the population
as a whole. The latter may also, of course, aid capital by lowering
the costs of labour-power, by increasing demand in the private sector
and so on, but we see this as a contingent rather than a necessary
function (e.g., the perceived need for a 'Great Debate' suggests
that much current educational expenditure does not aid capital;
there is little reason to suggest that council houses with garages
reproduce labour-power any more effectively than those without; and
so on).

Where it intervenes directly in the process of capital accumulation,
whether through provision of infrastructure, manipulation of tax
incentives, regulation of wages or whatever, the state can be seen
directly to affect the class relation between capital and labour, and
the realm of politics so designated (i.e., the 'production' function
broadly conceived) can thus be analysed in terms of class theory.
Put another way, political class struggles take place around the
productive interventions of the capitalist state and around issues
concerning the organisation of production in society.

State intervention in the sphere of consumption, however, does
not give rise to class struggles but to conflicts between what
Dunleavy (1979) terms 'consumption sectors'. In other words, when
people mobilise politically (whether by demonstrating, voting or
whatever) over questions of consumption, they do so not as members
of a class, but as consumers of a particular commodity or service;
as commuters, council tenants, parents, book-borrowers and so on.
The boundaries of these and other consumption sectors bear a
necessary non-correspondence to class boundaries (in Weberian terms
they are 'status groups'), nor do they necessarily exhibit any
significant degree of overlap with each other (e.g., those concerned
about the level of council-house rents may constitute a very
different social base from those prepared to mobilise over a
declining library service or a deteriorating pupil-teacher ratio).
Yet as Dunleavy's work indicates, they remain crucial factors in
determining people's political orientation in that privatised
modes of consumption (e.g., house and car ownership) may outweigh
even class location in significance as regards political alignments.

Now we are not suggesting that consumption struggles are
irrelevant to, or remain untouched by, class struggles, for they
clearly occur in the context of capital's over-riding requirement
for ever-renewed accumulation. To study (or, indeed, to engage in)
battles against welfare cuts without relating the cuts themselves
to the crisis of profitability in the private sector would be
ludicrous. However, we are arguing that it is misleading to
designate such battles as part of the overall class struggle since
the politics of social consumption are not class politics, and
classes do not mobilise politically in this field. (3)

Taking our argument one step further, we saw that the production
and consumption functions of the British state tend to be organised
through different modes of interest mediation such that the state's
productive activities are typically determined by means of corporate
strategies involving representatives of the (class) interests of

capital and labour, while consumption functions are more generally the product of competitive (non-class-based) political struggles. There is, in other words, a bifurcation of the political process with the crucial production policies insulated from the arena of popular democratic politics (elected assemblies, petitions, demonstrations) while consumption politics tend to be the subject of more open struggle and debate. As Middlemas (1979) shows, there has existed in Britain ever since the First World War a 'corporate bias' through which representatives of large capital and organised labour have negotiated directly with political and administrative leaders over key production policies.

This insulation of production and consumption is further reinforced through the division of functions between different levels of government such that production policies tend to be concentrated in central state agencies while local government now enjoys little responsibility outside the area of social consumption. As Friedland et al. (1977) have suggested, an important effect of this is that the most crucial aspects of state policy-making have been removed from the most accessible and vulnerable levels of the state apparatus. As the long history of local radicalism in Britain indicates (Clydeside, Poplar, the 'little Moscows', Clay Cross, South Yorkshire and so on), it is quite possible for non-capitalist and even anti-capitalist interests to gain control of local authorities, but their scope for action when they do is limited if crucial production policies are no longer located at the local level.

To the extent that production and consumption functions are located at different levels of the state apparatus, there also develops a tendency for different ideological concerns to focus on these different levels. In particular, local government becomes associated with questions of social need while regional and central state agencies become associated with private sector profitability. As Cockburn observes, 'we have been taught to think of local government as a kind of humane official charity, a service that looks after us "from the cradle to the grave"' (1977, p.41). In this way the two core elements of the dominant ideology within British society for the last 200 years, expressed in Bentham's principles of subsistence and security of property, tend to be divorced from each other - need versus profit, subsistence versus security, rights of citizenship versus rights of property. Such dilemmas are to some extent overcome through their insulation. Thus we demand the services to which we are entitled but we lose sight of the basic question of the legitimacy of private property's prior claim over social resources.

The conclusion which we draw from all this is that we may distinguish in ideal-typical terms between

(a)   a sphere of the politics of production ...
      in which capital and labour are directly represented as classes ...
      which negotiate with the state in a relatively exclusive corporate sector of the polity ...
      which is located mainly at central and regional government levels ...
      and whose prevailing ideological principle is that of private property and the importance of maintaining private sector profitability;

and
    (b)   a sphere of the politics of consumption ...
           in which a plurality of consumption sectors mobilise as
           non-class-based interest groups ...
           which battle with each other over specific issues in a
           competitive sector of the polity ...
           which can be found at central and local (though not regional)
           levels of government but most crucially at the relatively
           accessible local level ...
           where the prevailing ideological principle is that of
           citizenship rights and the importance of alleviating social
           need.

Our hypothesis is that (a) may best be analysed in terms of what may
be called an 'instrumentalist' theory such as that elaborated by
Miliband (1973), while (b) may better be approached by means of a
political theory of imperfect pluralism. We are arguing, that is,
for the abandonment of unitary theories of 'the' state and for the
development of a dualistic theoretical approach which seriously
takes account of the different political processes associated with
different types of state policy.

The reason why the state, seen as a unitary whole, appears to be
relatively autonomous from any one class is simply that, while the
interests of capital can generally prevail in the sphere of the
politics of production (for the reasons discussed by Miliband, 1977,
pp.68-74 - the class backgrounds of state personnel, the power
exerted by organised capitalist interests, and the recognition by
the state that capital accumulation must be safeguarded as a first
priority), other interests may come to prevail in particular
localities over particular issues in the sphere of the politics
of consumption. While more empirical work is needed to back up
these claims (particularly as regards the operation of capitalist
interests in the corporate sector of the central state), we would
nevertheless suggest that the paradox of the relative autonomy of
the state may be resolved through the development of a dual
perspective such as that we have outlined.

NOTES

1 This is an important difference between the concept of corporatism
   as outlined here and that of Winkler, who argues that the
   state's role is directive vis-a-vis private industry, and
   autonomous with respect to specific class or elite interests
   (1976, Appendix).
2 Winkler (1977) provides the best account of the differences
   between corporatist and bureaucratic forms of administration.
3 This argument has some important implications for the analysis
   of so-called urban social movements. According to Castells, for
   example, a crisis in the provision of collective consumption may
   lay the foundations for the development of broad popular class
   alliances since large sectors of the population extending far
   beyond the industrial proletariat may find themselves adversely
   affected by deteriorating state provision of housing, education,
   transport and so on. Our argument, by contrast, is that the

politics of collective consumption are inherently fragmented by
the plurality of consumption sectors, that mobilisation around one
issue (i.e., day nurseries) may go hand-in-hand with resolute
disinterest towards others (e.g., bus services), and that attempts
to encompass the wide scatter of consumer movements under the
umbrella of some class-based political party (which Castells sees
as crucial to the development of urban social movements) are
likely to founder, not because of poor organisation or stunted
political consciousness, but because people who may discover
common interests in one specific issue will find themselves on
opposite sides on another, and in any case will be unlikely to
endorse a political party to which they are otherwise antagonistic.

As regards current struggles against social consumption cuts,
therefore, we would suggest that campaigns may achieve success
on specific issues in specific localities, but that activists
are likely to be disappointed if they attempt to use such
campaigns as vehicles for achieving broader and more radical
objectives. Such a conclusion would seem to be supported by
empirical evidence of rent strikes, squatting movements and the
like, for most studies in Britain indicate the limited character
of such struggles.

Chapter 2

DE-INDUSTRIALISATION, CLASSES AND POLITICS
John Urry

In 'The Anatomy of Capitalist Societies' I argued that there were
three spheres of civil society, of circulation, reproduction, and
struggle, and these in some sense lie between the sphere of
capitalist production, on the one hand, and the state, on the
other (see Urry, 1981a, as well as Cooke, 1983). I suggested,
among other claims, that we can periodise the development of
struggles within capitalist societies into that in which the sphere
of circulation is dominant and that in which the sphere of
reproduction is dominant. In the first section of this chapter I
shall consider the consequences for social struggle of this
dominance of the sphere of reproduction. However, I shall go on to
consider some recent transformations of the British economy, which
can be loosely summarised as involving its de-industrialisation.
I shall argue that these developments imply (a) the inadequacy of
theories of post-industrialisation, (b) the importance of changes
in the appropriation of time-space by particular social forms, and
(c) the emergence of relatively novel patterns of struggle and
hence of civil society, especially on the level of each locality.
I shall argue against the claim that regions are particularly
significant foci of contemporary political struggle. I shall
therefore try to analyse the manner in which we should approach the
study of civil society and the state within a rapidly de-industrialising society.

THE SPHERES OF CIRCULATION AND REPRODUCTION (see Urry, 1981a, ch.8)

With regard to the development of the class struggle and the state
there are two main periods in the development of capitalist
societies: that in which the sphere of circulation is dominant
within civil society; and that in which the sphere of reproduction
is dominant. In the former, the relations of exchange dominate the
relations of distribution and consumption. It is essential for the
process of accumulation that commodity-capital is quickly realised
as money-capital and returns to the sphere of production. Thus,
there is a strong basis for the establishment of 'Freedom, Equality,
Property, and Bentham' (Marx, 1976 edn, p.280), for the establishment

of those conditions which permit the most efficient and fastest
circulation of commodities. But it is erroneous to suggest that
such conditions follow automatically from the dominance of the
sphere of circulation. The establishment of such conditions results
from particular social struggles without which such conditions will
not be established. As Blanks et al. say: 'The owner of labour
power as a free wage-labourer with the full and equal rights of a
citizen was able to develop only through long class struggles. In
no way does he [sic] arise from the surface forms of competition'
(Blanks et al.,1978, p.142).
     Where the sphere of circulation is dominant there are four main
forms of struggle. First, there is the attempt by the different
fractions of the nascent capitalist class to establish monetary,
measurement, and transportation systems within the national territory
appropriate to the developing exchange economy. They also seek to
establish legal procedures backed up by the state so that market
transactions can be contractually established, sustained and enforced,
and if necessary to establish procedures for sueing and being sued.
Second, there is that struggle, mainly pursued by popular and
working-class forces, to establish conditions in which all individuals
exchange commodities in a position of approximate legal equality.
The effect of such struggles if successful is to produce a set of
social relations within which formally free and equal juridic
subjects are constituted, subjects who take themselves to be the
authors of their own actions, who sue and are sued, who buy and sell
commodities, who alienate their own labour-power or purchase that of
others, and so on. Third, there is struggle around the conditions
which affect exchange, which determine the price at which different
commodities are bought and sold. In particular, with relation to
labour-power, there is struggle over the categories of worker
(male/female/child), the time they are available, their capacity to
organise, and so on. In situations in which the conditions are
highly unfavourable, then extensive mobilisation will be probable,
generally along the lines in which the systematic denial of rights
happens to exist. And fourth, there will be struggle by different
classes and social forces to extend the principle of exchange
equality into the political sphere, to ensure that they possess the
right to vote, to join a political party, to stand for election and
so on. There are a number of points to note about these struggles.
     First, the development and extension of the 'liberal' state,
safeguarding and extending the circulation of commodities, does not
follow directly from the nature of an economy characterised, as
this will be, by the production of absolute surplus-value. It only
follows through the effects, which are often unintended, of the
forms of struggle in which the various classes and social forces
in that civil society happen to engage. Furthermore, to the extent
that such struggles do have the effect of ensuring the extension
and elaboration of the system of generalised commodity exchange,
then this has the consequences, both of accelerating the rate of
accumulation, and shifting the dominant sphere of civil society from
that of circulation to that of reproduction. To the extent that
such struggles do not have these effects then the rate of accumulation will be lower and struggles will continue to be structured
within the sphere of circulation. Although the production of

relative surplus-value may be dominant, in cases through the
'importation' of such relations of production from other social
formations, it does not follow that the sphere of reproduction will
be dominant within civil society. There thus may be uneven development between advanced economic development and 'reactionary' political
forms oriented around the attainment of relations of formal exchange-
equality. In such situations there will be at times intense struggles
focussed upon the bases along which such formal exchange-equality has
not been established, along that of religion in Northern Ireland, for
example, or ethnicity in the USA. This also indicates that although
one may conceive how in general formal exchange-equality is established
in society, there will always be exceptions to this, the most noticeable
being, of course, that of women. Partly, the political significance
of this is obscured through the central involvement of women in the
sphere of reproduction, but this is not to deny the importance of
their labour-power within the market. Finally, the significance of
establishing formal exchange-equality for most sellers of the
commodity labour-power is considerable. It changes the parameters
of politics in the advanced capitalist societies and represents a
major gain for the popular classes. But there are two provisos to
this. First, such an achievement has to be protected since reversals
may well occur, as has happened in Latin America over formal political
rights. And second, it aids the development of relative surplus-
value with certain deleterious consequences, among which is the
shifting in the sphere of struggle to that of the dominant sphere of
reproduction. I will now consider some aspects of this situation.
    Unlike the former case where the central characteristic is the
establishment of exchange-equality in the present between buyers and
sellers of different commodities, in this case the central feature
is the emphasis placed on the distribution of wages and of surplus-
value, and on the consumption of commodities. Thus, distribution and
consumption are dominant. This can be seen from the viewpoint of
both capital and labour. In the case of the former, the tendency
for the rate of profit to fall is experienced in part as a series of
crises of realisation, so that the later stages of capitalism are
characterised by a tremendous emphasis on sustaining and enlarging
consumption. The growth in the concentration and centralisation of
capital increasingly means that the general conditions of production
cannot be provided by individual capital units - reproduction cannot
be therefore assured simply through exchange processes. Furthermore,
the growth in the scientific and technological character of
capitalist relations means that such skills have to be themselves
produced, or reproduced, among the bearers of certain kinds of
labour-power. And in the case of labour, the gains achieved through
the achievement of formal exchange-equality in the sphere of
circulation have a number of consequences in the period in which
the sphere of reproduction dominates: a commitment to the conservation of gains already achieved, a demand to extend them to other
areas, especially to the political, an emphasis upon extending
struggle to increase consumption, and a willingness to engage in
distributional struggles. The establishment of such formal legal
equality is important in leading each group in society to evaluate
how well they are doing with many other groups. Further, the fact
that the relations within exchange are less directly influential

means that patterns of distribution are a matter for struggle. They
are not simply determined and in part legitimated through the
market. They are much more the consequence of social struggles.
And a crucial lesson learnt in the sphere of circulation period is
that changes are achieved only through collective forms of struggle
and not through individual forms, in particular, through trade
unions, political parties and pressure groups of various sorts.

I will now consider the characteristics of struggle within the
sphere of reproduction. First, there is a proportionate decline in
the importance of class as opposed to other kinds of social struggle
(see Parkin, 1979). This is in part because certain groupings, such
as women or ethnic groups, will seek to establish conditions of
total exchange- and political-equality. But it is also because the
more such general formal equality is achieved, the greater the
variety of bases on which groupings will seek to establish a degree
of substantive equality. There is no reason why mobilisation will
only take place along class lines. This is especially so when a
particular kind of subject, such as women, youth, blacks, and so
on, undergo similar experiences in relation to the labour market
and their organisation by capital. The importance of the reproduction
of labour-power also means that there are substantial sectors of
labour-power either engaged in such reproduction (teachers and
lecturers, hospital workers, etc.) or in being themselves reproduced
(students, patients, etc.).

Second, once the sphere of circulation is no longer dominant
within civil society, then the likely forms of class struggle
generally become less intense (see Trotsky, 1934 edn; Giddens, 1973).
Of course, there are some exceptions to this, in part depending on
the rate and form in which formal exchange-equality and later formal
political equality is achieved. However, the attainment of basic
private and public rights dramatically weakens the effectivity of
class struggle. This is because a major determinant of that struggle
is that of the systematic denial of such rights to all workers; once
they are achieved or even partially achieved then a major basis of
class action disappears and other bases of social struggle become
as important. Wage-labourers may seek to reproduce their material
conditions of life in a variety of different kinds of social struggle.

Third, the reproduction of labour-power necessarily involves the
state. This is because the nature of capital is such that it is
rare for it to be in the interests of any particular capital-unit to
bear the costs of reproducing its own labour-power. This is at least
the case when there is a need for specialised forms of training,
medical care, sickness and welfare benefits, and so on. As the
sphere of reproduction assumes dominance it is the state which
ensures that all capital-units bear some of the costs of their
provision.

Fourth, this socialisation of the costs of provision clearly
reflects the growing demands from the wide variety of social groupings
within civil society. All such groupings seek the state to provide
for their reproduction - there are none of the limitations characteristic of the period in which the sphere of circulation is dominant.
Obviously this will also include the economically dominant classes
and fractions, the professional and new middle classes, as well as
wage-labourers of various kinds. The effect is that there is little

disincentive on any particular grouping to moderate the demands that
it places on the state, the regulation of such demands having to take
place through fiscal crises and dramatic cuts in public expenditure
(see O'Connor, 1973, on the fiscal crisis of the state).   Thus the
widely noted extension of the state in the later stages of capitalism
results in part from the large number of demands placed upon it,
demands which are difficult to resist stemming as they do from the
wide variety of social groupings in civil society. Politics in the
period of dominance of the sphere of reproduction increasingly
involves the state. Thus there is a changed relationship with civil
society. On the one hand, the state is far more subject to determination by the characteristic forces of civil society; and, on the
other hand, the state is enhanced in the degree and kinds of activity
in which it can engage. Yet to the degree to which the former occurs,
the effectivity of policies that are enacted is increasingly
problematic. There will at times be strong demands from different
groupings for a functional representation within the state in a
manner which transcends the limited effectiveness of parliamentary
representation. Any trends towards a corporatist relationship
between state and civil society must be in part understood in terms
of the demands articulated by the relevant classes themselves.   In
certain societies this will include the capitalist class, which will
benefit from the expansion of the state, especially where there is
a strong and active working class. Hence, the paradox that the
latter may result in an increased centralisation of the state, which
is then less responsive and which cannot be so easily shifted (see
Perez-Diaz, 1978, pp.44, 69-72).
    Fifth, there will be considerable conflict within civil society
and within the state over the form taken by the extensions of the
state.   There will be conflict and struggle between the adherents
of commodified and of non-commodified state policies. The former
involve those interventions by the state which work through, and
reinforce mechanism within, the sphere of circulation; these include
taxation changes, unemployment payments, cash forms of welfare,
profit, price and wage controls, health and education provision
through payment, regional and other subsidies to private industry,
etc. Non-commodified state policies involve the state providing
a use-value and not a commodity. Thereby, avoiding the sphere of
circulation to that of reproduction means that political demands are
increasingly oriented to non-commodified rather than commodified
policies. This is for two main reasons. First, with a commodified
and/or selective policy there is difficulty in ensuring that all
members of a particular category acquire the particular use-value
in question. It is easier to ensure this if the use-value does not
have to be purchased on the market. Second, many different social
groupings will be likely to support such non-commodified policy.
In particular, it will effectively mobilise popular democratic
sentiment oriented around the contradiction, the people: the state.
However, although it is likely that political demands from the
popular classes will take this form, it is also progressively the
case that the state will attempt to resist such demands, or at least
to moderate them often in a substantially significant manner. This
is because such a non-commodified programme will be more expensive,
and since it will be financed out of general taxation it will thereby

divert surplus-value that would otherwise be appropriated by capital. Therefore, much of capital, and probably also the traditional petite bourgeoisie, will struggle against non-commodified policy. Such opposition will often be sufficient to prevent the implementation of such a policy. It is only if such classes have in part been politically neutralised that a non-commodified policy may be implemented (see the discussion in Cooke, 1983, on the development of circulation-based state policies in the late 1970s in a number of Western economies).

Finally, the dominant elements in the sphere of circulation are those of consumption and distribution. This has two consequences. First, all groupings are implicated in a competitive struggle for maximising their share of distribution; there are few restrictions which prevent such a competitive struggle, which will obviously be heightened during crises. This means that the state cannot but be involved in mediating the various claims of the differing social groupings. Second, the importance of reproduction means that groupings are progressively involved, not merely in sustaining an income adequate for their reproduction, but in influencing the pattern of production itself. There is thus a shift in the focus of political demand, from (1) achieving formal equality of exchange conditions, which many groupings have only partially attained even in later capitalism; (2) struggling for an improving distribution of income and wealth; and to (3) ensuring that their reproduction can be assured through the consumption of particular use-values, and for a specific balance between the commodified and non-commodified form. That is, that the processes of exchange do not yield an appropriate balance of use-values.

However, this analysis, although important, remains at a fairly general level. In the following sections I shall consider how changes in the structure of the modern economy will transform social struggles and the relations between civil society and the state. I will begin by briefly considering the thesis of post-industrialisation, a thesis which during the 1960s was the most influential of interpretations of the economic and political development of Western societies.

POST-INDUSTRIALISATION AND DE-INDUSTRIALISATION

I shall not consider the theses of Bell (1964), Fuchs (1968), Touraine (1974), and so on, in detail here. Nor shall I consider the more general issues concerned with the supposed centrality of theoretical knowledge, or of the dominance of the scientific-technical elite, or of how the universities are to be viewed as the primary institution. As Miller ironically remarks: 'the post-industrial society was a period of two or three years in the mid-sixties when GNP, social policy programs, and social research and universities were flourishing. Things have certainly changed' (1975, p.28).

Post-industrial society theorists argue that there both has been and will continue to be a shift from the concentration upon capitalistically produced manufactured goods to the more socially conscious provision of services. Modern societies are less and less

capitalistic; they are increasingly involved in the provision of
human services which are necessary given that basic material needs
have been satisfied. As society gets richer new needs develop which
are more demanding of personal services for their satisfaction.

There are however two particular problems with these claims:
first, little adequate specification of the nature of supposed services
and just how they might therefore be provided; and second, no
evidence that there is in fact an increased consumption of services,
merely that there is increased employment in the service sector (see
Bell, 1974 for the clearest example).   However, once we realise
that (a) service employment may in fact be as much involved in
material production as in the provision of services; (b) so-called
service production can be as or more adequately provided via material
commodities; then (c) there is in fact no identity between the growth
in service employment and the growth in the demand for, and provision
of, services. This can be seen by considering the expenditure on
services directly. Is Bell right to extend Engels's law and argue
that as societies get richer, the proportion spent on necessities
like food decreases, and that spent on services increases?
Unfortunately, the data is ambiguous. If we consider cross-sectional
budget data, then, as one receives a higher income, the proportion
spent on services increases (see Gershuny, 1978, p.75). However,
if we consider time series data this does not appear to be the case.
Thus, if we compare 1974 with 1954 (in the UK), although the
proportion spent on food decreases, the proportion spent on services
remains almost constant. The category of personal expenditure to
show the most marked increase is that on domestic machines (TV,
domestic appliances, transport goods); when corrected for relative
price changes, it increased from about 4 per cent to 16 per cent of
total personal expenditure (see Gershuny, 1978, p.80).

So, as Gershuny shows, the most important increase in expenditure
is in fact not on services but on consumer goods so that we provide
ourselves with the service, transportation by car, entertainment
by the TV or video, food by electrical kitchen goods, etc. Gershuny
thus talks of the development of an increasingly do-it-yourself
economy with substantial capital investment taking place within
households (see Burns, 1977). And even if we add to the spending
on services the expenditure by the state on its services, particularly
education and health, the total still accounts for less than one-
quarter of all current expenditure, as compared with the proportion
of service employment of over 55 per cent (see Rothwell and Zegweld,
1979, p.39). How can we explain this disparity? Why hasn't service
expenditure risen pari passu with the growth in service employment?

There are three important and inter-connected reasons for this.
First, as a result of rising real incomes fewer people are willing
to 'service' others on a one-to-one basis. There is increasing
disutility of such work especially for indigenous, adult males.
Second, increasing numbers of such people will want such use-values;
and this means that their provision will have to be socialised,
either through the state, or through mechanisation. In the latter
case, the consumer obtains the 'same' service but it is not
provided directly by individual human beings, but rather through
the acquisition of mechanical means of reproducing such services.
And third, the production of these increasingly complex material

commodities necessitates a vast expansion in service employment, in planning, forecasting and marketing such commodities, and in the organisation of labour-power and money-capital (see Mandel, 1972, ch.2). Gershuny suggests that at least half of all those in service occupations are in fact engaged, either directly in primary or secondary industries, or indirectly in providing services related to the production of material commodities (see 1978, ch.6; Greenfield, 1966).

Thus, although post-industrial theorists are incorrect in arguing that there is a post-industrial society which is based on the predominant consumption of services, there is nevertheless a distinctive shift towards service employment in most of the major capitalist societies. By 1975 service employment exceeded manufacturing employment in all European countries except West Germany and Luxembourg (see Marquand, 1980, p.27). Incidentally, the UK is relatively distinctive in the degree to which its manufacturing sector has shrunk. Manufacturing output has decreased from a peak in 1973, while manufacturing employment has fallen by nearly two and a half million between 1966 and 1981 (see Singh, 1977; Barratt Brown, 1981; and Showler and Sinfield, 1981). Since 1970, while most economies have experienced job-less growth in manufacturing, Britain first experienced a period of job-destroying growth, then one of job-destroying zero-growth, and finally one of job-destroying manufacturing collapse (see Marquand, 1980, pp.28-30 for very useful comparative material).

This means that when we consider the de-industrialisation of the UK economy, this implies both the growth, relatively and absolutely, in service employment, and enormous increases in unemployment and under-employment. On the first, it is important not to see this growth as natural, as inevitably resulting from some natural history of economic change, in which first extractive, then industrial, and finally service employment, is dominant (see Sabolo, 1975; and Urry, 1981b, pp.7-13). We may at the cost of considerable over-simplification consider those factors which account for the apparently homogeneous expansion of the service sector: the extension of intermediate functions dependent upon the increasingly specialised division of labour; the increased need for workers to ensure the realisation of value within an epoch in which the opportunities for offsetting the falling rate of profit are minimal (e.g., market research); the extension of commodity production to new areas where all or almost all the labour is mental (e.g., producing computer software); the increased embodiment of conception away from labour and within separate organisations which can be seen as fulfilling functions for capital (e.g., operations research); the growth of new technology which permits the greater socialisation of pre-existing service work (e.g., audio-visual aids); and the expansion of the state and the resultant development of socialised forms by which to reproduce labour-power (e.g., health). The effect of these is to produce increases in recorded employment in the service sector, especially of so-called producer services. The fact that there are these different determinants of the increase thus means that there is no simple relationship which can be posited between manufacturing industry and the service sector. Each component of the latter will exemplify

a different structure and that employment change will be the
consequence of the particular forms of restructuring pertinent within
each of the aspects outlined above.

The second most obvious consequence of de-industrialisation is
to produce huge increases in levels of unemployment and under-
employment. The following are some of the main points to note:
(a) the level of registered unemployment is about 3 million and
likely to rise to 3½ million within the next six months or so
(February 1982); (b) according to the 1977 General Household Survey
we can add 25-30 per cent to this figure to indicate the number of
non-registered unemployed (see GHS, 1977 (1979), p.67, and Showler
and Sinfield, 1981, p.9 on the 'discouraged worker' effect); (c) the
majority of the labour force is rarely unemployed while a small but
growing proportion bears much of the impact (recently 3 per cent
have born 70 per cent of the weeks of unemployment in a single year;
see Metcalf, 1980, pp.25, 27); (d) however, even between 1976 and
1977 over 10 per cent of males had experienced some period of
unemployment in the previous twelve months (see GHS, 1977 (1979),
pp.57, 68); (e) there has been a very marked increase in the number
of long-term unemployed (those unemployed one year or more is now
over 1 million); (f) the supply of labour will continue to rise
with perhaps up to one million more in the labour force by the end
of the 1960s - thus without any decline in the demand for labour
there would need to be 800 new jobs created each day in order to
maintain the present balance of demand and supply of jobs (see
Showler and Sinfield, 1981, p.6); (g) there is a considerable
decline in the rate of economic activity in the UK: for example,
between mid-1979 to end-1980 the working population fell by one
million - in 1981 it was about the same as it had been in 1971;
(h) there is a decline in the proportion of people employed on a
full-time basis throughout the year - in the USA in most industries
only about 60 per cent of the employed population work full-time
for the whole year (see Castells, 1980, p.182).

At the same time, there is some evidence of an increase in the
informalisation of the economy. I am not suggesting that there
has simply been a corresponding development of the informal economy
in order to compensate those who have been excluded from the
formal economy. Indeed it is clear that access to the informal
economy is highly uneven and to some extent it will be connected
with access to certain elements within the formal economy. The
first set of evidence for the growth in a substantial informal
sector in the 1970s comes from the divergence between the GDPs
of income and expenditure. If the latter exceeds the former then
this will imply that there are fairly large amounts of income which
are unrecorded. During the 1960s this difference was only 1 per
cent (of GDP of expenditure) but by the 1970s it had risen to 3 per
cent (see Macafee, 1980, pp.84-5). We can take this as prima facie
evidence for some increase in the forms of irregular or hidden
sources of income. A second set of evidence relates to changes in
the taxation system. The introduction of VAT and the fact that
income tax is paid by most income-recipients, encourages numerous
forms of tax-avoidance and tax-evasion. Joel Barnett suggested
that the latter represented a loss of £3,500 million in 1980-1
(Guardian, 30 January 1981), while the chairman of the Board of

Inland Revenue calculates that income undeclared for tax may represent
at least $7\frac{1}{2}$ per cent GDP (Macafee, 1980, p.86). The effect of
reasonably high personal taxation (note the shift away from company
to personal taxation in recent years) is an inducement (a) to do the
job required oneself; or (b) to pay someone under-the-counter; or
(c) to get someone to do it free in exchange for some goods or
service one can provide; or (d) to pay for it using money acquired
irregularly within the household economy. Burns says that the effect
of high personal taxation is that initiative and incentive reappear
outside the market-place in the efforts of individuals and families
to create for themselves that for which they once paid (Burns, 1977,
p.163). And finally, we can anticipate that the growth of capital
investment within the household (see above, pp.30-1) enables many
people, who are either not employed, or only irregularly employed
within the formal economy, to engage in monetised or non-monetised
irregular work. Especially with the relatively rising cost of
services there is much incentive to provide the service oneself, or
to provide it for others on an informal basis. Burns suggests that
in the USA, even by 1966, the value of household property exceeded
that of private capital, and that it becomes increasingly rational
to work longer hours in the household economy and to use domestic
capital goods to replace paid services (see 1977, pp. 55, 191).

Connected to the development of a progressively de-industrialised
economy has been the very considerable expansion of employment by
the state, which has produced very considerable changes in the
economic structure of many localities. Such economies were once
dominated by a relatively small number of private manufacturing
firms, who were involved in numerous commodity and interpersonal
linkages with the locality and with the surrounding region. Now
these economies are dominated, or at least strongly influenced, by
large state employers. Relatively few large manufacturing
establishments remain and they have limited linkages with other
locally based capital. Small private employers will be substantially
dependent upon the expansion or contraction of state expenditure
(see Murgatroyd and Urry, 1982, on the effects in Lancaster).
Dunleavy argues that the realm of state employment is a crucial
cleavage within national and local economies, on a par with that
between the corporate and market sectors (see Dunleavy, 1980a,
1980b). Indeed he points out that the combined effect of state
employment, unemployment and underemployment (including early
retirement and so on) meant that even as early as 1976 only two
out of every five voters in the UK were employees of private
companies (Dunleavy, 1980a, p.367).

In the following section, I will try to clarify some of the
political consequences of these economic changes. However, in
assessing such changes it is important not to construct a misleading
picture of economic and political struggles prior to 'de-industrialisation'. Roughly speaking the most significant form of
oppositional struggle within the industrial period of British
capitalism was economic militancy, combined with support for
separate political struggle within the Labour party. This pattern
was found in the major industries - coal, steel, docks, railways,
engineering, automobiles, etc. In each case there were a number of
distinctive features: large numbers in each workplace, a high

proportion of male workers, some development of an occupational
community, and the centrality of that industry to the national
economy. Yet, at the same time, many areas and industrial sectors
were not economically militant. What we now have to consider is not
only what are the forms of politics characteristic of de-industrialisation, but also what the effects that this de-industrialising pattern
will have on *existing* patterns of accumulation and struggle within
each area. In other words, there is not a single form of politics
which will result from 'de-industrialisation'. We will thus try to
illumine how the impact of new patterns of private accumulation,
state activity, occupational change, and patterns of job loss, will
restructure existing forms of economic and political struggle. It
is important not to see these changes as simply undermining existing
forms of struggle.

This point can be illustrated by briefly considering Massey's
analysis of how industrial restructuring is a process of class
restructuring (1980). In particular, she considers the differences
between coal-mining localities, especially in South Wales, and
industry and politics in Cornwall. In the former case, it is not
difficult to see how a number of conditions ensured the pattern of
economic militancy: a relatively undifferentiated working class;
a single union; pride in the masculine character of mining and
steel work; the relative lack of a new middle class or a small
entrepreneurial capital; and the lack of alternative forms of labour
(Massey, 1980, pp.3-6; on masculinity and work, see Cockburn, 1981).
However, the decline in the mining industry and the arrival of
multinational plants and new forms of service employment has
threatened the power and dominance of especially the mineworkers.
There are the following effects: first, to increase the size of
the 'new middle class' and thus to blur lines of conflict between
labour and capital; second, to increase 'external control' of the
region and hence the difference between South Wales and more
'central' regions and to heighten the demand for more top management
and professional jobs within the region (rather than the regaining
of the functions of conception and control); third, to decrease
the average skill level and to increase semi- and unskilled labour
especially for women and hence to undermine the homogeneity,
uniqueness, maleness, income and status of the previous dominant
forms of labour; and fourth, to introduce capitalist or state wage-
relations to a relatively inexperienced and unorganised labour
force (Massey, 1980, pp.6-14).

Massey then considers the impact of similar industrial and
occupational changes on Cornwall. Here she suggests the following
opposite effects are to be found: first, to increase waged labour
and not to depress wage levels; second, to produce a more
homogeneous working class and other waged sectors; and third, to
threaten traditional capital with competition in both the labour
and commodity markets and hence to increase previously highly
blurred lines of conflict between capital and labour (Massey, 1980,
pp.14-16). Hence, the impact of a roughly similar pattern of
accumulation and state activity seems to have produced different
effects because it is articulated with a quite different pre-existing
structure. Massey convincingly shows that in order to assess the
significance of the trends to de-industrialisation, we cannot

characterise regions simply in terms of their present industrial/
occupational/class changes. In the next section I will consider how
to analyse such spatial transformations in the forms of social
struggle in more detail.

REGIONS, LOCALITIES AND FORMS OF STRUGGLE

I will begin here by making some general observations on relations
of time and space within contemporary capitalism. The most
distinctive feature of this period is an extraordinary increase in
the degree of what Giddens has recently called time-space
distanciation (see Giddens, 1981, ch.4). In particular, capital
has been transformed at the end of the last upward long wave
(especially during the 1960s) and during the onset of the downward
wave in the 1970s. New modes of control have developed which
transcend conventional limitations of time and space. Modern
capitalist enterprise is no longer dependent upon the immediate
presence of controllers. There are of course those who convey
decisions but it is generally clear that they are acting merely to
implement the structure of control whose locus may be spatially
located on the other side of the globe. The exercise of power does
not depend upon the presence of the controllers, or even the
potential presence of the controllers - and much of the effective
control will result from the devising of a corporate strategy
which simultaneously unifies the activities of spatially highly
differentiated units. The need for spatial proximity, which
resulted from the time taken to convey information or decisions,
has been transformed by the development of electronically transmitted
information. As a consequence, offices have been split off from
workplaces, and different workplaces themselves have been split
off from each other in terms of different labour-forces employed
and the resultant labour-processes.
    However, at the same time, there has not been a corresponding
transformation of labour. People still live in households which are
grouped together in various localities (of varying degrees of
density), which are defined partly in terms of the overlapping co-
presence of residents, and partly in terms of an attachment to the
built environment and its relationship to nature. Localities are
thus the prime site in which social practices are made and sustained,
social practices which constitute social systems (Giddens, 1981,
p.27). Hence, labour is organised into relatively self-sustaining
localities which are based on a much more limited degree of time-
space distanciation compared with capital. And although most people
live in cities in capitalist societies, cities have become
progressively less powerful. Indeed Giddens argues that they have
never been the dominant time-space container or crucible of power
within capitalist societies (see Giddens, 1981, ch.6). This is
assumed instead by the territorially bounded nation-state. This
therefore accounts for the manner in which the local state is
integrated within the overall national state structure (but see
Cawson and Saunders, Chapter 1 of this volume, for a partly contrary
view). Cities have also been weakened by the collapse of indigenous
manufacturing industry; and by the fact that it is the more rural,

less-industrialised areas in the UK which have expanded in population and employment in the recent period (see Fothergill and Gudgin, 1979, for details of this).

These spatial relations can be considered at three levels: first, the spatial patterns implied by the regularities and routines of everyday life - what Pred terms the 'weaving dance through time-space' (1977, p.208; and see 1981 for more general discussion); second, the spatial relations implied by a given social structure, such as the relatively separated organisations of households within civil society; and third, the spatial effects of the relations between distinct social (and hence spatially and temporally located) structures, such as that between worldwide forms of capital accumulation and relatively bounded, immobile and individualised households of civil society. Moreover, these effects are also interrelated temporally. Thus, the consequences of a particular social practice depend upon the manner in which distinct social structures are spatially interdependent over time. Assessment of such spatial effects thus depends upon analysing the particular temporal relations between the causally pertinent social structures. Hence, certain transformations in particular social structures and in their consequential spatial and temporal interdependences produce distinct spatial effects; namely, new variations in local systems of strati-fication, an increased significance of regional or local deprivations of one's own stratification structure vis-à-vis one or more other structures, and a heightened importance of struggles centred around the locality vis-à-vis other local/regional/national structures. What then are the transformations in the particular social structures and in their consequential spatial and temporal interdependences which produce these particular spatial consequences? There are two particular transformations that are important here.

First, the increased concentration and centralisation of capital (see Prais, 1976), which has, as we have noted, the effect of dramatically increasing the time-space distanciation of modern capitalist societies. Internationally organised capital can therefore redistribute its activities in order to take advantage of all possible variations in the price, organisation, skills and availability of the relatively immobile local labour force (see discussion in Westaway, 1974; Massey, 1981; Urry, 1981c). In particular, it is argued by Fröbel, Heinrichs and Kreye (1980) that the following three developments have greatly increased the likelihood of industrial production being established in 'world-market factories' in the Third World: first, some capitalisation of Third World agriculture, so releasing a huge industrial reserve army; second, the above-mentioned fragmentation of the production process which enables certain sub-processes to be carried out by very briefly trained unskilled/semi-skilled workers; and third, the development of a globally efficient transportation and communications technology (see the critical discussion in Jacobson, Wickham, Wickham, 1979). Thus a world-wide market for labour has been established in which workers from all capitalist (and in part state-socialist) countries compete with each other. To some degree a new hierarchy of economies has been established and this depends in part upon the relative cheapness and availability of labour (see Cohen, 1981, on the effects of this especially on the urban hierarchy).

Second, the increased role of state employment and expenditure.
There are a number of interrelated aspects: the enlarged range of
functions including especially the productive as well as the
allocative (see Offe, 1975); the development of the state as the
manager of the everyday-life of individuals within civil society
(see Castells, 1978); its centrality in the employment structure of
very many localities and regions (see Cooke, 1980, on South Wales,
for example); some heightening of the separation between the local
and central state (see Cawson and Saunders, Chapter 1 in this volume,
as well as the extensive discussion in Cooke, 1983); the centrality
of struggles within civil society both to affect the state directly
and to use the state to affect the location of capital (see the
discussions in Carney, Hudson and Lewis, 1980); and finally, although
there are these significant extensions of state activity, it remains
very firmly national with a particular structured relationship to
civil society within a given territory (see Giddens, 1981, ch.8,
on the nation-state).

We will now consider some of the spatial consequences of these
processes, beginning with the development of new local variations in
contemporary local stratification structures. There are a number of
significant recent changes whose impact varies considerably from
locality to locality: (a) decline in size of the 'capitalist class',
of those owning and controlling capital; (b) decline in the inter-
linkages between local capitals; (c) increase in the tendency for
the owners of capital to be resident outside the locality and to
be uninvolved in local politics; (d) heightened separation between
local/regional capital and national/international capital; (e)
extensive developments of the service class and of deskilled white-
collar workers, especially employed by the state; (f) increased
feminisation of the labour force, especially of deskilled white-
collar workers; (g) decreased size of the working class, both male
and especially female; and (h) rapid growth in a substantial under-
class of unemployed and under-employed (see Abercrombie and Urry,
1982, ch.7 on many of these points). The interrelation between
these changes means that there is a heightened variety of local
stratification structures. To illustrate this the following are
four important types (I am using local here ambiguously as referring
to any non-national structure; I am also ignoring ethnic differences):

1 Large national or multinationals as dominant capital – small
   service class and deskilled white-collar workers – large working
   class, either mainly male or female, depending on supposed
   skill levels.
2 State as dominant employer – largish service class – many
   deskilled white-collar workers – declining working class –
   high employment of women.
3 Traditional small capitals as dominant employers – large petit
   bourgeois sector – small service class–few deskilled white-
   collar places – largish male working class – lowish female
   employment.
4 Private service sector capitals as dominant employers – large
   service class – many deskilled white-collar workers – many
   female workers – smallish working class.

Thus far I have argued that important changes in contemporary
capitalism will produce significant variations in local class

structures. I will now consider how such differences may give rise
to local or regional deprivations. This issue has been explored
by Buck (1979). He points out that, although in certain countries
there was some lessening in regional inequality in the 1970s, there
was no obvious reduction in the 'regional sense of grievance' (1979).
Buck argues that it is important to consider, not the quantifiable
economic indicators such as regional income, growth or employment
levels, but rather the 'deeper' class structures present within
capitalism (Buck, 1979, p.518, and see Buck and Atkins, 1978). Thus,
even if there were a full equalisation of economic indicators across
all regions within capitalism, there would still be substantial
class inequalities. Moreover, these class conflicts may assume a
spatial form if class interests are localised. In particular, Buck
analyses the consequences which follow from the imbalanced distribution of classes between regions which produce a sense of regional
grievance. If particular classes are overwhelmingly concentrated
in some regions rather than others, then there will be grievance
experienced in these regions relatively deprived of dominant class
locations. And this will be increasingly the case as its inter-
nationalisation enables capital to appropriate space in an ever
more subtle and complex manner. Buck points out that there is
increasing concentration of higher order activities within the
centre (of 'orientation', 'planning and development') and of routine
industrial processes (both clerical and manual) within peripheral
areas (also see Buswell and Lewis, 1970, and Leigh and North, 1978).
This process has been clarified by McEnery who points out that
between 1965 and 1977 the south-east increased its proportion of
service workers from 56 per cent to 67 per cent (1981, p.27).
Indeed, this increasing concentration of service employment is seen
as having produced a 'sociological trap' in part caused by the bias
of regional policy against service industry.

Buck goes on to postulate that the more pronounced is this
centralisation of 'higher-order' service activities the greater
will be the ensuing sense of regional deprivation. In his analysis,
he finds that in terms of a number of measures, Britain and France
exhibit fairly high regional variations in the proportions of 'high
order to total male allocable employment' (Buck, 1979, p.521).
Germany and Australia by contrast exhibit much lower rates of
dispersion of the proportions of higher-order to total male
employment. Thus the reason why France and Britain exhibit higher
rates of regional grievance is because there is a more unequal
class distribution between the different regions in these two
countries. He summarises:

> regional grievances in Britain and France are correlated with
> a high degree of regional concentration in high-order jobs,
> i.e. public and private sector control is heavily concentrated
> in regions such as the southeast of England and Paris at the
> expense of peripheral areas like the north of England and France
> Nord (Buck, 1979, p.523; for detailed changes in different
> regions in Britain, see Buck and Atkins, 1978, p.214).

One difficulty in this otherwise interesting argument is that
Buck concentrates on the spatial allocation of male occupations
and ignores the significant changes in female occupations referred
to earlier. However, the main difficulty concerns the widespread

presumption that all those problems and issues which concern the distribution of activities within the geographical area of the nation are to be viewed as 'regional'. Buck does refer to the imbalances within regions (Buck, 1979, p.522), but concentrates in his analysis purely on the differences between regions. In the following, I shall argue that the concept of region is not well established and that we should consider the 'local social structure' as an equally salient unit of analysis (see further discussion in Urry, 1981c).

We can begin by noting that there are two rival principles by which an area might be designated a region (see Brown, 1972, p.27f). The first is that of homogeneity - that the area contains a particular set of shared economic, cultural and political features which mean that it should be treated as a unit. The second is that of self-sufficiency - that the area contains a set of relatively self-contained and complementary activities which justify its treatment as a self-sufficient unit. These principles may be antithetic - the former leading to the isolation of areas sharing some characteristic (e.g., dependence on a particular industry like textiles) - the latter leading to the isolation of areas which embrace a number of different characteristics (the inter-dependence of different industries). The main problem, however, is that the nature of the spatial distribution of activity and population at any one time is in part the outcome of a whole series of previous rounds of accumulation each with its own spatial division of labour superimposed on the other (see Massey, 1978). And each round of accumulation is itself the effect of a large number of determinants, including the patterns of class and popular struggle, and of state action. And the effect of these successive spatial divisions of labour does not now generally produce coherent economies on either principle mentioned earlier. In particular, contemporary spatial divisions of labour are not based upon regional specialisation. Hence, the attempt to impose 'regions', distinctive entities defined in terms of supposed homogeneity or self-sufficient interdependence, is not a plausible project. It results from the way in which the state has attempted to devise non-national economic policies. So although there are spatial problems, there is no coherent concept of 'the region'. What we find is that there are a variety of patterns in terms of which capital appropriates time and space. The superimposition of these different patterns gives rise to spatial inequalities but there is no warrant for treating these as 'regional'. So although Buck's account of analysis of spatial inequality is of interest it is necessary to develop further understanding on the basis of in part non-regional spatial concepts.

These changes within contemporary capitalism mean that the organisation of local labour markets are of singular significance in structuring the patterns of industrial location (see Urry, 1981c, for further discussion; more generally see the excellent discussion in Cooke, 1983, ch.8). Large mobile capital operating on a world-wide scale is able to identify different labour markets in relation-ship to its various fractional operations, and in relationship to small-scale subcontracting capital. These operations will not all be located in particular regions but rather in terms of the range of different labour markets available. It is the local labour

market which is relevant to capital, not the overall region.
International capital (that which enjoys 'international spatial
elasticity', Hamilton, 1978, pp.37-8) may have no other interest
in the region. This further means labour markets are in part
spatially segmented, as well as segmented in a variety of other
forms (see Kreckel, 1980). Thus, in the process by which capital
rotates in and out of particular sectors, the segmentation between
what may be spatially contiguous labour markets will be important
in allowing the existence of plants which occupy different places
within the spatial division of labour within a particular industrial
sector. However, it is important not to overemphasise the mobility
of capital here. It is necessary also to consider the changing forms
by which capital is restructured within each sector, and the
consequential demands for different kinds of labour-power which are
therefore required (see Murgatroyd and Urry, 1982, on the effects of
different forms of restructuring upon a local economy).

These are clearly complex issues. I will now consider some of
the consequences for local politics. First, it will be to decompose
further national classes, and in particular to undermine the regional
basis of conventional working-class politics (as in South Wales,
the North-East, etc.). And second, especially while the economy is
being de-industrialised, this central importance of the local labour
market will heighten the significance of non-class-based politics
which are focussed around the axis, the local social structure vis-à-
vis capital and the state. Clearly, the local basis of potential
mobilisation will vary, from being conurbation-wide (as in the case
of the 'Save Merseyside' campaign) to being town or city-specific
(see 'Local Socialism', no.6, February 1980, on the 'Save Consett'
campaign). In either case, however, there may well be disparate
struggles directed against either or both large-scale capital and
the state, from the perceived consequences of how 'external control'
is undermining the strength of the local economy. As the 'Merseyside
in Crisis' report put it:

As the traditional industries continued to contract, the
penetration of the multi-nationals created a further vulnerability.
The future of Merseyside's workers was more often than not in the
hands of companies whose power centres were continents away. And
if not Detroit or Tokyo, then London (Merseyside Socialist
Research Group, 1980, p.41).

In some places this has generated something of a 'local social
movement' based on protecting the locality (broadly defined except
in the case of conurbations in terms of the local labour market)
against capital and the state. This 'movement' may well be highly
disparate, it will include a number of distinct social forces which
are on other issues opposed to each other (local labour movement
and local small capital), and it will employ a variety of tactics
(from marches, strikes and sit-ins to lobbying MPs, entertaining
potential employers, etc.). Supposedly like 'urban social movements',
there is a 'growing homogeneity in the interests of all popular
classes' (Castells, 1978, p.61). However, in this case it is an
homogeneity that does not transcend the locality but is one which
is based on the specific differences between that and other
localities. The homogenisation is only local (see the discussion
of local struggles over 'reproduction' within Denmark, in Jensen

and Simonsen, 1981). So although there is often considerable
mobilisation of popular forces, and these may well provide much of
the original impetus for the local social movement, this mobilisation
can do little but to fragment social classes and to prioritise non-
class based political movements (the journal 'Local Socialism' is
a very interesting effort to prevent this). These local struggles
are not generally intended to abolish capitalist relations but to
increase the capitalisation of that locality, in order in effect to
sustain its reproduction. They are also intended to increase, or
at least to prevent any decrease in the manufacturing base of the
local economy; that is, to counter its de-industrialisation and the
growth of both services and the informal economy. However,
paradoxically, the struggles to sustain manufacturing employment
will increase the likelihood that that locality will be further
deskilled, and to be treated as a repository of secondary labour,
perhaps on a par with many Third World economies (this is a summary
of part of Urry, 1981c; see the articles in Crick, 1981, for details
of the de-industrialisation of various local/regional economies).

There are two other political consequences which in part follow
from processes of de-industrialisation. First, one of the effects
of the relative cheapening of domestic capital goods is to encourage
new or revised forms of household enterprise. In particular, we
may anticipate an extension of petit bourgeois activity, resulting
in part from the positive rejection of waged employment within the
formal economy, whether of large corporations, or the state.
Contrary to the arguments of Braverman or Mandel on the 'universal
market' (see Braverman, 1974, and Mandel, 1972) it would seem that
there is a rotation by capital in and out of different departments
and commodity sectors. As a result profitable openings are available,
in rotation within different sectors, to small-scale capital or to
a kind of counter-cultural petit bourgeoisie (see Gershuny and
Pahl, 1980, on these developments). They are able to use relatively
cheap household capital goods, they can save on overheads, they
are funded in part through the state (directly or through transfer
payments), and they can serve local markets. This possibility of
extending the household and informal economy has potentially an
important consequence in commodifying, individualising, and
marginalising particular political struggles.

Second, this development can be seen as one aspect of the more
general shift in political forms, partly away from the politics of
production to the politics of consumption. Gartner and Riessman
(1974) argue that (a) the industrial worker is no longer the leading
force for social change and that this role is now played by youth,
women, the minorities, and the 'educated affluents'; (b) the major
movements now are related to consumer-oriented issues - the environment, participation, inflation, taxation, the quality of life;
(c) a new dimension of politics has emerged which de-emphasises
electoralism and traditional organisations, and focusses instead
upon movements, boycotts, publicity, legal actions, consciousness-
raising and community action; and (d) the basis for these politics
is a new consumer consciousness which stems from the unique
conjuncture by which individuals are consumers both of the
sophisticated products of capitalist production and of the services
especially of the state (see Gartner and Reissman, 1974, especially

ch.3; as well as the discussion in Miller, 1975). Two particular
features of a progressively de-industrialised capitalism have
contributed to this: on the one hand, because a considerable
portion of the population will not have to work within the industrial
work force it will be more open to a variety of alternative
consumption and value orientations; and on the other hand, the
profitable production of capitalist commodities requires that
consumers are constantly stimulated to feel dissatisfied with last
year's product and to seek new forms of commodified satisfaction.
The workings of these factors generate particular contradictions
for those groups who are least able to enter those occupations
yielding the incomes necessary to obtain such commodities and
services. Exploitation has then in part shifted to the sphere of
circulation and is expressed through rising taxation, inflation,
faulty commodities, declining provision of services, and so on.
Struggle shifts to this domain of consumption and is reflected both
in the formation of specifically consumer bodies, and more generally
in what Dunleavy (1979) terms 'consumption sectors'. Saunders
(1979, p.136) talks of the development of 'consumer trade unionism',
namely, limited, piecemeal, reactive and localised expressions of
solidarism and dissent which may affect small shifts in resources
but which do not entail larger-scale conflicts and struggle.

Cawson and Saunders (Chapter 1 in this volume) have tried to
systematise this distinction between production politics and
consumption politics. They present this in terms of two ideal
types. On the one hand, there is the sphere of the politics of
production. Here capital and labour are directly represented as
classes and they both negotiate with the state in the corporate
sphere of the polity. Such politics are conducted mainly at the
central and regional levels. And on the other hand, there is the
sphere of the politics of consumption. In this case a plurality
of consumption sectors mobilise as non-class-based interest groups.
They battle with each other over specific issues within the
competitive sphere of the polity. These struggles are conducted in
part at the central level but mainly at the more accessible local
level. The latter struggles are fragmented by the diversity of
consumption sectors, mobilisation is likely to vary greatly from
issue to issue, and the possibilities of generating widely based
local struggles, let alone national struggles, are highly limited.
Local politics and regional/national politics are relatively
separated (see Saunders, 1981a, pp.265-75).

There is, however, one particular difficulty with this formulation.
It is surely not the case that local struggles necessarily revolve
around the politics of consumption. The de-industrialisation of an
economy effects a substantial restructuring of the politics of
production. This is partly because production is put back on the
political agenda (if every it went off) but in a manner in which
struggles revolve around the re-capitalisation of localities.
Furthermore, various kinds of inter-regional and intra-regional
conflict are heightened, partly focussed upon the unequal spatial
distribution of industries and occupations. Struggles are oriented
around the form taken by capitalist/state activity. The consequence
of the imposition of new rounds of accumulation, with 'service'
industry as the leading sector, will tend to disrupt working-class

politics, partly because of the decline in the absolute and relative
size of the traditional working class, and partly because of the
increased local effectivity of service sector employees. This thus
means that there are local struggles focussed on production, but
often these will not take a directly class-structured form. However,
at the same time, increasing numbers of workers in Britain will not
be employed within capitalist enterprises. To the extent there is a
growth of informal forms of economic organisation then there will be
a further development both of consumption politics and of struggles
to push back even further both capitalist and state forms of
production. There is then an important realm of production struggles
generated within capitalist Britain, but these are progressively
focussed upon the optimal relationship between the formal and
informal economies and between the state and private industry. We
can anticipate that the growth of the household as a unit both of
consumption but more particularly of material production will further
encourage struggles of a non-labourist, individualist kind - what
Banfield terms in another context 'amoral familialism' (see 1958).
Certain of these struggles may even involve opposition to capitalist
relations but often in a manner which involves opting out of
regular, sustained, and full-time employment within capitalist
enterprises or within the state.

CONCLUSION

I have thus tried to detail some of the important political
consequences of de-industrialisation - namely, that in certain
regions conventional trade uhion and labourist politics will be
undermined, although perhaps developed elsewhere; that crucial
importance is to be attached to localised, disparate forms of
struggle, especially to efforts to re-capitalise the locality; that
the household is an important determinant of political practice and
that varieties of household economic and social relations will
fundamentally affect political responses; and that the growth in
service employment, however related to capitalist production, will
generate alternative forms of limited, transitory and shifting
struggles particularly within the politics of consumption. We do
seem to be moving out of the heavily industrialised era of Western
capitalism - but not into a post-industrial society. Neither the
conceptual apparatus sociologists employ for industrial capitalism,
nor that generated in the optimism of 1960s post-industrialism, seem
appropriate to the task of understanding contemporary Britain which
appears more akin to a non-industrialised country, but one with
much of the structural and cultural heritage of a former industrial
country - perhaps we will increasingly talk of FICs, 'former
industrial countries'. But to the extent to which the elaboration
of civil society and the extension of the state depended upon the
growth of capitalist production, then if that production declines
within any particular nation-state, the basis for civil society and
the state will also be threatened. As a result former industrial
countries will polarise around two kinds of oppositional struggle:
one to increase capitalist activity, especially at the local level;
the other to protect the social practices of civil society and the

state which were developed when the sphere of reproduction was
dominant.   Thus, it will be increasingly the case that the sphere
of struggle will not be determined by either the sphere of circulation
or of reproduction.   Rather, fragments will be formed around the two
kinds of oppositional struggle just mentioned.   Conventional political
parties will find enormous difficulty in articulating these disparate
struggles in late capitalist, former industrial societies, of which
the UK is the prime example; but, at the same time, there seems to
be little to be gained by characterising contemporary politics as
simply 'corporatist'.

Chapter 3

POWER, POLICY AND THE CITY OF LONDON

Michael Moran

DOES THE CITY EXIST?

The apparently plain language in which we conventionally discuss
interest group politics actually contains many curious assumptions.
The common categories used to distinguish great interests - organised
labour, manufacturing industry - involve at best striking simplifications, at worst gross distortions. Such simplification is a
particular danger in discussing the City of London. In many accounts
of economic policy-making in Britain 'the City' is treated as a
clearly distinguished and united interest; on occasion it is even
pictured as synonymous with the financial community. Yet such
usage involves serious distortion, for that conventional phrase
'the City' suggests a set of interests both more precise and
distinct than is the case in messy reality.

   'The City' in practice means a variety of things. Precisely and
historically it refers to a geographical area defined by the
boundaries of a local government unit. Within this area much of
the nation's financial business has traditionally been done, though
it is only in the present century that financial institutions have
come utterly to dominate the geographical City (Dunning and Morgan,
1971). There is much to be said for such a restricted geographical
definition: it is precise and it reflects the common observation
that concentration into a small physical area has fostered special
attitudes among financiers. Yet in a world where financial markets
are increasingly organised on a supra-national scale, where a market
is commonly a set of points on a telecommunications network rather
than an institution with a central physical location, and where
individual financial institutions increasingly disperse their
operations beyond London, a geographical definition has declining
use.

   Against this narrow and precise definition may be set the common
practice of identifying 'the City' with the whole financial
community. This was always an illegitimate practice, for there
never was a time when all British financial institutions were
controlled from London; but what a generation ago would only have
been an annoying imprecision is now a great distortion. This is
because one of the most significant economic developments of the

last two decades has been the rise to prominence of financial
institutions not traditionally connected to the geographical City.
The most obvious of these are the building societies which dominate
the market in housing finance and challenge traditional City
institutions, like the clearing banks in the market for personal
savings. Even where newly significant institutions are located in
the City - as is the case, for instance, with many pension funds -
their connections with government, and thus how they set about
interest representation, are very different from traditional City
ways of going about things.

As a compromise between the precise narrowness of a geographical
definition and the looseness of treating London as if it were
synonymous with all financial institutions, we may sensibly work
with a picture of a series of institutions trading within and out
of the historical City of London. Almost all trading done by such
City institutions is carried on in financial markets: that is, it
involves dealing in financial claims rather than in physical goods.
Trading takes place in a variety of financial instruments, and the
conventional institutional outlines of the City largely reflect
these different instruments. Thus the Stock Exchange is a market
specialising in company securities and public debt; Lloyds trades
in insurance and reinsurance claims; a range of markets organise
buying and selling of claims to large tranches of money; a number
of less important markets - notably those in commodities - are
apparently markets in goods but are in practice another way of
trading financial claims.

Picturing the City as a series of markets has the considerable
advantage of alerting us to one of the most significant features of
modern financial life, its extraordinary capacity for innovation:
new markets, new instruments and thus new interests are constantly
being created. Yet even this definition involves simplifications
on a heroic (or foolhardy) scale. Many City institutions do a good
deal more than trade in financial claims, and their diverse
activities cannot be parcelled out in discrete sections. The
obvious examples are the clearing banks which trade in many City
markets but also provide a nationwide money transmission system
and numerous customer services in their retail branch networks.
An even more dangerous simplification is involved in treating a
host of separate and specialised markets as if they were linked by
obvious common interests and ways of defending those interests. The
most casual observation soon dispels the illusion that there exists
in the City either a community of interests or agreement on tactics.

Similar problems of defining the character and boundary of common
interests of course exist in examining other groups such as the
professions, labour or manufacturing industry, but the difficulties
are especially stark in the case of the City because of the unusual
way in which financial markets have practised interest representation.
The characteristic instrument of representation used by most great
interests is the peak association or the trade association. Consequently, the best studies of individual interests have been able to
avoid the trickier questions of definition by focussing on the
policies and tactics of such associations (Eckstein, 1960; May, 1975;
Grant and Marsh, 1977).

No such solution is possible in studying the City for one of its

most distinctive features has been a reluctance to practise the open
and formal representation characteristic of other interests. The
practical consequence is that there exists no peak association
speaking for the City. This contrast between the common forms of
interest representation and the forms practised by financial markets
provides the theme of this chapter. I begin by sketching in the
pattern of pressure group politics, and follow this by describing
the very different pattern traditionally existing in the City. In
this traditional distinctiveness lay the special, and often elusive,
power of London's financial institutions. The last two decades
have, however, seen important changes in the way City markets
practise interest representation. These changes have also accompanied
a decline in the City's traditional power. The result is that while
the influence of individual institutions and markets remains great,
it is doubtful if the City can any longer be pictured as a cohesive,
corporate interest.

THE CITY AND INTEREST REPRESENTATION

The characteristic way in which powerful interests have influenced
policy-making in modern Britain may be summarised in one word:
they have done so *bureaucratically*. Their chief instrument has been
bureaucratic organisation: labour, industry, the professions have
all created formal, specialist institutions with a paid staff
designed to represent members' interests. These institutions in
turn have stimulated a bureaucratic style of lobbying: developing
close contact with civil servants in Whitehall; intervening
continuously in the policy process at the stages where official
advice and proposals are being prepared; participating in a wide
variety of official advisory committees and executive bodies.
These institutional manifestations of a bureaucratic style have
been matched by a more elusive development: associations in
continuous contact with Whitehall have taken on bureaucratic styles
of argument which emphasise the formal presentation of a case
supported by systematic evidence. Out of bureaucratic organisation
and a bureaucratic style have come an emphasis on bureaucratic
implementation: in other words, the chief purpose of interest
representation has been to affect formal policies, notably those
given force by legislation.
     The City's peculiarity was that until very recently it rejected
forms of interest representation involving bureaucratic organisation,
style and implementation. Formal institutions like trade associations and other regulating bodies were, true, common in the markets;
indeed in many cases they were central to organising economic
activity, but the trade associations had few bureaucratic features.
They were often no more than a letterhead, rarely employed full-
time staff and had few written rules. When the officers of the
London Discount Market Association told the Radcliffe Committee that
they were only 'a small, haphazard Association' they were expressing
a common indifference to formality (Radcliffe, 1960a, p.258). Bodies
with a more elaborate regulatory role, like the Stock Exchange
Council, could not be quite so indifferent, but in regulation the
City was nevertheless marked by a conscious rejection of formality
and precise rules.

The consequence was that interest representation depended much more than was the case elsewhere on links between the authorities and particular firms and personalities. Indeed the very notion of a separate activity called 'representation' would have made little sense to most people in the City a couple of decades ago: consultation and the expression of views occurred as a by-product of doing business and mixing socially. This informality was possible because the City community was small in numbers and was located in a compact area. As the Governor of the Bank of England remarked in 1957: 'If I want to talk to the representatives of the British Banks, or indeed of the whole financial community, we can usually get together in one room in about half an hour' (Radcliffe, 1960b, I, p.52).

This rejection of bureaucratic organisation plainly helped the City to reject also the prevailing bureaucratic style of interest representation common elsewhere. The simple institutional sign of this was that until as recently as the late 1960s most City markets had little direct contact with Whitehall, preferring both to receive official views and to communicate their own views through the Bank of England. In the case of some key institutions – such as the clearing banks and the discount houses – the Bank was not only the chief channel, it was the only channel between the markets and central government. In turn the Bank preferred to cultivate personal and informal contacts between its own officials and individual bankers rather than to gather City opinion by any formal apparatus.

This insulation from the bureaucratic world of Whitehall was reinforced by the way the Bank of England organised its own relations with central government. Until the 1960s these relations were shaped by a reluctance to be drawn into a wide range of dealings with central departments and a consequent desire to use the Treasury as the Bank's chief point of contact (Moran, 1981a). This choice was connected to the Bank's reluctance to be drawn into the world of committees which were such an increasingly important part of the machinery of policy-making in Whitehall. By restricting contacts largely to the Treasury and by keeping such connections personal and informal, the Bank hoped to preserve its independence of action and outlook. Separation protected its officers, in Sir Leslie O'Brien's words, from being 'impregnated with Ministers' enthusiasms and aspirations', a fate which Sir Leslie believed commonly befell civil servants (Select Committee on Nationalised Industries, 1970, p.131).

This institutional isolation was matched by a rejection of the bureaucratic style of argument common in central government. Because the Bank suspected excessive formality in organisation, it suspected also the marks of excessive formality in putting arguments. Thus it preferred the experienced judgment of practical men over what it saw as the theoretical arguments of those with formal technical qualifications. This is one reason why the Bank only reluctantly conceded the case made by the Radcliffe Committee (Radcliffe, 1959, pp.301-3) for putting more resources into acquiring better information (in the form of more statistics) and better expertise (in the form of more economists).

The City came to reject bureaucratic organisation and a corresponding style of lobbying because of a complex range of historical experiences and social forces; but the chief immediate reason for rejection was a determination to avoid bureaucratic implementation. Other great interests tried to influence the content of legislation and formal government decisions; the City's objective was to keep law and formality out of its markets.

The successful rejection of bureaucratic interest representation was the key to much of the City's traditional power. Other great interests sought to influence policy by entering into the bureaucratic politics of Whitehall or the partisan politics of Westminster; the City succeeded in removing numerous sensitive issues from these arenas. This success was summed up in the widespread acceptance of the idea of 'self-regulation', a doctrine which presumed that devising and enforcing rules governing the conduct of business in financial markets should be the independent responsibility of participants in those markets.

Self-regulation took numerous issues out of 'politics' as conventionally understood, and thus allowed the City to settle many important questions independently of central government. The balance to be struck between free competition and restrictive practices, for instance, was left to the markets and to the Bank of England. Until the 1960s that balance decisively favoured restrictive practices: in money and banking, on the Stock Exchange and in Lloyds the competitive urge was hemmed in by numerous limitations. The reason was directly connected to self-regulation, for the voluntary restraints which its successful operation demanded depended on offering to those admitted to markets a decisive competitive advantage over outsiders. That is why City markets became dominated by a web of cartels and other restrictions.

These restrictions were reinforced by the fact that another set of key questions - concerning who should be admitted to markets and what degree of ownership concentration was allowable - were also settled inside the City. In the case of banking, for instance, it was the Bank of England which effectively controlled the terms of mergers between institutions, and it was the Bank also which determined whether, and under what conditions, a new enterprise could be admitted to the banking community. Important questions about the rules which should govern the prudent and honest conduct of business were likewise decided by the City itself.

The most obvious public sign of this independence was the way financial institutions were long able to stem the rising tide of company law from flowing into the City: banks, for instance, were effectively exempted from many of the disclosure requirements of the 1948 Companies Act. The tricky question of what constituted a prudent allocation of banking assets and liabilities was likewise left to conventional agreements between the Bank of England and the banks. In the securities industry it was still conventional wisdom as recently as the late 1960s that the Stock Exchange's system of self-regulation was preferable to legal controls.

By rejecting the conventional bureaucratic model of interest representation, and by emphasising the primacy of self-regulation, the City gained an extraordinary independence from central government. Its great power was elusive because it rested, not on the crude capacity to influence overt policy, but on the fact that issues vital to the interests of financial markets - the extent of competition, the definition of honesty and prudence, the distribution of

ownership - had become 'non-decisions': they were matters not
thought to be the concern of bureaucratic politics in Whitehall or
partisan politics in Westminster.

This capacity to transform important issues into matters of
apparent mere technicality extended also to areas where Whitehall
was nominally supreme. Thus in managing the gilt-edged market and
the foreign exchange markets the Bank was formally only the servant
of the Treasury, but in practice it enjoyed great tactical freedom:
in the case of the gilt-edged market, for instance, in the 1950s the
Bank only gave a weekly, informal report of its dealings to senior
officials in the Treasury.

This great freedom was a direct product of the rejection of
Whitehall's prevailing bureaucratic style. By insisting that
financial markets could be understood only by those with long practical
experience the Bank and the City discounted any intellectual weight
or formal expertise which Whitehall could muster. In this way an
attitude of deference was induced in the Treasury. The idea that
the Treasury elite would defer to anybody may seem extraordinary,
but that such was indeed the case is perfectly illustrated by the
evidence given to the Radcliffe Committee by Lord Bridges, a former
head of both the Treasury and the civil service. Bridges explained:
'The high officials of the Bank of England ... have long and intense
training and experience in their particular field. They are
specialists who have risen to the top through their skill and
experience in dealing with financial matters'. By contrast, he
continued: 'officers of the Treasury are laymen in the sense that
most of them do not spend much of their lives becoming experts in
any particular subject' (Radcliffe, 1960b, III, p.47).

The power traditionally exercised over policy-making by the City
was therefore both special and potent. It was special because it
surrounded financial markets with a great mystique, thus repelling
the attentions of outsiders. It was potent because it rested on
none of the crude pressures associated with orthodox lobbying.
Indeed to those with practical experience, in Whitehall or the City,
it hardly looked like an exercise in power at all: it simply
seemed that a variety of issues were conventionally defined as the
legitimate concern of the financial markets alone.

This special and potent power was nevertheless weak in two ways.
It rested, first, on a fragile set of understandings about the
appropriate division of labour between central government and the
City. This fragility was amply demonstrated in the 1960s when
Whitehall began to challenge the notion that financial markets should
independently control their own affairs. The second weakness was
even more serious. Separating the City from the bureaucratic
politics of Whitehall preserved the autonomy of financial markets,
but it also separated City interests from key areas of policy-making.
The City did not participate in the world of 'government by
committee' - to use Wheare's famous phrase - which was such an
increasingly important part of the machinery of central decision-
making. It consequently did not have the opportunity to make its
voice heard in those important parts of Whitehall where labour
market policy, industrial policy and even fiscal policy were being
made.

The City's special strength, and its special weakness, may thus

be briefly summarised: rejecting conventional bureaucratic interest
representation kept Whitehall out of the City; but it also kept the
City out of Whitehall, and in doing so excluded the City's voice from
important areas of policy-making.   This conclusion will surprise some,
for it has been conventionally believed that in the Bank's relations
with the Treasury the City enjoyed unique access to the vital part of
the policy-making machine.   Yet to imagine that access to a
chancellor or a permanent secretary gives special control over policy
betrays an outmoded notion of how modern government works.   When
government is a large and complex organisation intervening in a wide
range of social and economic affairs, policy-making becomes a
bureaucratic business: decisions are ground out of a network of
committees, not independently made by a few highly-placed individuals.
Obtaining access at the highest levels can produce spectacular
coups, but it is no substitute for shaping the terms of policy
argument by intervening at the point where alternatives are first
being formulated, and where details are being settled.

This is why some of the most apparently impressive instances of
the City's power actually signify points where it was weak.   Thus
memoirs of the Labour government's early months in office after
October 1964 recall how the Governor of the Bank of England (Lord
Cromer) repeatedly complained to the prime minister about the
administration's fiscal policies (Wilson, 1971, p.34; Williams, 1972,
p.36).   In fact these complaints, and the governor's public out-
bursts, reflected exasperation at the Bank's and the City's inability
to shape fiscal policy.   This inability was born of separation from
the Whitehall machinery where the details of tax burdens and spending
decisions were made: the standard study of the politics of public
spending decisions in Britain does not make a single reference to
the Bank of England (Heclo and Wildavsky, 1981).

Lord Cromer's complaints in the 1960s were one small sign of the
City's weakness.   A more obvious indication was the collapse in the
same decade of that fragile understanding which had taken issues out
of 'politics' and spirited them into the hands of the City.   By the
1960s this understanding had already been challenged in one key area,
official interest rate policy.   Before 1914 'bank rate' was pictured,
under the rules of the gold standard, as the automatic outcome of
the workings of an impersonal economic mechanism.   By the 1920s
control over bank rate was an issue of contention between chancellors
and the Bank (Sayers, 1976, I, p.120).   By the 1960s decisions about
interest rates were totally politicised, shaped by the politics of
economic management and the electoral considerations produced by the
rise of a cheap credit lobby among mortgaged owner-occupiers in the
housing market.

During the decade, this transformation of issues previously the technical concern of the City into matters which were the concern of central
government happened on an extensive scale.   The Bank and the City's
right to shape competition policy in the banking industry was
challenged in 1966, when bank charges were referred for investigation
to the National Board for Prices and Incomes.   The Board's Report,
published and widely discussed in the following year, went well
beyond its precise terms of reference: it contained a wide-ranging
and hostile analysis of the structure of the banking industry,
examined the technical management of monetary policy and criticised

the way in which cartels and restrictive practices in banking had
become an important part of the means of monetary control (National
Board for Prices and Incomes, 1967).

A year after the appearance of the NBPI Report the City had an
even more traumatic experience. Since 1918 it had been accepted that
mergers between banks should be controlled by the Bank of England,
subject to consultation with the Treasury. In 1968 the Bank,
apparently under the impression that no objections would be raised
in Whitehall, assented to a series of mergers between the large
clearing banks, only to find the proposals referred by Whitehall to
the Monopolies Commission, which in turn recommended rejection of
some of the mergers (Monopolies Commission, 1968).

This episode was a triple blow to the traditional way in which
the City went about defending its interests: it suggested that
relying on informal soundings in Whitehall and the City gave rise
to misunderstandings about what had been decided and was insufficient
to cope with a bureaucratic environment; it indicated that the key
question of ownership in banking was no longer to be decided inside
the City; and the Commission's Report yet again contained criticisms
from outsiders of restrictive practices in banking. Politics - the
bureaucratic politics of Whitehall and the partisan politics of
Westminster - were an increasing intrusion.

At the very same time a corresponding change was occurring in
the relations between the Bank and central government. During the
1960s the Bank's traditional isolation from the committee machinery
of Whitehall, its hesitation about going beyond the Treasury into
the wider world of central departments, and its reluctance to put
its relations with Whitehall into formal connections, were all
superseded. By the end of the decade it was becoming increasingly
integrated into the machinery of central government (Moran, 1981a).
The notion expressed by Lord Bridges that the Bank was the unique
possessor of expertise in managing markets was also challenged:
under Mr Jenkins's chancellorship the Bank was compelled to manage
the gilt-edged market under close Treasury scrutiny (Brittan, 1971,
p.388).

The Treasury was also at work trying to prise open the Bank for
public inspection. According to the Crossman Diaries it was an
important influence behind the moves to subject the Bank to public
scrutiny by the Select Committee on Nationalised Industries (Crossman,
1976, pp.276 and 666). The Committee's highly critical report began
a process which has subjected the Bank's internal affairs to an
unprecedented amount of parliamentary examination and Treasury
control (Select Committee on Nationalised Industries, 1970 and 1976).

This growing incorporation into the Whitehall bureaucracy
inevitably affected the Bank's style. During the 1960s it
increasingly adopted the technical and professional outlook of a
public bureaucracy. The publication of a 'Quarterly Bulletin' -
begun in 1960 after the recommendations of the Radcliffe Committee -
inaugurated a steady increase in the attention given to collecting,
analysing and publishing technical data; while during the rest of
the decade the Bank hired growing numbers of professional economists
to both carry out technical tasks and to provide policy advice.
In a phrase, the Bank became increasingly bureaucratic.

These internal changes in organisation and outlook were also part

of a wider change which came over the City. In the 1950s and 1960s
financial markets, unlike most other parts of the British economy,
experienced an economic miracle. There was a great increase in the
amount of business done, many new markets were created and London
re-emerged as a leading world financial centre. This burst of
innovation and expansion magnified the size and diversity of the
City, and brought a great increase in the ferocity of competition
for business. As a result the restraints on which effective self-
regulation depended were seriously weakened.

Economic change was not only transforming the City; it was also
altering the whole financial community, and as a result was affecting
the relationship between City institutions and other financial
intermediaries. The large joint stock banks found, for instance,
that their pre-eminence in the mass market for retail deposits was
increasingly challenged by the building societies. This in turn
had repercussions for interest representation, since the societies -
whose historic origins and modern strength lay in the provinces
rather than in the City - had developed direct links with Whitehall,
by contrast with the clearers' reliance on the Bank of England as
an intermediary. During the 1970s the clearing banks were to return
time and again to the argument that the building societies had
secured concessions from central government which gave them an
unfair competitive advantage.

The rise of the building societies was itself part of a wider
shift in the balance of the financial community away from traditional
City institutions. In the securities market, for instance, the
period after the late 1950s saw the rise of institutional investors:
by the end of the 1970s institutions dominated the market in company
stocks and in gilt-edged securities. Institutional share ownership
in turn was dominated by the insurance companies and by the pension
funds. Though these bodies had much closer connections with the
City elite than had building societies, the political and regulatory
environment in which they lived was very different from that common
in the City: the insurance industry and the pension funds were
closer to Whitehall than to the Bank, and lived under regulatory
regimes shaped more by statute than by doctrines of self-regulation
(Moran, 1981b).

TRADITIONAL POWER PASSES AWAY

Under the impact of all these powerful forces the traditional methods
of practising interest representation in the City have largely
passed away since the late 1960s. In their place has developed a
system which increasingly resembles the orthodox pattern of bureaucratic representation practised by other great interests. The
change can be illustrated by examining in turn the three elements
in bureaucratic representation: organisation, style and implementation.

In the last two decades the organisation of the City has become
more bureaucratic, whether that word is used precisely or loosely.
Financial institutions have been bureaucratised in the precise
Weberian sense that in recruiting and promoting staff, 'merit' -
measured by technical competence and the possession of special

skills - has commonly superseded ascription. This shift is in turn a reflection of changed styles in conducting business and presenting arguments. As markets have grown in scale, and business has increasingly been conducted impersonally between strangers rather than between fellow members of a small community, so technical competence has come to matter more than enjoying a precise social place in that community.

The shift to Weberian bureaucracy has been accompanied by bureaucratisation in a looser sense: the institutions traditionally trading in City markets - enterprises owned and controlled by family dynasties and specialising in particular kinds of business - have been increasingly replaced by large financial conglomerates, often operating on a multinational scale and controlled by professional managers.

This transformation was wrought in manufacturing industry half a century ago, but the forces creating the original revolution in ownership and control are still recognisable in the financial community: the search for economies of scale, the ambitions of large firms to buy out competitors, the need to match the scale of activity elsewhere in the economy. Everywhere one looks in the City the pattern is remarkably similar. In the banking industry in the late 1960s a pattern of ownership which had been stable for half a century was finally disturbed by a series of mergers between clearing banks. Fourteen years later a renewed pattern of stability has yet to be established, but in the intervening period the clearers have been changed from relatively specialist institutions operating largely on a national scale into multinational corpora-tions providing a diversity of services. On the Stock Exchange amalgamations have drastically reduced the numbers of jobbing and broking firms, and in the case of brokers in particular have produced large organisations offering a diverse range of financial services (Wilson, 1980). In insurance broking and underwriting, in accounting and auditing, the pattern is repeated: the replace-ment of owner-controlled family dynasties by managerial bureaucracies.

These changes in organisation are, not surprisingly, also evident in the narrow field of interest representation. The traditional reliance on informal contacts between key individuals in the City and in the Bank of England has given way to the use of specialist lobbying organisations. The banking industry exemplifies this trend. The turn to organised lobbying was stimulated in banking by a series of failures in the old means of representation. In the mid- and late 1960s it became painfully clear to bankers that Whitehall was unwilling any longer to accept the traditional division of labour under which the organisation of the industry was the independent concern of the banks and the Bank of England: that was the significance of the intrusions by the Prices and Incomes Board and the Monopolies Commission. In addition the misunderstandings produced by the Bank's soundings in Whitehall before the proposed mergers in 1968 showed how vulnerable were the old informal methods in a world of large-scale bureaucratic policy-making. The problems experienced in operating the traditional system partly account for the decision in 1971 to dismantle many restrictive practices which had been administered by the Committee of London Clearing Bankers (CLCB).

The clearers took the opportunity offered by this change to alter decisively the purpose of the CLCB: it was turned from a small institution primarily carrying out limited functions as a trade association into a professional lobbying organisation (Committee of London Clearing Bankers, 1978). In the succeeding year the British Bankers' Association was similarly transformed from a semi-moribund state into a lobbyist for the whole banking community, with a particular brief to represent British banking in Brussels on the country's entry into the EEC.

In 1974 the bankers' conviction that they needed to practise a more formal style of interest representation was strengthened by their experience with the Consumer Credit Act which was passed in that year. The Act as originally drafted put a heavy burden on the clearing banks, because one of its provisions required those advancing consumer credit to state the true rate of interest on loans. Since banks have traditionally advanced loans to private customers by the highly flexible overdraft system this implied that banks would have to perform the administratively complex and expensive task of calculating and stating the true interest rate on all overdrafts. Relying on traditional informal methods of representation, the clearers approached the Bank of England with the problem. The Bank in turn made soundings in Whitehall, and apparently received the impression - which it communicated to the banks - that the difficulty would be solved by re-drafting. This was never done, and when the measure became law the clearers found themselves required to state and calculate rates of interest in the same manner as other providers of consumer credit.

This apparently trivial episode rankled with the banking community for many years. As late as 1979 it was a recurring complaint in bankers' contributions to the debates surrounding the Banking Act which was passed in that year; indeed the Committee of London Clearing Bankers used the bargaining during the final parliamentary stages of that Act to tack on an amendment exempting the banks from the 1974 Consumer Credit Act. More significant than the substance of the issue was the impetus which the banks' defeat in 1974 gave to the shift towards formally organised lobbying. After it, the CLCB appointed for the first time an adviser on public affairs, whose identity plainly signified a willingness to go out of the City into the world of politics in Whitehall and parliament: he was Mr Brendon Sewill, a former head of the Conservative party's Research Department and between 1970 and 1974 an adviser in the Treasury to the chancellor of the exchequer.

By the late 1970s the conversion of bankers to interest representation through a large-scale bureaucratic organisation was complete: the CLCB's evidence to the Wilson Committee paints a picture of a complex, organised machinery operating over seventy committees and working parties scrutinising every aspect of government policy affecting the banking industry (Committee of London Clearing Bankers, 1978).

It is not surprising that clearing bankers have led the way in adopting formally organised interest representation, for the central part played by the joint stock banks in the economy makes them very vulnerable to changes in public policy. But the greater formality marking the clearers' lobbying activities is only a more highly

developed version of a change which is occurring generally throughout the City. Thus in 1973, following prolonged debate about how
financial markets should be represented in policy-making, the Bank
of England sponsored the formation of a series of committees drawn
from the most important sectors of the City. These bodies - they
include a City Liaison Committee and more specialised groups
covering subjects like taxation and company law - are an important
organised means by which financial markets can now intervene in
both policy debates and in the details of policy formulation and
implementation.

The rise of bureaucratically organised lobbying in turn has been
connected to an important change in the style of representation
practised by the City. Traditional informal and personal contacts
funnelled through the Bank of England, which in turn tried to
preserve some distance from the bureaucratic machinery of Whitehall,
have been increasingly replaced by more bureaucratic ways of going
about things. We have already encountered some of the signs of
this change: the complex internal machinery developed by the
Committee of London Clearing Bankers, and the network of City
committees, are both signs that allusions and understandings between
individuals are being replaced by a world of formal reports and
systematic argument.

Another qualitative indication of the change in style which has
occurred can be gained by comparing the City's evidence to the
three great public investigations of the financial community
conducted in this century: the Macmillan Committee's investigation
into the financing of industry completed in 1931; the Radcliffe
Committee's examination of the monetary system published in 1959;
and the Wilson Committee's scrutiny of financial institutions which
appeared in 1980. The City's evidence to Macmillan was cursory
and came largely in the form of oral evidence by leading personalities in financial life. When Radcliffe gathered submissions the
various institutions and trade associations presented some systematic
evidence, though it was brief and largely confined to describing how
markets worked. By the time Wilson came to gather material the
situation was transformed. The evidence presented by the various
representative institutions and associations was massive (the
clearing banks' main submission was so long that it was published
separately from the official evidence); was technically highly
professional; and was shaped into a sophisticated defence of
financial markets against the charge that they were not serving the
needs of the economy at large.

These changes in style undoubtedly have much to do with the fact
that the City is being increasingly drawn out of its isolation into
the world of Whitehall; and as it is drawn into that world, so it
has adopted bureaucratic modes of argument. The end of the City's
isolation from the central machinery of policy-making is in turn
due, above all, to the changing role of the Bank of England. Under
the kind of interest representation traditionally practised by the
City the Bank was the habitual point of contact with Whitehall;
for a number of key institutions - notably the clearing banks and
the discount houses - it was long accepted as the only legitimate
avenue of communication. The Bank's primacy had, however, been
established under conditions which by the 1960s were rapidly passing

away. Its monopoly in representation dated from the period of
Montagu Norman's governorship (1920-44) when the City was a comparatively small community which could be organised in an informal way
and when the Bank was unambiguously a City institution with weak
formal links to Whitehall.

During and after the Second World War the Bank's position changed
considerably. Its nationalisation in 1946, though in itself a
comparatively unimportant event, signified the growing extent to
which it was being used by Whitehall as an instrument of control over
financial institutions. The most obvious cases concerned the control
of bank lending, where after 1940 the Bank channelled to the clearing
banks 'requests' about the volume and direction of lending which
were effectively instructions from the centre. During the 1960s
the Bank's significance as an instrument of government began to be
reflected, as we have seen, in a growing participation in Whitehall's
internal committee machinery. These developments produced a tension
between the Bank's executive roles as a public institution and its
role as the City's voice in government. In the last decade this
tension has been increasingly resolved at the expense of the Bank's
position as the City's spokesman.

The growing willingness of City interests to organise formally
for the purpose of interest representation was prompted in part by
a recognition that the Bank's capacity to express City views was
being limited by its public role. This is why the shift to formally
organised interest representation in the City has been accompanied
by a growing willingness to by-pass the Bank in favour of direct
contacts with Whitehall. This latter development is admittedly
far from complete. The Bank remains, rather in the manner of a
conventional sponsoring department, an important means of expressing
City interests in government. Some sections of the old City elite
who have historically been very dependent on the Bank - such as the
discount houses - remain comparatively insulated from Whitehall.
But no significant City interest now feels it necessary to approach
central government only through the Bank of England; and the powerful
clearing banks, who a couple of decades ago would not have ventured
into Whitehall except in its company, now look upon it as just one
way among many of influencing public policy.

Going into Whitehall has meant more for City interest groups than
merely lobbying for particular policies. As groups elsewhere in the
economy have found, central government is highly sympathetic to
organised interests and tries to incorporate them into policy
formulation and implementation. This process of incorporation is
nicely illustrated in the City's case by the history of its relations
with the National Economic Development Council (NEDC). When NEDC
was first established the Bank still insulated the City from central
government. Although a City representative first sat on the main
Council in 1965, both the Bank and the markets long resisted any
detailed involvement: there never has been, for instance, a 'little
Neddy' (an Economic Development Council) for the City. During the
1970s this isolation was effectively ended: the NEDC Committee on
Finance for Investment (and its successor the Committee on Finance
for Industry) after 1976 effectively carried out the functions of
an EDC for the City (Roll, 1978).

The growing traffic between Whitehall and the City has not been

one way, for at the same time that financial interests have begun
to make their voice heard in central government, Whitehall has begun
to intervene directly in the life of the City. This development
reflects perhaps the most profound institutional change of all to
have occurred in recent decades: the rise of bureaucratic implementation. Control was traditionally exercised in the City by a set of
informal mechanisms inadequately summed up in the phrase 'self-
regulation'. Traditional interest representation in turn was bound
up with self-regulation. The City's success in preserving its
markets from the intrusive influence of the statute book and the
civil service shaped the form of financial politics. Financial
markets were able to keep their distance from central government
because self-regulation allowed the City itself to settle key
questions about the conduct of business. But for over two decades
now self-regulation has been in difficulties. In the 1970s these
difficulties reached crisis proportions. Coping with crisis involved
irreversible changes which in all markets have greatly increased the
formality of the City's own regulatory arrangements and led to
growing external regulation by the state. In some cases the changes
have been so great as to raise doubts as to whether anything but
the rhetoric of self-regulation remains. Since representation and
self-regulation were bound together, these changes have inevitably
transformed the way individual markets now have to defend their
interests. The nature of the transformation can be illustrated from
three sectors: the banking industry, the securities industry
organised by the Stock Exchange, and the insurance and reinsurance
markets organised in Lloyds.

Traditional regulation in banking might better be described as
'self-policing' than as 'self-regulation'. The decisive controls
were exercised, not by an independent association, but by the Bank
of England. But the Bank in turn tried, with some success, to keep
formal control and surveillance to a minimum: the law was largely
kept out, while the Bank itself engaged in little detailed scrutiny
of the internal affairs of banks, preferring to trust them to conduct
business prudently and honestly.

This system of trust worked because the Bank, by using its
considerable authority and economic power, determined who entered
the banking community. In this way it created a 'primary' banking
system populated by a small elite who refrained from 'excessive'
and imprudent competition in return for the status and privileges
which the Bank of England dispensed. This informal system of
control was destroyed in the two decades after the mid-1950s. The
chief forces of destruction were the extraordinary innovations in
the financial system, abetted by the effects of public policy. As
financial markets developed rapidly, so there also developed a
variety of institutions performing many banking functions which
were nevertheless excluded from the 'primary' sector. The rise of
these institutions in the 1960s was helped by the fact that the
Bank, acting as the instrument of Whitehall, was imposing a variety
of restrictions on the primary banks' ability to compete for
business. By the end of the decade there consequently existed
alongside the primary banks a thriving, highly competitive and
largely uncontrolled secondary banking system.

In response to all this the Bank of England, in September 1971,

dismantled many of the restrictive practices common among the primary
banks (Zawadzki, 1981). The next two years saw a ferocious burst of
competition, and a great rise in what turned out to be highly
imprudent lending, especially to the property market. This was
succeeded at the end of 1973 by what is conventionally called the
'secondary banking crisis' which was in reality a crisis of the
whole banking system allied to a wider crisis in international banking
markets (Channon, 1977).

The results of this crisis have considerably diminished the
importance of 'self-policing' in favour of formal surveillance and
the application of legal rules. After 1974 the Bank of England
greatly increased both the range of institutions which it supervised
and the detail with which scrutiny was conducted. In order to
accomplish this it created for the first time a Supervision Division
staffed by specialists, and put increasing resources into the
activity of supervision (Blunden, 1975). In 1979 it reinforced these
controls with the Banking Act, which gave it wide legal powers to
control entry to the banking system and to intervene in the affairs
of individual enterprises. The details of that Act show the Bank
to be still attempting a retention of traditional self-policing, but
the workings of the new regime suggest that this is a vain hope.
The system now controlled by the Bank is simply too big to be
managed by the old informal means: under the 1979 Act the Bank has
so far authorised over 270 banks and issued licences to over 280
other 'deposit-taking' institutions. The evolution and implementation
of banking regulation under the 1979 Act has taken on the bureaucratic forms common in other policy areas: the preparation and
circulation of formal consultative papers, and the use of representative associations to transmit the views of different banking interests
on those papers. The preparation and passage of the 1979 Act also
opened the details of banking regulation up to a variety of groups
whose intervention in such matters would have been unthinkable a
couple of decades ago: civil servants, ministers, lawyers, even
parliamentarians.

The brutal impact of the great banking crisis of the mid-1970s
produced a dramatic change; by contrast, in the securities industry,
there has been since the late 1950s a slow draining away of the
authority exercised by the Stock Exchange's system of self-regulation.
The first signs of difficulty came in the take-over battles at the
end of the 1950s. The defects which these battles revealed in the
system of regulation led to the preparation in 1959 of written
guidance by a committee convened by the Bank. Though the guidelines
were tentative, their existence was an unusual mark of formality at
that time. Since then the increasing complexity of the securities
industry, and the continuing inventiveness of financiers in devising
new business practices, has forced a perpetual increase in the
formal elaboration of rules and in the formal creation of institutions.
The 1960s, the decade of the asset-stripper, drew to a close in 1968
with two significant increases in formality: revision of the 1959
guidelines into a much more elaborate City code on take-overs, and
the foundation of a Panel on Take-Overs and Mergers which was given
full-time staff to administer the code (Panel on Take-Overs and
Mergers, 1979).

The next decade nevertheless saw a succession of scandals which

were publicly dissected in successive reports by Department of Trade
Inspectors (Clarke, 1981). The Inspectors' Report on Ferguson and
General Investments contains, for instance, a devastatingly critical
account of how poorly the Take-Over Panel performed when faced with
a clever and unscrupulous financier (Department of Trade, 1979, p.133).
These scandals explain why in 1978 the Panel was incorporated into
an enlarged Council for the Securities Industry (Wilson, 1980). The
Council pictures itself as an agent of self-regulation, but it
operates in an environment where the informality and independence of
the old methods are passing away. The continuing inventiveness of
financiers in devising new strategems has forced the Council to
perpetually elaborate new rules to match new practices; the problems
created in 1981 by 'dawn raids' are a striking illustration of the
process at work.

     At the same time as nominal 'self-regulation' has come to lose
its distinctive traditional features, the influence of Whitehall and
of the law has grown. The institutional signs of this change include
the Joint Review Body for the Securities Industry which includes the
Department of Trade, and thus gives Whitehall a continuing right to
intervene in the details of regulation. The legal sign of the change
is in the extent to which practices traditionally thought to be the
independent concern of the Stock Exchange (for instance, control of
'insider dealing' in company shares) is now the subject of company
law. The role of the law will almost certainly grow in the future.
In January 1982 the Department of Trade published a discussion
document on investor protection by Professor L.C.B. Gower, one of
its senior legal advisers. Professor Gower scathingly summarised
the defects of the present system of regulation in the following
terms:

     complication, uncertainty, irrationality, failure to treat like
     alike, inflexibility, excessive control in some areas and too
     little (or none) in others, the creation of an elite and a fringe,
     lax enforcement, delays, overconcentration on honesty rather than
     competence, undue diversity of regulations and regulators, and
     failure to achieve a proper balance between Governmental
     regulation and self-regulation.

In the light of these judgments it is not surprising that the
Professor concluded by recommending a significant shift towards more
legal controls, in the form of a Securities Act (Gower, 1982, pp.
137-9).

     The decline of self-regulation is common throughout the City,
but the rate of decline has varied in different markets. By contrast
with the slow draining away of authority on the Stock Exchange,
until the mid-1970s self-regulation in Lloyds seemed stable and
effective; that stability was indicated by the fact that the powers
of the governing body rested on private legislation passed as long
ago as 1871. In the second half of the 1970s, however, Lloyds was
afflicted with a series of scandals and failures which called into
question both fundamental features of market organisation and the
adequacy of existing means of regulating the way business was done.
These scandals and failures were both publicly embarrassing - in
one case the conduct of the markets was even raised on the floor of
the House of Commons - and internally divisive, as was clear from
the unprecedented introduction of litigation into the affairs of

Lloyds. As a result of these embarrassments an internal committee, chaired by Sir Henry Fisher and containing representatives of the main interests in the market, was set up to examine the existing system of regulation. Its report recommended important changes in market organisation, a sweeping reorganisation of the governing body and a considerable increase in the powers of that body.

The attempt to implement the Fisher Report has fundamentally changed the politics of Lloyds. Until recently it was an institution whose regulation was private, informal and largely separated from the law. The Fisher Report, by raising important questions about regulation and market organisation, opened a series of important arguments: between different economic interests in the market which would be affected in different ways by reform; between different interests which find it difficult to agree on the powers and composition of a new governing body; and between supporters of reform and those who see change as abandoning fundamental features of self-regulation.

These divisions have been widened because, in order to implement the Fisher proposals, a new Private Bill is necessary. At the time of writing (March 1982) this Bill is still undergoing an argumentative and delayed passage through parliament. The necessity of legislation has had several important effects. It compelled the governing body of Lloyds to consult with the Department of Trade over the proposed Bill. It sharpened internal divisions, by stimulating the formation of competing pressure groups within the market to lobby backbench members of parliament. It allowed backbench MPs to intervene in the details of market organisation: the Commons Committee examining the Bill refused to sanction its further passage without amendments which committed Lloyds to important changes in the relations between different parts of the market.

Growing formality and institutional complexity; the increasing intrusion of Whitehall, parliament and the statute book; the rise of organised pressure groups concerned to lobby over the preparation and implementation of policy: these are the signs of a widespread decline of traditional self-regulation in the City. They are also the reasons why interest representation has increasingly been concerned with bureaucratic implementation. The decline of self-regulation can be expected to continue, for it is caused by features deeply embedded in modern financial markets: their great scale, which destroys the social cohesion on which self-regulation traditionally rested; their fiercely competitive character, which destroys the voluntary restraints so essential to self-regulation; and their extraordinary capacity for innovation in the pursuit of profit, which constantly creates new practices and new problems for regulators.

THE DECLINING CITY?

Capitalists make bad pressure group material. The competitiveness which is at the heart of the market system divides enterprises, creating common suspicion and only the most limited and contingent perception of united interests. Capitalists thus suffer seriously from the universal problem of organising collective action: it is not necessarily rational for any individual businessman to devote time and expense to defending the interests of business as a whole. That is why business pressure groups are so prone to desertion and secession, and why stable groups generally organise a limited and distinct sector, and offer clear selective benefits to members. A characteristic successful group will be an association operating restrictive practices which powerfully discriminate against non-members.

The City was traditionally a political force to be reckoned with because it had evolved highly effective solutions to the problems of organising collective action. The social solidarity of City markets - grounded in the practice of recruiting the City elite from a narrow social stratum - encouraged a sense of community at the expense of suspicion. More brutally, a network of cartels and other restrictive practices in financial markets diminished the suspicions and uncertainties which competition brings. These restrictions were also powerful disincentives to free-riding, or to other deviant behaviour, since to be accepted into the markets was to be offered significant economic advantages. Finally, in the Bank of England the City possessed precisely the kind of powerful organising institution needed to maintain solidarity: the Bank policed the markets to exclude undesirables, sponsored and defended restrictive practices, and distilled from competing interests a common City view which it put in Whitehall. Its functions were exactly those which a Marxist might expect: it defended 'the common interests' of the whole City community, both against other groups in the economy and against the self-interested behaviour of individual financiers.

That the common interests of a group may be very different from the selfish individual interests of its separate members was no great difficulty in the City as traditionally organised: the Bank's authority to speak as its voice was unchallenged, while the community itself was relatively small and cohesive. But as the Bank became an increasingly bureaucratic institution, and thus began to respond to other interests in Whitehall, its account of the City's common interest became suspect. At a mundane but important level clearing bankers, for instance, began to wonder what was so advantageous about arrangements which turned them into the Bank's agents for the conduct of monetary policy, while other institutions outside the Bank's magic circle were taking up profitable business turned away by the clearers under official pressure. The rise of these competitors was a sign of the other forces destroying the City's solidarity: the growing scale of markets which was diminishing the influence of social cohesion, and the spread of competition which was everywhere destroying the disciplining effect of cartels and restrictive practices.

These changes make it sensible to speak of 'the City' as a declining political force. This is not at all the same as saying that the power of financial institutions generally, or of particular financial markets, is in decline. On the contrary: there is convincing evidence that innovation and inventiveness are putting some markets beyond stable control, including control by those who take part in them. 'The declining City' refers rather to the decline of a certain collection of interests given unity by a particular

conjunction of forces which are now ebbing away. In place of the old
cohesive City is left a series of separate sectors displaying
varying levels of organised cohesion and effectiveness. They vary
from sophisticated and influential lobbies (the clearing banks)
through institutions of declining significance (like the London
Discount Market Association and the Accepting Houses Committee) to
bodies like Lloyds, who are just beginning to learn the hard lessons
of pressure group politics.

Those within the City who want to restore its old unity are
therefore chasing a historical mirage. There will continue to be
City-wide co-operation (as in the various off-shoots of the City
Liaison Committee) but it will have the contingent and unstable
quality common to collective action by diverse groups of businesses.
There are obvious particular parts of the City (such as the Stock
Exchange) where the institutional foundations also exist for similar
limited co-operation. As the City splits into a diversity of
formally organised groups the lines of cleavage will be determined
by the usual complex mixture of forces which shape the organisation
of business interests elsewhere: the extent to which ownership
becomes concentrated; the divisions which emerge between enterprises
of different size and specialisms; the kind of demands for pressure
group organisation made upon markets by central government; the
expansionist ambitions of existing established groups, and the
success with which they are pursued.

Against these uncertainties may be set more definite prospects.
The traditional British division between the City and industry is
being closed. In a like manner pressure group organisation will
increasingly span the divide. Large multinational financial
institutions (many of which already belong to the CBI) will find it
convenient to enter alliances with multinational capital in other
parts of the economy. The City is no more likely to exhibit a
continuing capacity for collective action than is the dispersed and
incoherent collection of interests recently discovered by Metcalfe
and McQuillan to be common in other sectors of business (Metcalfe
and McQuillan, 1979). The problem of definition with which we
began will thus become intractable. It is time to dissolve the
City into its constituent markets and institutions, and to study
how those markets and institutions are connected to other interests
and to government. The City as a traditional interest - private,
cohesive and anti-bureaucratic - is passing away.

NOTE

The largest part of the paper which I gave at the original conference
on Capital and Politics was published as Moran, 1981b. At the
conference most discussion of the paper concerned the concluding
section on the power of financial institutions. It quickly became
clear in this discussion that my original argument was highly
unsatisfactory, and the whole section was omitted when the paper
was published. This chapter has been an attempt to restate and
elaborate my original argument in a more satisfactory way. I am
grateful for the many comments offered at the original conference,
and for the opportunity to try out my ideas further on the Department

of Government seminar at the University of Essex. The material
reported in these pages was partly gathered in interviews conducted
in the City as part of a larger study of the politics of money and
banking. This is an appropriate place to thank the many busy people
who talked to me.

Chapter 4

REPRESENTING CAPITAL: THE ROLE OF THE CBI

Wyn Grant

The task of representing capital is not an easy or straightforward one. It is not a simple matter of mobilising dominant values to attain clearly apparent and easily obtainable objectives. The political objectives of capitalists cannot be simply deduced from an analysis of their apparent interests, for businessmen are divided both over political goals and the strategies and tactics to be used in their pursuit. Even the size and resources of the CBI are as much a handicap as an asset, giving the organisation a stifling breadth that limits its capacity for effective action.

The analytical strategy used in this chapter will be to examine the organisational and political objectives of the CBI. The nature of these objectives is not always readily apparent, and the objectives themselves may frequently be lost sight of in the press of daily representational business. Nevertheless, the assumption that the CBI as an organisation has some long run goals which can be subjected to scrutiny is not unreasonable, although one must be careful not to exaggerate the sense of identity and common political purpose possessed by businessmen, even in collective representation.

There is, of course, a sense in which the CBI is a sideshow. As Offe has pointed out, 'Whereas capital can bring its obstructive power to bear even *if it is not* organised as an interest group, the withdrawal of labour power can function as an instrument of power only if it is practiced *collectively*, that is, if it is organised in at least a rudimentary way' (Offe, 1981, p.147). In so far as business needs a political capacity, the very large businesses which are of such crucial importance in the British economy may deal direct with government, rather than through an intermediary such as the CBI (Grant, 1981). Nevertheless, the resources that businessmen put into the CBI (time being more important than money as a scarcer resource for this group) and its ability to exert a significant influence on government policy on occasions suggests that the CBI is worth examining in its own right.

THE CHOICE OF STRATEGY

Even if industrialists can agree about what is in their interests,

which is by no means easy, there is often disagreement about the way
in which those interests should be defended. There has always been
a tension within the CBI, more apparent at some times than others,
which mirrors two clusters of capitalist opinion identified by
Westergaard and Resler. According to Westergaard and Resler (1976,
p.238), one cluster of opinion

> has favoured cutting concessions to labour, and relying more on a
> combination of market forces and penal law to ensure labour
> discipline. The other school of thought has sought both to extend
> state activity in aid of business ... and to secure the partner-
> ship of organised labour for these ends through concessions and
> through firm institutionalisation of ostensibly voluntary
> collective bargaining.

The two clusters of opinion can be identified within the CBI: neither
position has ever been without its supporters, although the lines of
division are often complex with, for example, personnel managers
taking a conciliatory line in the industrial relations committees
while their superiors on the board argue for a hard line in the
economic policy committees. Nevertheless, up to 1974, the conciliatory
line could be said to have been dominant. It enjoyed a golden dawn
in the first years of the 1964-70 Labour government, but then became
more difficult to maintain as the government's promise of improved
economic performance was not fulfilled. As labour relations
deteriorated, and the government resorted to greater intervention
in the economy, relations between the CBI and the 1964-70 Labour
government became increasingly strained. The CBI's general adherence
to the approach to industrial relations that culminated in the
Conservatives' Industrial Relations Act might seem to represent a
victory for the hard-line strategy, although it may be questioned
whether the CBI and industrialists in general were as united behind
this line as appeared to be the case at the time.

In any event, the difficulties that the attempt to implement
a hard-line strategy in industrial relations encountered led to a
'golden age' for tripartism with the CBI, particularly under the
combined leadership of a 'liberal' president (Sir Michael Clapham)
and a 'liberal' director-general (Campbell Adamson) from 1972 to
1974. The Prime Minister, Edward Heath, had also become a convert
to tripartism. As Viscount Watkinson (1976, p.85), a CBI activist
at the time who later held office as president, has recalled:

> No prime minister has ever devoted as much care and patience
> as Edward Heath did to seeking to bring about tripartite agreement
> between the CBI, the TUC and the government on the cure for
> Britain's economic ills. Had the Industrial Relations Act not
> soured relationships, the initiative might well have succeeded.

The failure of Heath's experiment in neo-corporatism brought
about its repercussions in the CBI. The organisation faced an
internal crisis brought about in part by Campbell Adamson's publicly
expressed reservations about the Industrial Relations Act a few days
before the February 1974 general election which led to a number of
firms resigning or suspending their memberships of the CBI. The CBI
also faced an external crisis brought about by rapidly rising rates
of inflation, the election of an apparently socialist Labour
government, and mounting signs of social breakdown such as the
formation of 'private armies' and the appearance of a number of new

organisations drawing support from the more marginal members of the
middle class (King and Nugent, 1979). The CBI reacted to these twin
crises under the presidency of Ralph Bateman (1974-6) by adopting a
more combative attitude towards the government.

However, it was the subsequent presidency of Viscount Watkinson,
who established a successful partnership with the director-general,
the late Sir John Methven, that really set the organisation on a
new course. The CBI became much more concerned than it had been in
the past with influencing public opinion, a change of emphasis
symbolised by the introduction of an annual conference in 1977. The
idea of such a conference had been rejected in the past, largely
because of the fear of exposing internal divisions within the CBI
(not to mention the damage that could be done to the organisation's
image by its more reactionary members), but these worries were now
swept aside in the search for television time and column inches in
the press. It is doubtful whether the conference has made much of
a constructive contribution to the policy-making process within
the CBI - indeed some of the resolutions adopted have been a positive
embarrassment to the leadership - but it has become an annual media
jamboree, which even if it is a less exciting event than the party
conferences or even the TUC conference, nevertheless attracts some
useful publicity for the CBI.

Along with the Conservative party in opposition, the CBI embraced
the 'hard-line' policies that emerged out of the intellectual
regrouping of the British right after 1974. The collapse of
technocratic corporatism left a vacuum, but something had to be
found to replace incomes policy as a central totem, a gap filled,
of course, by control of the money supply. In the first of a series
of comprehensive policy programmes published in 1976, the CBI made
it clear that, 'We would prefer a consistent monetary policy
appropriate to the fight against inflation, even at the cost of
relatively high interest rates' (CBI, 1976a, p.22). This commitment
did not prevent the CBI expressing concern about the levels of
interest rate experienced after 1979.

Although the Conservatives were elected in 1979 on a programme
very similar to that advocated by the CBI, industrialists became at
first uneasy; then worried; and, by the autumn of 1980, alarmed
about the impact of the government's policies on the British economy.
The CBI stifled its misgivings about the initial cuts in regional
aid because of its desire to lend general support to the government's
economic policy, but by 1980 the CBI's regional councils were
starting to openly express criticisms of government policy. The
regional councils are a useful 'safety valve' in this respect;
they allow industrialists to express their frustrations about
government policy without committing the whole organisation to a
particular policy position.

By the autumn of 1980, the restiveness within the CBI about
government policy could no longer be contained. Resolutions submitted
for the 1980 conference showed that the state of the economy and the
effects of the government's policies had largely replaced industrial
relations and pay bargaining as a subject for concern. As one
commentary noted, 'What was particularly striking was the extent to
which the resolutions called for government intervention in contrast
to the calls for "freedom from interference" in the past' (Income
Data Services, 1980).

The growing importance of the CBI conference as an event in the
political calendar was shown by the efforts of the government to
reassure industrialists and defuse anticipated criticism by the
hasty announcement of a 6 per cent pay limit for the public sector
and a promise of concessions on energy prices. In another move to
rally Conservative loyalists among industrialists, a meeting of ten
top industrialists was held on the last day of the 1980 Conservative
party conference by the party's deputy chairman, Alistair McAlpine.
The 1980 CBI conference was, of course, dominated by the speech by
Sir Terence Beckett, the new director-general, in which he talked of
a 'bare knuckle fight' with the government. Five major companies,
all with staunch Conservatives as chairmen, resigned from the CBI
in protest at these remarks.

The standing of the CBI leadership was not improved when, the day
after the conference, the president (Sir Ray Pennock) and the
director-general went to see Mrs Thatcher to inform her of the
worries of industrialists, only to emerge on the pavement of Downing
Street empty-handed and declaring that Mrs Thatcher's performance
was 'magnificent'. As one of the resigners, Babcock chairman, Sir
John King remarked: 'They went in like Brighton rock and came out
like Turkish delight.'

Sir Terence Beckett, who was away from his post for some time
because of illness, subsequently admitted that he may have gone too
far and said that he was putting on his gloves. Sir Ray Pennock as
president managed to develop an effective working relationship with
Mrs Thatcher, although one member complained that the CBI 'seems
able to win small concessions from the government, but nothing very
major'('Financial Times', 2 November 1981). The underlying problem
was that, in many ways, a Conservative government poses more
strategic problems for the CBI than a Labour government. On the
one hand, Labour governments (in the past at any rate) have been
more than open to influence from the CBI, as the experience of the
1974-9 Labour government shows. Indeed, the more right-wing members
of such governments may see the CBI as a welcome ally in their
battles against the left. Of course, in the 1974-9 parliament,
the CBI was helped by the fact that the government, for most of the
parliament's life, did not have a majority in the House of Commons.
The government's lack of a parliamentary majority enabled the CBI
to win the support of Liberal, Ulster Unionist and Nationalist MPs
to modify legislation, particularly taxation legislation. Even
when this particular tactic is not possible, experience shows that
the CBI can 'shift' Labour governments, even if only on matters of
detail, and these achievements can be duly publicised to the
membership. When a Labour government will not give way, it can be
attacked as an incompetent group of socialists who do not understand
the needs of industry, and the CBI members are satisfied in a
different way.

Conservative governments pose different problems. In many
respects, they are more likely to do what the CBI wants, and there
are therefore fewer areas in which policy can be 'shifted' in such
a way as to produce tangible benefits which can be displayed as
trophies to the membership. In other respects, when they do not do
what the CBI wants, they tend to be less open to influence than
Labour governments. There are a number of reasons for this tendency:

because Conservative ministers are more likely to have boardroom
experience, they feel more confident about asserting what industry
really needs; Conservative governments are anxious not to be seen
in the pockets of big business for electoral reasons and, if anything,
they are more likely to listen to the City than the CBI, whereas the
Labour party has a special respect for manufacturing industry.
Fidler (1981, p.229) reports a number of complaints from the
businessmen he interviewed about the influence of the City on the
Heath government, although much of City opinion was ultimately
disenchanted with what the Heath government achieved (Moran, 1981b,
p.391). The problem the CBI faces is that it is difficult to attack
a Conservative government openly for fear of upsetting those CBI
members who are loyal Conservative supporters. It should also be
remembered that, whatever worries and reservations businessmen have
about a Conservative government's policies, they regard any
Conservative government as preferable to a left-wing Labour government.

The CBI's difficulties with the Conservative government were
compounded by its own internal organisational problems. The impact
of the recession and, so the CBI claimed, its rate bill from Camden
Borough Council, led the CBI to declare thirty-one staff redundant
in May 1981. These redundancies, combined with a freeze on
recruitment, led to a reduction in staff from around 500 in 1979 to
360 by the end of 1981. The recession also made it difficult to
find a president to succeed Sir Ray Pennock in 1982. The job is
almost full-time and it was not easy to find a senior industrialist
with enough public standing and spare time.

The CBI's 1982 budget submission represented a delicate political
balancing act, combining a call for unchanged policies with some
quite robust criticisms of government policy. It must be stressed
that the tripartite conciliatory tendency has never been completely
submerged within the CBI, as is evidenced by the two to one vote
at the 1978 conference in favour of proportional representation.
It is not without significance that the CBI's 1980 conference saw
the launching of a new group for industrialists supporting the cause
of electoral reform. Among the supporters of the new group were
Sir John Sainsbury, Lord Plowden, Sir Adrian Cadbury, Evelyn de
Rothschild, Joseph Rank, Sir Fred Catherwood MEP, and Sir Maurice
Laing.

The CBI also knows that there are some industrialists who see the
Social Democrats as offering a new political hope for the future and
it has talked to the Social Democrats without being identified with
them. Moreoever, one commentator reported that ('Financial Times',
op.cit.)

> a lot of the [CBI] staff have joined the Social Democrats from
> both the right wing of the Labour party and the left wing of the
> Conservative party. This does not mean that the organisation is
> going 'pink' .... But it does illustrate the belief in consensus
> among many people concerned with industry who are tired of the
> polarisation of the main parties' policies.

If the Conservative government continues to be obdurate in the face
of mounting difficulties for industry, the CBI may once again move
towards a more conciliatory strategy. Another possibility is a
continuing revival of a new enthusiasm for protectionism which has
been evident among some sections of the membership, particularly

those industries hardest hit by import penetration such as footwear.
As a resolution from the Southern Regional Council submitted for the
1980 conference stated, 'This conference believes that the Confederation of British Industry should constantly remember that it is
British.'

ORGANISATIONAL OBJECTIVES OF THE CBI

The CBI was set up in 1965 to create a more effective and unified
organisation for employers. Industrial capital (or employers more
generally) cannot evolve an effective political strategy (or what
some might call 'class consciousness') without a common organisational
framework which facilitates the mediation of internal conflicts of
interest or ideology and allows the production of an agreed policy
around which members can unite. This task must be carried out
without resorting to a 'lowest common denominator' policy which is
so vague that it is unlikely to influence anyone, least of all
government. It is therefore important to consider any potential
internal divisions within the organisation, apart from those on
strategy which have already been discussed.

The transition from the three predecessor organisations of the
CBI to one unified organisation was achieved remarkably smoothly.
Perhaps the major problem was posed by the number of small firms
who had previously been in membership of the National Association
of British Manufacturers. Some of these smaller firms split away
from the new organisation to form a Society of Independent
Manufacturers, later the Smaller Businesses Association and
eventually the Association of Independent Businesses. However,
most of the small firm members of the predecessor organisations were
effectively coralled within the CBI in what eventually became a
Smaller Firms Council, led in 1981 by the Hon. Fiennes Cornwallis
of the Country Landowners Association. Nevertheless, as Viscount
Watkinson has emphasised, the CBI 'primarily revolves at present
around the pivot of the top one hundred manufacturing companies'
(op.cit., p.146). However, despite occasional complaints from
small firm members about the organisation being dominated by a
'Shell-ICI mafia', the CBI has been remarkably successful at
integrating smaller firms into what is essentially a representative
organisation for large industrial firms.

One of the organisational characteristics of the CBI which 'for
the outsider ... comes rather as a surprise' (Abromeit, 1980, p.45)
is the presence of all the major nationalised industries as members
with the exception of Rolls-Royce, the state-owned aero-engine
manufacturer, which resigned in 1982 because it did not believe
that it had been getting value for money from its £20,000 a year
membership fee. The nationalised industries had not been members
of the Federation of British Industries, but were allowed to join
the CBI (at first as associate members and in 1969 as full members)
because

There were many areas where the interests of the boards of
nationalised industries as large employers of labour and as
concerned with a wide range of managerial functions, coincided
with the interests of privately owned industry, and ... advantage

would accrue to both from their common membership of the CBI (CBI, 1965, p.7).

There have been tensions from time to time between private and public sector members, although these have been offset by such organisational devices as having separate committees patrolling the border between the public and private sectors and promoting better relationships between them.

In general, the nationalised industries have had a moderating influence on the CBI. A number of nationalised industry chairmen have played an important part in the work of the organisation. The late Lord Melchett was a close associate of Campbell Adamson and Sir Derek Ezra was for many years chairman of the CBI's Europe Committee. Nevertheless, the fact that all the specific problems of the nationalised industries cannot be dealt with by the CBI is indicated by the formation of the separate Nationalised Industries Chairmens' Committee. Originating as 'Alf Robens's lunch club', the group gradually acquired a more formal structure and its own tiny secretariat. It should not be seen as a competitor with the CBI with which it has close links; perhaps its main function is to enable the nationalised industry chairmen to forge a common solidarity in the face of government policies. Of course, it could provide the basis for a separate organisation for nationalised industries if a future government ever decides that the nationalised industries must leave the CBI.

The CBI also created a new category of membership for banks, finance houses, advertising agents, etc. on its formation, and in 1969 they were admitted to full membership. With the aid of a series of recruiting campaigns, the CBI has considerably increased its membership in the City and in the retail sector (although the Retail Consortium is not a member). However, although there has been some talk of the CBI becoming, in effect if not in name, a Confederation of British Business, such a title would not really be an accurate description of the organisation's role. The CBI is still essentially an organisation for manufacturing industry (see Tables 4.1 and 4.2). All its presidents have been drawn from industry, and the chairmen of its major committees have generally been drawn from the manufacturing sector. Most City institutions are content to use their traditional links with government through the Bank of England or devote their energies to their own growing trade associations. When the chairman of the Stock Exchange was asked why that institution had joined the CBI, he replied, 'I find that a difficult question to answer. I can't join the TUC, can I?' ('Financial Times', 22 January 1980). For the majority of financial institutions, CBI membership is a gesture of solidarity or, at most, a means of keeping in touch with industrial opinion.

A common conception of British capital is one which portrays financial interests as dominant over those of industrial capital. It is claimed that the interests of finance capital have been pursued at the expense of industrial capital, e.g., in the over-valuation of sterling in the 1960s. However, if there is such an objective clash of interest, it rarely comes to the surface, at any rate in the CBI. The CBI's evidence to the Wilson Committee on Financial Institutions could not be said to contain any fundamental criticisms of the operations of finance capital. Indeed, the

TABLE 4.1   CBI membership by category (per cent)

	1965	1970	1975	1979
Industrial companies (including construction)	98.5	96.4	93.5	77.6
Commercial companies	-	1.6	4.5	17.4
Associations	1.5	2.0	1.8	4.7
Public sector	-	0.1	0.1	0.3
(Total membership)	100	100	100	100

Source: CBI Annual Reports

TABLE 4.2   CBI subscription income by category, 1979 (per cent)

Industrial companies, over 1,000 employees	51.9
Commercial companies	14.1
Industrial companies, 201-1,000 employees	11.2
Associations	7.7
Industrial companies, 51-200 employees	5.3
Public sector	4.5
Industrial, 1-50 employees	2.7
Construction companies	2.6
Total	100

Source: CBI Annual Report, 1979

subject could not be said to be one which interests CBI activists very much.   At its 1978 conference the CBI overwhelmingly carried a motion which stated that

This Conference, recognising the interdependence of British industrial, commercial and financial sectors, in which each sector contributes to, and draws from, the success of the others, rejects any suggestion that there is a basic conflict between the requirements of industry, financial institutions and the national interest.

Perhaps more significant than the vote on this anodyne motion was the lack of interest that delegates displayed in the subject.   As the CBI admitted, 'The session on industry, commerce and finance clearly did not hold delegates' interest' (CBI, 1978a, p.41).

One possible explanation for this absence of conflict where many observers would expect it is that the significant dividing line is not between the City and industry, but between finance capital and large companies with extensive overseas interests, on the one hand; and medium-sized and smaller companies, with largely domestic

interests, on the other. It is, of course, the larger company with
transnational interests that tends to be dominant in the CBI. One
such company interviewed by the author stressed the importance to
its business strategy of maintaining good relations with the City.
The company was interested in expanding through negotiated acquisitions,
rather than highly publicised takeover battles, and the success of
such a strategy was highly dependent on good working relationships
with City institutions.

However, even if the boundaries of finance capital have to be
re-drawn to encompass the major transnationals, one must be careful
not to overstate the conflict between that sector and the rest of
industry. There are conflicts of interest between the City and its
transnational friends and the rest of industry, but these conflicts
are often sharpened in the perception of those who see the export
of capital overseas as one of the fundamental causes of Britain's
economic weakness. The absence of open conflict between finance
capital and industrial capital may not be a case of 'false consciousness', but may rather represent a realistic recognition by both
sides that what unites them is more important than what divides
them. After all, the CBI's view is that it is not a shortage of
external finance that has limited industrial investment but rather
a lack of confidence that industry will be able to earn a sufficient
return, a problem the organisation sees as related to such factors
as an increase in the bargaining power of labour and increased
government intervention.

The fact that both individual firms and trade associations and
employers' organisations are members of the CBI is another aspect
of the political organisation of industrial capital in the UK which
causes some puzzlement abroad. Certainly, the sector associations
make a relatively small contribution to the organisation's financial
costs, and the CBI often has to provide the smaller organisations
in membership with quite considerable assistance in the form of
services and even representational help. However, it would seem
that the CBI values their membership because it enhances the
organisation's claim to representativeness and allows it to keep in
touch with all industrial sectors. Membership for the industry
associations may also perform a control function: a trade association outside the CBI could, for example, run an extremely embarrassing
protectionist campaign; an employers' organisation might conclude a
pay deal which contained provisions which would set an example that
unions in other industries might attempt to imitate. The CBI cannot
stop such an organisation doing what it thinks is best for its
members, but it can have a restraining influence.

The real problem with the sector associations has not been the
conduct of their relations with the CBI, which have generally been
good, but in the chaotic nature of the system of industrial
representation below peak level. An attempt was made to reform this
system through the work of the Devlin Commission on Industrial
Representation which was sponsored by the CBI and the Association of
British Chambers of Commerce. However, very little came of the
Devlin Report, in part because the CBI was not enamoured of that part
of its conclusions which concerned the CBI, in part because there was
no real impetus for change at the sector or product level. On the
one hand, many of the more important industries (such as chemicals

and motor vehicles) already have highly effective trade associations; on the other hand, many of the small product associations of which Devlin was so critical, are highly cost-effective from the viewpoint of the individual industrialist. This still leaves some sectors in which representation is fragmented, often largely for historical reasons, into a series of medium-sized associations which cannot afford the kind of specialisation that modern industrial representation demands. The CBI now seems to have largely given up trying to restructure this secondary system of industrial representation, in part because it was disheartened by its earlier failures, and in part because it can no longer spare the resources for such an exercise.

POLITICAL OBJECTIVES

One of the characteristics which separates organisations like the CBI and TUC from other pressure groups is their wide range of concern. Apart from 'moral' issues like abortion and capital punishment, there is little that escapes the CBI's scrutiny. Clearly, the organisation's principal interest is in economic policy, but this includes a substantial interest in areas of social policy like education. The CBI's policy programmes, starting with 'The Road to Recovery' published in 1976, are comprehensive statements of preferences, backed up by relevant research evidence. However, as well as the 'broad sweep' of policy strategy, the CBI has concerned itself with a wide range of detailed issues such as running a campaign on water charges; criticising Health and Safety Executive regulations on dangerous substances; and opposing Private Bills sponsored by local authorities. Indeed, as rising rate demands have taken a larger share of declining profits, the CBI has displayed an increasing interest in the affairs of local authorities.

Clearly, however, there are some issues which have been of central concern to the CBI throughout its existence. Each of these central policy areas will be examined to see how successful the CBI has been in attaining its broad objectives. Such an approach does have serious limitations. It is open to the objection that the whole economic, social and political system is biased in favour of the interests represented by the CBI, although the CBI and its members would not see it that way. Thus, at the 1979 CBI conference the president spoke of the 'last call for dinner' for the market system in Britain and the director-general spoke of 'drinking in [the] Last Chance Saloon'. There is no doubt that many CBI members believe that Mrs Thatcher's government is all that stands between them and a rapid slide into a down-market version of the German Democratic Republic.

A further problem is that much of the CBI's influence does not come in the form of obtaining dramatic reversals in government policy, but rather through a 'drip, drip, drip' process, a gradual wearing away and modification of government programmes so that the final version bears little resemblance to the original intention. For example, the CBI fears that much pressure for environmental legislation is in essence a disguised attack on the profit system. However, its strategy has been to accept that some changes in the

statutory framework are both inevitable and desirable, but also to
ensure that such changes as do take place occur at a pace and in a
fashion that does not impose an excessive burden on industry. Hence,
the CBI's tactics are undramatic and its success difficult to
measure. Year by year, the CBI works quietly away on environmental
legislation, screening Private Bills and Private Members' Bills to
see that they do not contain clauses which damage its members'
interests; securing detailed amendments to legislation in Commons
committees (or more often) the Lords; and endeavouring to modify
the delegated legislation that often puts environmental measures
into effect through detailed negotiations with the government
department concerned. It is all very unspectacular, but it does
bring results which benefit the CBI's members.

A third problem with the approach adopted here is that the CBI's
stance on some issues has been ambiguous or has changed over time.
Industrialists are not always sure where their real interests lie.
This is true of one of the central issues of British politics over
the last fifteen years, prices and incomes policy. Certainly,
industrialists do not like controls over prices, although the CBI
did try its own voluntary prices initiative in 1971-2 with unhappy
consequences (Grant and Marsh, 1977, pp.192-7). However, what
about a government incomes policy? On the one hand, this could be
seen as an unwarrantable interference in the freedom of the
individual industrialist to fix wages. More pragmatically, firms
with full order books and needing skilled labour in short supply
might object to a policy which prevented them paying the rate
necessary to attract such labour. On the other hand, industrialists
recognise the importance of labour costs and the desirability, from
their point of view, of restraining them. If one has a statutory
incomes policy, the blame for a low offer can be transferred to
the government.

It is not surprising that the CBI has often found it difficult
to formulate policy on this issue, with its public sector members
often being more enthusiastic supporters of some kind of incomes
policy. The CBI supported the Heath government's incomes policies
and the CBI's economic director has argued in a retrospective
article that if the incomes policy had survived the test of the
1973-4 miners' dispute, 'many of our subsequent troubles would have
been avoided' (Glynn, 1978, p.31). However, the CBI did not oppose
the 1974 Labour government's abandonment of pay controls, partly
because of a desire to step away from what had come to be seen as a
policy of confrontation, and partly because 'many employers sought
an opportunity to restore pay differentials and remove pay anomalies
which had arisen under the incomes policy' (ibid., p.32). In May
1975, concerned about inflation and its impact on profits, the CBI
once again called for pay limits and 'an agreed analysis between the
CBI and TUC staffs played a significant part in leading to the
adoption of the £6 limit' (ibid., p.33). In their 1976 policy
document, the CBI found themselves unable to advocate a definite
policy position on incomes policy: 'we have decided that precise
proposals at this moment might not be helpful to our long-term aim
of securing a radical reform of our pay determination system' (CBI,
1976a, p.72). In 1978, the CBI plaintively stated: 'Employers do
not want to choose between moderation and freedom; they want both'

(CBI, 1978a, p.41).   The absence of a comprehensive pay policy under Mrs Thatcher's government helped to make the issue easier to handle for the CBI.   It was prepared to back the government's tough stance on public sector pay, although urging flexibility for its nationalised industry members, and discreetly encouraged its own members to restrain wage rises.

Any attempt to assess the success or otherwise of the CBI's efforts in the industrial relations field – apart from the complexity of the issues in this policy arena – is also complicated by the fact that its members have been divided on whether the best strategy is a 'co-optive' strategy which builds bridges with the unions or one that relies largely on penal labour laws.   When the CBI was formed, it was the first strategy that was emphasised, but towards the end of the 1970s the second strategy appears to have won more support within the organisation.   The CBI greatly resented the 1974–9 Labour government's industrial relations legislation which it saw as one-sided and biased against employers, although the CBI did manage to obtain some concessions on what became the Employment Protection Act.   The organisation's shift towards a harder line was marked by the introduction of the term 'employer solidarity' into the leadership's speeches: in his preface to the 1978 annual report, the president told members, 'employers must find ways of working together for greater solidarity, so that they are not picked off one by one.   This is one of the major themes on which we in the CBI will be working this coming year' (CBI, 1978b, p.3).   In practice, employer solidarity proved hard to develop.   CBI plans for a strike fund for employers had to be shelved for a combination of technical reasons, fears of its exploitation by 'rogue employers' and a general lack of support from member firms.

Despite its flirtation with the notion of employer solidarity, the CBI has generally adopted a more moderate approach to changes in industrial relations law than organisations such as the Institute of Directors.   The CBI's 1980 conference passed a motion endorsing Mr Prior's 'softly, softly' approach and recommending a cautious approach to any further proposals for changes in employment law. Summing up the debate on employment law at the 1981 conference, Mr Chris Walliker, chairman of the CBI's Midlands Region, stated that may industrialists were worried about changes in industrial relations law coming too far from the extreme right.   In the West Midlands the closed shop was not high on the agenda at meetings of personnel managers or CBI representatives and he hoped that the new Employment Secretary, Mr Norman Tebbitt, 'does not put as much emphasis on the closed shop as the Conservative associations of Cheltenham Spa or Ascot do' ('Financial Times', 5 November 1981).

One of the objectives which it was hoped that the formation of the CBI would achieve was the building of closer links with the TUC than had been possible on the part of the rather secretive British Employers' Confederation which dealt with industrial relations before 1965.   Some progress was made in establishing better relations with TUC, but the whole climate was soured by the Heath government's Industrial Relations Act and its aftermath.   Relations between the two organisations subsequently improved, but suffered a further setback in 1980 when the CBI Council failed to endorse a provisional agreement between the two bodies dealing with the introduction of new

technology in individual companies. Although many CBI members
welcomed the document as a statement of good practice, others felt
that it would do more harm than good by providing a platform on which
trade union demands could be built in individual companies. The
agreement would have been the first one between the two organisations
for eight years and the TUC had hoped that it would pave the way for
consensus on broader issues. TUC leaders were disappointed by what
they saw as a failure of the CBI leadership to 'sell' the agreement
to their 'backwoodsmen'. Private dinner meetings between the two
leaderships continued for a while, but relationships subsequently
underwent a further deterioration because of disagreements over the
Thatcher government's policies.

One of the CBI's main campaigning efforts during the lifetime of
the 1974-9 Labour government was its opposition to the Bullock Report
on industrial democracy. The CBI ran what it described as a 'sustained
campaign' against the report in the media, taking the view 'that the
proposals were not about so-called "industrial democracy", but about
power, particularly trade union power'. The CBI claims that, 'As a
result of the campaign led by the CBI, the government scrapped its
plans for the introduction of a Bill based on Bullock in the 1976/77
session of parliament' (CBI, 1977, p.6). Undoubtedly, the CBI
campaign did play a part in the outcome, but claims of this kind are
difficult to assess. Would the CBI have been successful if the
union movement had not been divided on the issue, and if right-wing
members of the Cabinet had not been lukewarm about the whole idea?
Perhaps the CBI was pushing at a door on a very weak latch.

The CBI also ran a vigorous campaign against the 1974-9 Labour
government's devolution proposals. Business reaction to this
prospect sometimes appeared to be a little excitable. Some Scottish
businessmen started to register their companies in England and the
vice-chairman of the Scottish CBI argued that devolution would lead
to the break-up of the United Kingdom. If it came to separation,
he declared, Scottish businessmen would do best to take the next
train to the border town of Carlisle ('Guardian', 6 May 1977). Some
businessmen with experience of countries with federal systems such
as Australia found the CBI's opposition to devolution somewhat
perplexing. Nevertheless, the Scottish CBI supported the 'Scotland
is British' campaign which 'entailed considerable support for, and
contact with, the campaign which advocated a "No" vote in the
referendum for a Scottish Assembly' (CBI, 1979, p.18). The CBI
was naturally pleased with the referendum result, although again
it is difficult to measure how much it was due to the CBI's efforts.

The CBI has placed increasing emphasis on what it sees as the
need to cut public expenditure and reduce taxation. In its 1978
policy programme, the CBI called for a 6 per cent reduction in
government expenditure as a proportion of GDP (from 44 per cent to
38 per cent) between 1976/7 and 1981/2. On taxation, the CBI called
for a basic income tax rate of 28 per cent and a top rate of 60 per
cent on earned income. The Conservative government's first budget
in 1979 'saw income taxes closely in line with CBI recommendations'
(ibid. p.7) particularly benefitting the higher paid. The CBI was
less enthusiastic about the way in which the burden of public
expenditure cuts fell on capital rather than current spending, thus
adversely affecting industries such as construction.

One area of government expenditure which poses problems for the
CBI is that of industrial policy. The CBI certainly had no time for
the highly interventionist policies advocated by the Labour government when it came into office in 1974. Aided by opposition to these
proposals within the highest levels of the Labour government itself,
the CBI quickly succeeded in watering down the original proposals
for extensive intervention in industry. Indeed, the National
Enterprise Board was made so acceptable to the CBI that the organisation was prepared to countenance its survival, albeit in a modified
form, at a time when the Conservative opposition was demanding its
abolition. Although many industrialists regard government intervention in industry as ideologically intolerable, many firms derive
considerable benefits from government assistance. On the whole,
the CBI has taken a much more generous view of regional assistance
than it has of national selective schemes which have tended to be
more discretionary in their operation compared with the 'automatic'
regional development grant. After he became director-general, Sir
Terence Beckett tried to persuade the CBI to develop a more positive
industrial policy that would recognise the need to help 'sunrise'
industries, but a lack of enthusiasm for these policies among the
membership led to them being dropped from a CBI discussion document.

The CBI has been a consistent supporter of British membership
of the European Community, although it has had serious misgivings
about policy developments in a number of areas. For example, in
1976 it published a critical review of the Community's industrial
policy which it said had been subject to 'delay and uncertainty'
(CBI, 1976b, p.1). However, although the overwhelming majority
of firms, particularly those with trading links with Europe, supported
continued British membership, the CBI has expressed concern about a
lack of enthusiasm for Community membership among some firms.

The CBI has enjoyed a number of significant policy successes
since its formation, although in many ways the 1979 Conservative
government has been harder to influence than its Labour predecessor.
Moreover, the CBI is worried about public attitudes towards business
in Britain and this had led it to launch what some people would
probably call an 'ideological offensive'. The CBI has expressed
its fear that 'there is still far too much ignorance and even
hostility towards industry not just in the schools but also in
polytechnics and universities' (CBI, 1976a, p.13). In 1976, the
CBI launched the 'Understanding British Industry' project, run
through a separate charitable trust. By 1978 it had raised £1.2
million, although by 1981 it was encountering cash flow difficulties
and it was reported that it would need £500,000 a year from 1983
to allow its work to continue. Aimed at 13-16-year-olds, the project
provides teaching materials which give 'young people the opportunity
to learn about the nature and functions of industry and commerce,
including their social and economic contribution, and the basic
elements of business economics' (ibid., p.13).

Despite the improved organisational capabilities of the CBI, and
its various policy successes, it should be noted that British
industry has continued to suffer from a continuing decline in its
rate of profit. The net rate of return at current replacement cost
for manufacturing companies declined from 13.3 per cent in 1960 to
2.0 per cent in 1980 ('British Business', 18 September 1981).

Although comparing the rate of profit across different countries poses technical problems, it would appear to have fallen faster in the UK than elsewhere (National Economic Development Office, 1980). This serious decline in profits does suggest that there are severe limits to the extent to which the CBI has been able to persuade politicians to create an economic climate favourable to business activity.

CONCLUSIONS

What does the task of 'representing capital' actually involve? Like many representative organisations, the CBI faces a membership that is quiescent and inactive for much of the time, despite the organisation's considerable efforts to bring about more member involvement through an expanded regional structure. This means that in practice most policy has to be made by a network of specialist committees working closely with the CBI's permanent staff. As far as broad strategy is concerned, the relationship between the president and the director-general is of crucial importance. However, such are the potential tensions within the organisation that there are limits to the leadership's freedom of manoeuvre set by the need to maintain at least the semblance of unity. Moreover, both Campbell Adamson and Sir Terence Beckett learned the hard way that there is a distinction between what businessmen say in private and what they are prepared to hear their spokesmen say in public.
    Representing capital requires a complex organisational structure to deal with a mass of issues, each of which may influence the ability of at least some businessmen to make a profit. It requires on the part of the leaders of the representative organisation an ability to forge policy positions which transcend the limited visions of some members without sacrificing their support. Representing capital involves being a trustee of the rather ambiguous values and conflicting interests of businessmen, but it is a trusteeship subject to recall by a membership not slow to respond to anything it regards as a breach of trust, even though the leadership of the CBI generally lacks any clear mandate from its members. Such a mandate cannot be provided by the conference which lacks any representative character; the largest delegation at the 1979 CBI conference was the entire works council of Fasson Adhesive Products on its annual outing with six more representatives than the team from ICI. Nor can a mandate be provided by the CBI Council, an unwieldy body of some 400 members which, at best, provides a mechanism for sounding out the mood of the membership. Ultimately, the CBI is governed by consensus, but it is a consensus which rests on an interpretation of what the membership, particularly the more influential of them, want, rather than on any clear statement of policy preferences by them. As Viscount Watkinson has commented, 'it is surprising ... that the CBI actually represents anything. Its structure ... is not well suited to the making of long-term policy or instant reaction to events' (op.cit., p.146).
    Nevertheless, the CBI does represent a more effective organisational framework for the representation of the interests of industrial capital than the three predecessor organisations; and

the CBI has grown in maturity, sophistication and organisational
capability in the first fifteen years of its existence. What is
the wider significance of this growth in the organisational strength
of the CBI? Middlemas (1979, p.452) has stated that

> a marxist analysis might suggest its role expanded as a
> consequence of an awareness among the capitalist class as a whole
> that its position was becoming increasingly insecure, not least
> because of the declining significance of the parliamentary system
> in general and the Conservative party in particular.

In the last resort, the CBI may not be able to determine its own
future; it will simply have to plot a path as best it can between
the treacherous sandbanks formed by the swirls and eddies of changing
economic trends and shifting political opinion. However influential
the CBI may be, it is weaker in terms of coercive and organisational
resources than the state and weaker in terms of political legitimacy
than the political parties. The CBI has stressed that it is a non-
party political organisation that does not model its activities on
those of the TUC. However, many of the decisions that ultimately
affect the prospects of its members are taken within the parallel
power system of the political parties. The combination of a
Conservative party apparently indifferent to the fate of industry
and a Labour party shifting leftwards does not augur well for the
CBI and its members. Some businessmen find the prospect of a
centrist government appealing, while others are staunch in their
Conservative loyalties in the face of what some of them see as
unavoidable adversity. A general belief in the desirability of
maintaining a capitalist economic system conceals many differences
of opinion among businessmen and gives little guidance on the
strategies and tactics to be used. The apparent strength of the
CBI can be deceptive, its task is a hazardous one, and its chances
of success are uncertain.

Chapter 5

CO-OPTATION AND STRATEGIC PLANNING IN THE LOCAL STATE (1)

Rob Flynn

INTRODUCTION

The relationship between governments and business is at the core of much political science and sociology and has been the source of considerable theoretical controversy. The identification and measurement of power pose fundamental questions, and in the case of urban policy-making and influences on local government there has been a variety of explanations ranging from community power through urban managerialism to neo-Marxist accounts of the local state in capitalism. Generally, empirical work is fraught with epistemol logical and methodological difficulties over the concept and estimation of power, and disputes about the nature and degree of state autonomy. This is particularly true in the analysis of the incorporation and representation of capitalist interests in local state policies (Saunders, 1979; Dunleavy, 1981a).

The role of the state within capitalism is obviously an enormous theoretical (and practical) puzzle. Most writers now acknowledge that the state is not merely an instrument for dominant class interests, and that it is neither homogeneous nor integrated. There is, moreover, awareness that there are distinct fractions of capital, and that the capital/state relation reflects the changing balance of class power, even though there are different views about the importance of economic and political forces (Holloway and Picciotto, eds, 1978; Urry, 1981a). At the more mundane local level it is also increasingly recognised that state policy is often, in Preteceille's words about urban planning, 'multiple, contra-dictory and torn between different exigencies' (Preteceille, 1974; 1976, p.74). The position adopted here is that we cannot simply assume a priori that the state is able to operate as a unified or efficient guarantor of the general interests of capital accumulation, or that class interests are totally determinant of, or directly reflected in, policy outputs. Rather, we need to be aware of the internal complexity of the state, the contingent and dynamic nature of state/society relations, and the variable nature of the mediation of control. More specifically we must, as Offe argues, investigate the manner and extent to which different state administrative organisations manage different functions and political

interests, without necessarily assuming that they are capable of
success or are functional (Offe, 1975).

This approach broadly corresponds with that advocated by Cawson
and Saunders above, who argue for the necessity of a dualistic
model of state structure and political representation (see also,
Saunders, 1979, 1981a). They suggest that, ideal-typically, social
consumption and social investment functions and policies are located
at different levels of the state, and are correlated with distinctive
political interests and types of political participation. Thus
social investment (e.g., state provision of physical infrastructure,
land, roads) is so important for capital accumulation that it is
the subject of political mediation in which large capital, central
state and organised labour (or 'corporate') interests predominate,
and is based in non-local institutions removed from popular pressure.
On the other hand, social consumption (e.g., public rented housing,
education, health, welfare services) tends to be decentralised, and
is the focus for local pluralistic (or 'competitive') politics and
especially working-class demands. Accordingly, 'questions regarding
the relative openness of different state agencies to different types
of groups in different areas must be answered through empirical
research' using different kinds of theory (Saunders, 1981a, p.271).
As we shall see below, there are problems in operationalising
this model, but it does provide a useful heuristic framework.
Moreover, it correctly emphasises the complexity of the form and
extent of capitalist involvement and influence in local government.

There is in fact little recent evidence of direct involvement
by capitalists in local government, notwithstanding the literature
on recruitment and social origins of councillors, and the existence
of commercial and industrial pressure groups in urban politics.
Several reasons may account for this apparent lack of involvement.
Local government affairs may not be directly or immediately relevant
to business and industrial activity, or central government policies
may be more important; and/or capitalist groups may actually
exercise influence over councils but covertly and informally through
community networks and unofficial participation in decision-making;
and/or their interests are effectively safeguarded in taken-for-
granted assumptions and non-decisions, which obviates the need to
participate in official politics. Whatever the reasons, the
conventional wisdom about low levels of involvement is being
questioned in the light of increasing examples of collaboration
between councils and industry, local authority intervention in
economic and urban development, and controversies about local rates
and the effects of fiscal crisis. Although central government
reductions in expenditure and restrictions on local government have
increased recently, local authorities still retain some discretion
over the disposition of powers, resources and services which afiect
the local economy directly and indirectly (see Broadbent, 1977;
Cockburn, 1977; Minns and Thornley, 1978; Young et al., 1980).
Given the potential relevance of the local state for both capital
accumulation and political legitimation, we therefore must explain
the pattern and processes by which different economic and political
interests affect council policy.

This chapter considers one aspect of this general problem: the
incorporation of capitalist interests in the formation of strategic

planning policy by a local authority. It describes the process by
which certain industrial groups were co-opted in the preparation
of a county structure plan, and analyses some of the implications
of the co-optation. There are several reasons why such a case-study
is relevant. First, structure plans are explicit statements of
strategic policy concerning a range of economic, physical and social
matters as they affect future patterns of land use and urban
development. In principle they represent one of the few formal and
public exercises resembling corporate planning in English local
government. Moreover, structure plans are intended to co-ordinate
plans for urban development and relate them not only to local,
regional and central government policies, but other public agencies
and private sector economic activity over a fifteen-year period.
They are, therefore, one of the many ways in which the local state
can attempt to influence capital and vice versa, and so require close
scrutiny.

Second, the case-study has a direct bearing on the question of
whether a new form of 'municipal corporatism' is emerging. Various
writers have shown that major local elites and business and
industrial groups play an influential or even dominant role in
statutory public participation procedures in structure planning
(Boaden et al., 1979; Darke, 1979, 1981) and others have suggested
that there is growing evidence of corporatism in town planning
(Simmie, 1981; Cawson and Saunders, chapter 1 in this volume). There
is disagreement, however, about whether land-use planning can be
regarded as an element of, or subject to, corporatist politics
(Cawson, 1977, 1978, Reade, 1980). There is even greater disagreement about the general validity of corporatism. It is a problematic
concept and discussion has centred on macro- or societal questions
about the integration of organised labour and capitalist groups in
central or national government decision-making. A major division
of opinion exists between those who regard corporatism as a
distinctly new or alternative economic and political system (Winkler,
1976), and those who merely view it as an extension of advanced
capitalism (Panitch, 1980). Corporatism is variously used to refer
to an ideology, a process, or a strategy, and there is uncertainty
about whether it describes a particular set of organisational and
political arrangements or their concrete outcomes. These ambiguities
add to the difficulties of identifying corporatism empirically.
However, if we adopt the broad, generic concept of corporatism
recommended by Crouch, then it would appear, superficially at least,
relevant to the case-study discussed below (Crouch, 1981). For
Crouch, corporatism consists of the institutionalisation of interest
representation: key groups are given privileged access to the
state, and play some part in policy-making, because they are
representative of interests which are potentially threatening to
the state, and because once incorporated they can regulate the
conduct of their members. The process of co-optation described
here resembles this general definition or pattern of corporatism
but provides further evidence of its problematic nature.

Finally the case-study points to the continued importance of
organisational and ideological factors in the explanation of
consultation and collaboration between industry and local government.
Any comprehensive analysis of the relation between capital and

and politics must include some examination of the role played by
bureaucrats and professionals in state agencies and inter-organisational relationships. Although there are inevitably constraints on
their autonomy and influence, state officials are located at the
interfaces between different levels of the state, local politicians,
fractions of capital, pressure groups and client populations (Pahl,
1977a). It is therefore necessary to assess the importance of
bureaucratic strategies and professional ideology in agenda-setting,
mediation between interests, coalition formation and the implementation of policy (Flynn, 1981). In addition, ideological factors are
relevant in accounting for the legitimacy accorded to state policies
and procedures, and the salience of tacit understandings between
councillors, officers and commercial, industrial or landowning
interests. However, as always, the major problem is that of
discovering relationships between intentions and outcomes, and
tracing the connections between subjective perceptions and material
interests. This chapter cannot resolve the latter problem, but it
does provide empirical material relating to the other issues. First,
there is an outline of the preparation of the case-study structure
plan, its aims and objectives. Then there is an account of the
emergence of a planning strategy geared to wealth creation, and the
arrangements for liaison between industrialists and the local
authority. The nature of local capitalist demands and the capacity
of the council to implement policies is considered, and finally
some of the contradictions arising from attempts at co-optation are
analysed.

Evidence is drawn from research conducted several years ago as a
participant-observation study of the role of planners as urban
managers (Flynn, 1979). (2) The project was based in a large non-
metropolitan county council controlled by the Conservative party.
Fieldwork extended over two years and involved direct observation,
interviews and documentary analysis. The main data sources used
here comprise official minutes, officers' memoranda and published
documents, together with observational notes from committee and
official meetings, and interviews with senior officers and councillors.
It must be stressed that much of this material is secondary,
fragmentary and largely related to structure planning. Moreover,
the case-study format restricts the extent to which wider generalisa-
tions can be made. Nevertheless, the evidence does provide insights
into the relatively unexplored process of co-optation and the links
between capital and the local state.

THE PRODUCTION OF STRUCTURE PLAN POLICIES AND OBJECTIVES

Structure plans are essentially formal statements of strategic policy
which, after examination-in-public and ministerial approval, act as
the main statutory framework for town and country planning in a
county area. Producing structure plans involves a large amount of
technical survey work and elaborate consultation procedures specified
by legislation and government advice, as well as intensive political
debate within a county council. As in most authorities, the task
of preparing reports, devising alternative strategies, and designing
policies in the case-study council was undertaken by a specialist

team of structure planning officers in the county planning department.
Research reports were drafted by middle- and upper-tier officers,
and work was co-ordinated by a steering group of senior planners.
There was also an extensive network of inter-departmental and inter-
authority (county/district) officer working parties which collated
information, considered draft proposals, and debated alternative
strategies. Regular reports to county councillors were made at
planning committee meetings and at chief officer briefings with
committee chairmen and other senior councillors. At several stages
of plan preparation, county councillors held joint meetings with
district councils to discuss the structure plan. In addition, the
formal public participation exercise included consultation at two
stages to consider public reaction and comment on alternative
options and the final draft plan. Throughout this process there
was a widespread circulation of documents to numerous official
bodies, a large number of public meetings and exhibitions throughout
the county, a household attitude survey, and publicity inviting
representations. The whole procedure took about four years from
inception to submission of the final documents to central government
and the examination-in-public.

Professional planners played important policy-making and mediating
roles in the production of the structure plan. As in all complex
organisations they adopted conventional strategies for bargaining
and persuasion, and invoked specific rationales to obtain commitment
to, and compliance with, a consensus on policy both within the
county council and between the county and other state and private
bodies. This consensus, and the planners' activities, can be
interpreted sociologically as creating a culture in which political
values were translated into technical policies, and which supplied
a normative framework to regulate future inter-authority, inter-
professional, and local state/private sector relationships (Flynn,
1981). The core assumption of that framework, from which detailed
objectives and tactics were derived, was that the strategic plan
should assist economic growth and wealth-creation in the county.

The county's philosophy and approach to planning, and detailed
proposals, were contained in their structure plan written statement
submitted to central government. In that document it was noted
that the plan, as well as providing a basis for local plans and
development control would also provide a 'guide or context within
which investment decisions taken by various public and private
agencies involved in the development process can be coordinated'.
Most importantly, the principal aim was to seek a gradual increase
in the growth of economic activity in the county by 'realising
economic potentials'. The structure plan, it was claimed, would
establish a suitable framework to encourage economic activity and
employment creation, and would work with industry's locational
preferences as far as possible. Accordingly, policies were designed
to encourage land, infrastructure and housing provision to assist
economic growth. However, the council stressed that the structure
plan and other local authority programmes were faced with several
major constraints: national and regional economic and planning
policies; existing land allocations, planning permissions and
established policies; limits on public sector resources; and great
uncertainty about future changes. Despite these problems the whole

thrust of the plan was towards policies which maximised the creation
of wealth and economic expansion.

Obviously there was a vast range of detailed policies proposed to
implement this strategy, but four major components can be identified.
First, the strategy involved concentration of land allocation,
housing, physical infrastructure and services in selected 'growth
points' in the county, and a decision to steer mobile industry to
those areas. Second, there was to be a moratorium on further land
for housebuilding: fresh land for housing would only be released
in exceptional circumstances for specific local needs. Third, in
certain areas employment growth would be encouraged but no further
housing or associated development would be permitted. Finally,
some areas in the county were to be protected from urban development
and were designated as 'restraint areas'. Over and above these
policies the county were anxious to introduce a 'corporate approach'
to implementation by establishing linkages with public utilities and
private sector groups.

The idea of explicitly gearing structure planning towards economic
expansion represented a significant evolution in county policy.
Previously, the dominant concern in planning had been to contain
urban growth and relatively little attention had been paid to
economic or employment matters. However, various factors seem to
have precipitated a shift in attitude and ideology away from a
negative approach towards positive planning. An alteration from a
basically conservation stance towards the goal of wealth-creation
can be linked with national economic recession, public expenditure
reductions, reduced population migration into the county, and a
realisation that, previously, housing growth had outpaced local
employment growth and service provision.

In addition to these external factors there recently had been
internal political changes in the council due to the changed
composition of the long-dominant Conservative party group (Liberal
and Labour representation was extremely small). The majority group
during the 1970s was predominantly composed of councillors with
backgrounds in business, industry, finance and the professions.
Detailed evidence is not available, but there are signs that changes
in councillor values and orientations altered the climate within
which the structure plan emerged and underpinned the move away from
conservation towards fostering economic growth.

However, changed political preferences and exogenous factors
were not the only stimulus towards an economically-based strategy.
Documentary, interview and observational data suggest that planning
officers were also influential. Clearly an osmotic relationship
normally exists between senior officials and leading councillors,
so that professional advice is conditioned by political expectations.
Nevertheless, senior planners initiated and guided much of the
explicit debate within the council about the need for a change in
direction for policy. Officers stressed the necessity to adapt in
the face of changing economic conditions and a revised regional
strategic plan. According to one senior planner, the economic
crisis had accelerated the review of county attitudes and once
councillors had been briefed they eagerly endorsed a shift in
planning policy. Similarly, at an early stage of plan preparation
the chief executive urged that economic objectives should be paramount

and that the plan should integrate and co-ordinate public and private investment. Thus, in a 'policy review statement', the chief executive recommended that the county must act 'in concert with industry and not in opposition to it ... we must find a way in which it can play its full part in the creation of wealth'.

So both political and professional attitudes converged and focussed on the need for planning to work with certain market trends, particularly in supporting manufacturing industry. In an interview the council leader explained that the structure plan's economic goals 'emerged naturally' out of the survey and analysis work done by the planners. Councillors had been alerted to the fact that while previously the county had accommodated the export of people and jobs from the adjacent conurbation, economic decline and demographic trends had removed these sources of growth. They were determined therefore not to allow any decline in the major industries in the county, not least because of their importance for employment and rates revenue. The structure plan's growth point proposals were thus entirely congruent with councillors' main priorities: first, because local authority service provision was to be more efficiently concentrated in specific zones with economic potential for growth, and, second, because other areas and towns could be conserved and protected in line with conservationist preferences.

However, within this broad strategy there were many political and professional uncertainties and dilemmas. The balance between different economic objectives (wealth-creation versus job-creation, employment versus housing development) and the effects of this on the future of different areas was the subject of continuing argument and debate, particularly with those district councils who either resisted designation as a growth zone, or rejected a conservation and restraint policy for their area. Such common contradictions arise out of an inherent tension between different capitalist demands and interests, particularly conflicts between manufacturing industry, commercial employers, small businesses and retailers, and landowners, developers and housebuilders. We shall consider some of these contradictions later, but now turn to the process by which some industrial groups were incorporated in the structure planning machinery.

LIAISON WITH INDUSTRY: CONSULTATION AND CO-OPTATION

At a very early stage of the structure planning process, and as part of their routine research, county planners undertook a survey of local labour market conditions. In several areas planners conducted the survey in collaboration with local productivity associations (comprising groups of employers in different industries and businesses). This work was used in preparing structure plan reports and was linked with other consultation exercises in which the county council sought views and comments from a large number of public and private organisations. General publicity and circulation of draft documents outlining the plan's functions led to the receipt of representations not only from local productivity associations but also from major industrial employers in the county, the local branch of the CBI and other employer and business groups. As a

result of this response, senior planners then held discussions with
various company chairmen, managing directors and chief executives
of large manufacturing firms, and other employer representatives.
    Documentary data from these meetings show that the employers'
main concern was for the 'needs of industry' to be fully taken into
account in the plan. They were also concerned about specific skilled
labour shortages in some areas, and difficulties in securing adequate
housing for employees. Officers stressed the limitations on county
powers and resources generally and restrictions on structure planning;
they also emphasised the importance of the conservation lobby in
influencing county policy. None the less, in one speech to employers,
the chief planner was noted as suggesting that the key issues for the
plan was employment and economic growth, and the main question was
whether to 'back the winners' (i.e., economically buoyant areas)
or attempt to stimulate growth elsewhere in the county.
    A desire to incorporate industrial interests more formally in the
planning process seems to have emerged out of these initially informal
officer-employer discussions. In officer notes for a meeting with a
local CBI branch, planners welcomed closer links between industry
and the county council and suggested that such contacts were one of
the best achievements of the structure plan. Moreover, it was
observed that the views of industry had not previously been sought,
that the creation of wealth was a mutually shared goal, and that
the council and industrialists would benefit from detailed discussions
about policies for land, labour and transport. Other documentary
evidence indicates planners' growing interest in the direct involvement of industrialists in discussions of policy options, and there
appears to have been a gradual acceptance of a move away from mere
consultation towards co-optation.
    Although legally required to conduct extensive consultations with
numerous organisations, the county was not statutorily compelled
to set up special machinery for liaison with industrialists. However,
county planners made positive and successful efforts to establish
regular meetings between industrialists and the council. A senior
planner's notes for a speech to one group of employers stressed the
necessity for the county to consult those organisations which were
likely to be major clients for the plan. It was suggested that
dialogue between planners and bodies regarded as customers or
instigators of activities affected by the plan would be very useful.
Mutual understanding between planners and industry was regarded as
especially helpful because there might then be better comprehension
of labour supply and demand, the scope for industrial expansion,
and how and where planning could assist industry.
    Within the department planners were generally agreed that by
engaging industrialists and employers in regular discussions during
the formation of policy, the county's subsequent influence would be
strengthened. The tacit assumption was that a high degree of
congruence between industrialists' priorities and the structure plan
strategy was desirable, and that common aims would make implementation of policies easier. Incorporating employers into the policy
process would increase the chances of gaining their confidence and
commitment, and so reduce the chances of opposition or conflict
subsequently.
    Clearly, certain local employers also felt that it was worthwhile

being involved with the structure plan, and useful to participate in
a liaison committee with the county council. Two 'industrial
liaison groups' were established, based on geographical divisions
of the county. One group was composed of chief executives, managing
directors and chairmen of major manufacturing firms spread across
the electronics, engineering, paper and cement industries. The
other group comprised employers of comparable status but from a wider
variety of industry including services. County council representatives
included the council leader, the planning committee chairman and
other leading councillors, the chief executive, chief planner, chief
highways and transport officer, and other specialist officials. Both
sides regarded these liaison groups as 'very high-powered'. Meetings
were conducted informally and held about every six months.
     Departmental memoranda indicated that the groups' objectives and
terms of reference were:
(a) to develop a dialogue between the county council and industry;
(b) to examine matters of joint concern;
(c) to bring to the county's attention the needs of industry in
    so far as they were affected by county policy and action;
(d) to inform the council of changes in industrial circumstances
    particularly land use and land requirements;
(e) to bring to the county's attention the views of industry
    on any relevant council policies and their long- and short-
    term effects on local industry.
It seems that these terms of reference were drawn intentionally wide
so as to encompass a broad range of local authority and industrial
activities. However, agendas for initial meetings were concerned
largely with structure plan matters. It was anticipated that liaison
group members would discuss labour availability, housing provision,
education and training, land allocation for local firms, road
construction priorities and public transport, and policy on industrial
location and the growth of distributive trade and office employment.
However, while the original impetus for collaboration and consultation
emanated from structure planners and was primarily concerned with
structure plan policies, the liaison groups actually went on to
function as meeting points for major employers and senior county
politicians and officials and dealt with a wider spectrum of issues.
     Planners' records of meetings showed that industrialists were
preoccupied with several major issues. The alleged negative effects
of central government regional and industrial development policies
appears to have been a major concern and cause for complaint among
industrialists both in discussions before and after the liaison
groups were convened. Employers criticised the procedures and
criteria for awarding industrial development certificates (IDCs:
permits to allow firms to expand their plant and factories) because
they prevented local firms from growing. County councillors and
officials assured employers that the council had consistently
criticised IDCs and had lobbied central government to adopt a more
flexible attitude. They referred to recent official county deputa-
tions to the minister and subsequent meetings at which Department
of Industry regional officials explained the operation of IDC policy
to local authorities and firms in the county. Central government
policy on diverting industrial growth to the depressed regions had
remained unchanged, and county officers argued that despite

industrialists' pleas for an easing of controls, and despite county
assistance for local firms, IDCs were largely outside the county's
influence. Planners reminded employers that the structure plan was
a general strategy, and that many factors were beyond their control.
However, opposition to IDC policy and pressure on the county to urge
a change in government policy continued and seems to have figured as
a regular issue for discussion in the liaison groups.

Industrialists were also worried about shortages of skilled labour
in certain areas and linked this with the problem of restricted
housing opportunities. They asserted that one of the reasons why
employers experienced difficulty in obtaining a supply of suitable
labour was that suitable housing was not readily available. Skilled
workers, they claimed, were often unable to break into relatively
expensive owner-occupation and/or were ineligible for council
housing; or they found it too expensive to move to the area from
outside the county. Planners seem to have acknowledged this as a
serious problem. Structure planners raised the issue with Department
of Environment regional officials and asked whether it was possible
to include policies in the plan which attempted to link industrial
employment growth with local authority housing programmes. Central
government officials advised them that the structure plan must
relate predominantly to land use and should avoid statements about
council housing allocation procedures, because these were district
council matters.

Nevertheless, county planners continued to press for policies
which would enable a greater match or fit between labour supply and
housing supply. Eventually a meeting was arranged between county
officials, employers' representatives and district councillors and
housing officers. Discussions centred on the extent to which
greater priority could be given to 'key workers' in the allocation
of council tenancies. Whether this led to any real changes in
policy is not known; county planners seem satisfied, however, that
district housing officials had been made aware of housing and labour
supply as a 'strategic' issue. Industrialists too were noted as
having expressed satisfaction with districts' statements that they
would adopt more flexible approaches in future.

A number of other themes were reiterated by county planners in
successive meetings of the industrial liaison groups. Officers'
notes reaffirmed the importance to the county of growth among
existing local employers, justified the structure plan strategy
in terms of benefits flowing from concentration of investment and
public infrastructure in a few growth points, and promised an
adequate supply of land for industrial expansion. Planners invited
industrialists' views on site requirements and employment prospects,
but also asked generally how the county could provide help for
industry. Two further demands emerged and re-appeared at most of
the minuted liaison group meetings: education and training, and
transport. Regarding education there appears to have been some
anxiety about school-leavers' skill levels and general criticism
of the educational system because it did not encourage positive
attitudes towards industry. In relation to transport, several
industrialists complained about low levels of investment in major
roads throughout the county, and urged greater priority for new
construction and improvements on specific routes.

The county council appears to have been disturbed by these
criticisms of local schools. In a published 'corporate review'
document the chief executive observed that: 'It is not only in the
planning field that the county council has heard the voice of the
industrialist. The message about attitudes, training and standards
from the industrial community has come through loud and clear.'
In a parallel report to the Policy and Resources committee, the chief
executive informed councillors that there had been criticisms by
industrialists about the quality of school leavers seeking jobs,
about lack of relevance in curriculum to the needs of industry, and
failures among career advisers to stimulate interest in industry.
It was subsequently decided to set up meetings for industrialists
to discuss these points with county educational officials, teachers
and local employment officials. Whether these talks had any practical
consequences for education cannot be determined, but they represent
a clear willingness by the county to respond to employers' complaints.

Transportation was an issue upon which planners and industrialists
shared virtually identical views. Senior planners recognised and
accepted many of the complaints firms made about road conditions,
traffic congestion and the need for new highway investment. However,
policies on roads and public transport were affected by different
pressures and demands in the structure plan. While planners
advocated expenditure priorities which assisted economic and
industrial growth, they were also aware that certain towns and
villages outside growth areas required relief by-passes and other
improvements. Central government control over (and reductions in)
transport expenditure was a crucial determinant of the highways
programme from the outset. While these constraints were readily
acknowledged by planners in talks with industrialists, a further
important constraint was not made explicit. Policy on transportation,
and the formulation of annual expenditure, was primarily the responsibility of a separate highways department, and county planners (and
thus the structure plan) had little direct influence over highways
staff, plans or expenditure.

Thus, the industrial liaison groups were a means for direct
communication and negotiation between major industrial employers and
senior council policy-makers. They were a new mechanism for
industrialists to express their demands and were superimposed on the
pre-existing pattern of consultative and political relationships.
They also provided a forum for planners to explain the logic and
implications of the structure plan strategy and other county policies,
as well as the constraints and difficulties encountered by the
authority. From the officers' viewpoint, such collaboration would
ultimately facilitate co-operation in the implementation of policies
and add some leverage to their own professional influence inside
and outside county hall.

Evidently officers and councillors regarded it as imperative to
establish special links and seek some kind of understanding with
industrial employers in the county. Small business and commerce
were not accorded so much political significance or explicit
attention; in any case, they were already indirectly represented
on district councils and through bodies like local Chambers of
Commerce. Trades unions and trades councils had been circulated with
publicity documents and invited to make representations but were not

formally involved as a group in the structure plan discussions. The
divisions of interest between fractions of capital and their
reflection in county/district political relationships cannot be
adequately treated here because of the research design and insufficient
data, but were nevertheless important. One aspect of the fragmentation
of capitalist interests can, however, be highlighted: the structure
plan embodied proposals which were intended to encourage employment
but minimise further housing development. Builders' and developers'
interests thus appeared to have been effectively subordinated to those
of industrial (and to a much lesser extent commercial) capital. Not
surprisingly this was a source of contention, and county planners
endeavoured to persuade builders and developers of the merits of the
plan through a separate liaison committee which we shall now briefly
consider.

Prior to the preparation of the structure plan, county planners
had established a liaison committee with representatives from both
small and large housebuilding firms (members of the National
Federation of Building Trades Employers) to discuss matters of mutual
concern. During the preparation of the plan, this committee met
several times and debated various policies together with other aspects
of local planning. At one of the observed meetings (at an early stage
in the structure plan) different housebuilders spoke of problems in
the construction industry caused by economic recession, and they
claimed that planning policies on residential land allocations were
exacerbating those problems. They were especially critical of the
Community Land Act (CLA), alleging that planners were causing
excessive delays in bringing land forward for development. County
planners agreed that recession had reduced housing demand and posed
problems for builders, but they suggested that the growth-point
strategy in the structure plan would encourage employment growth
and thus stimulate local housing demand. County planners denied
responsibility for delays in land release, and pointed out that
district councils were 'in the driving seat' since they were the
planning authorities with power to implement the Community Land Act.

After publication of the draft structure plan, housebuilders
repeated earlier criticisms and rejected the plan's proposals on
land for housing (i.e., in effect a freeze on further allocations).
Builders stressed that the CLA had restricted the flow of land for
development to an unacceptable degree, and pressed for membership
of the joint committee to be widened to include district planners
so that they could address the relevant officials. The latter
proposal was eventually agreed by county planners, but they refused
to modify structure plan policies on housing land.

Housebuilders dismissed planners' claims that sufficient land
(or planning permissions) was already available, and they informed
the planners that they would challenge the policy and dispute their
statistical data at the plan's examination-in-public. Planning
officers repeated the strategic justifications for the policy but
also indicated that the plan was very flexible and could change if
circumstances changed - if housing needs caused pressure in specific
areas, then the policy could be relaxed. But they stood by their
basic argument that urban development and housing would in future
be 'employment-led', and private housing would be linked to economic
expansion in selected areas in the county. The county council was

thus firmly committed to intervention in residential land development.
Two major arguments were repeatedly used by planners to de-fuse
builders' objections: an appeal to the overall 'rationality' of the
plan, arguing that its economic objectives would have local multiplier
effects on the housing market; and a reassurance that policies were
'contingent' or flexible and would be modified if necessary. The
builders and developers were not convinced, however, despite continued
discussions with planners in the liaison committee. Eventually
residential land availability became one of the major issues debated
formally at the examination-in-public, and the planners' efforts at
co-optation did not secure the compliance they desired.

These examples illustrate the familiar but crucial point that
capitalist demands and interests are neither uniform nor continuous.
The relative balance between fractions of capital, types of industry,
and stages of economic growth and decline will all obviously affect
the demands made on the local state. Demands will vary in nature
and degree and will probably be expressed in different ways in
different areas. Furthermore, the political composition and structure
of local authorities may not entirely coincide with, or consistently
reflect, discrete interests, and this will affect the way in which
councils acknowledge, or respond to, particular pressures. In this
case, industrialists' interests were regarded as strategically pre-
eminent, and likely to be undermined by the dissipation of public
resources which would result from unchecked private housing growth:
manufacturing industry thus took precedence over private housebuilding.

Formal liaison machinery was used as a device to secure some
agreement on the implications of this order of priority, but it was
also used to legitimate the local authority's directive powers. In
discussions with industrialists and housebuilders, county planning
policy was presented as facilitating selective economic growth and
smoothing out some of the dysfunctions of the market. However, it
was also emphasised that a rational, co-ordinated approach entailed
substantial strategic control and the ultimate sanction of intervention, through development control or withholding of local authority
services. 'Contingency planning' was offered as a means for
maintaining discretion and flexibility but in effect it also provided
for a form of putative relative autonomy in implementing the structure
plan.

Uncertainty about implementation is a general feature of structure
planning, but in this case it was especially important in that it
made county/industry liaison even more problematic. The difficulty
consisted in the fact that even assuming total agreement with
industrialists' complaints or support for their claims, the county
council could not guarantee the translation of the agreement or
commitment into action. Industrial employers had requested local
government assistance with what can broadly be described as both
production-related expenditure and policies (e.g., land, roads,
regional policy) and consumption-related services (e.g., local
authority housing, education). But even with a favourable local
political climate, the capacity of the county council and the
structure plan to provide this assistance was limited, uncertain
and variable. Many facilities and services required by employers
could not be directly supplied by the county council; for example,
council housing was a district responsibility, and public utilities

infrastructure was controlled by nationalised industries or
statutory undertakings (water supply, sewerage, gas, electricity).
There were of course statutory and procedural limitations on the
power of counties and structure plans, and the county could only hope
to persuade agencies to conform to the structure plan in many
instances. Moreover, central government through the rate support
grant, industrial development certificates and a host of other
measures also set the parameters within which local authorities and
employers worked, and so influenced the effectiveness of strategic
planning for economic activity. Within the county council, putting
the plan into effect also required a substantial degree of corporate
organisational integration and sustained political commitment. This
was obviously dependent on the extent of co-ordination among officials
and departments with differing bureaucratic and professional responsibilities and orientations, and the maintenance of political consensus
among the councillors. Finally, the structure of local government
and division of functions between county and districts added to the
uncertainty: ambiguity and disagreements not only about development
control and local plans but other issues ensured that county/district
relationships were complicated.

 As in all local authorities there were inevitably organisational
and political limits on the capacity and willingness of the county
to carry out their strategy. Co-optation of industrial groups can
be seen as a response by councillors and planners to their lack of
direct powers and their desire to influence industry. By contrast,
the county probably possessed sufficient legal powers to enforce
its policy on private housebuilding, and therefore did not need to
engage in such intensive co-optation of builders and developers.
However, the very process of incorporation revealed to industrialists
the constraints and limitations on county planning policy. This
raises two major questions - why the county undertook the co-optation
of industrial groups when it apparently demonstrated their limited
usefulness to industry, and why industrialists nevertheless were
prepared to collaborate and continue the liaison?

CONTRADICTIONS OF CO-OPTATION

There are many reasons why a local authority should go out of its way
to consult interest groups (see Dearlove, 1973; Newton, 1976;
Saunders, 1979). Political support must be won and opposition pre-
empted or contained if policies are to be successful. Where those
policies depend on voluntary compliance by organisations in the
external environment then local governments must secure acceptance
of and commitment to those policies through various methods. Active
attempts to co-opt important (i.e., potentially threatening or
autonomous) external groups and organisations in policy-making, to
involve or incorporate them in the decision-making process, is one
of these methods.

 Co-optation has long been recognised as a strategy in inter-
organisational relations in which groups strive to control their
environment by persuading rival agencies to collaborate in joint
activity (see for example Selznick, 1949; Elkin, 1975; Benson, 1978;
Pfeffer, 1981). According to Selznick, co-optation is a process of

absorbing new elements into the policy-determining structure of an
organisation as a means of averting threats to its stability. He
argued that it might take different forms, depending on whether the
main aims were securing legitimacy and respectability (formal
co-optation) or reacting to specific political pressures and interest
groups (informal co-optation). He also noted that there was likely
to be a persistent tension between the pragmatic necessity to
incorporate, and unwanted encroachment on, or sharing of, actual
power. The evidence reviewed above indicates that the division
between formal and informal co-optation is not clear-cut (see also
Moran's discussion of styles of incorporation, chapter 3 in this
volume) but it supports Selznick's view that co-optation is
administratively and politically expedient.

The practical (and theoretical) difficulty about co-optation is
that there is an inherent ambiguity about the sharing of power and
uncertainty about its outcomes. That indeed may render it expedient
but it also leads to contradictions. Token participation in
decision-making may offer some ideological and symbolic benefits
but eventually a co-opted group may demand material rewards and an
effective role in policy. Any attempt to subordinate co-opted
participants' interests, emasculate their influence or suppress
protest (c.f. corporatism) will almost certainly be unsuccessful
unless co-optation yields some important rewards for the co-opted
group. Similarly, even where there is no explicit intention to
subordinate an external group or the relationship is more akin to
partnership, there is still the risk that collaboration will
stimulate demands and expectations with which both parties are
unable or unwilling to comply. Thus, for example, this case-study
suggests that even though the local authority generally supported
industrial interests there was a dilemma, in that the council wished
to aid industry, yet it could not guarantee to deliver the decisions,
resources and services industry required. There was also a basic
tension between the county's political commitment to wealth creation
and assistance for industry and their affirmation of their powers
to intervene through strategic planning controls.

Obviously the conversion of capitalist demands or inputs into
local state outputs is extremely complex and empirically variable,
and the local state's capacity to respond to and service capitalist
demands is subject to different constraints. Inevitably, therefore,
difficulties arise when we try to determine whether this case of
industrial incorporation was merely window-dressing, or more symbolic
than substantive. In order to estimate the extent to which different
industrial demands were met and to assess the degree to which the
county and its structure plan effectively influenced other local
government actions, we require an elaborate conceptual model of
interests, causality and power, and a methodological approach which
accounts for non-decisions and enables the measurement of influence
over a period of time. These ideal theoretical and empirical
conditions cannot be met here because of the initial research
design and objectives, but, nevertheless, the data allow us to make
some general observations about the advantages and disadvantages
of co-optation for both industry and the local authority.

From the perspective of industrial capital several points can
be made. First, it is possible that industrialists initially

believed that participation in official liaison committees would
eventually result in council policies which fulfilled their demands,
but subsequently found this naive or mistaken. Second, it is
possible that industrialists appreciated the constraints on the
county and the problems of structure planning, but nonetheless hoped
that their involvement would be useful if the county could be used
as a spokesman, or acted as an agent representing their interests
with central government, district councils and other public agencies.
This is partly supported by evidence of county efforts on regional
policy, council housing and roads. Finally, consultation and
incorporation might simply have been regarded by industrialists as
a token return on their local financial investment - employers as
major ratepayers often complain about taxation without representation.
    The latter point is significant and should not be underestimated.
It is relevant to our awareness of the long-term and indeterminate
benefits which accrue from regular interaction or collaboration
between capitalist groups and local state agencies. The process of
incorporation is partly a reciprocal relationship, in which
participants may experience a mutual adjustment of attitudes and in
which some consensus on values may be expected to develop. The
value of this consensus, or what Saunders has described as
institutionalised friendship or political communion (Saunders, 1979,
pp.300ff), is considerable because it can affect future relations
between local authorities and capitalist groups. If collaboration
results in a stock of common assumptions and shared values, then
investments in goodwill can be expected to be capitalised when
specific needs or problems arise. Policies and decisions can thus
be shaped or even pre-empted by the taken-for-granted understandings
which emerge from such a process.
    If we consider the benefits of co-optation or incorporation from
the county council and planners' perspective, there are comparable
advantages. First, discussion actually produced some concrete
results in the form of information relevant to policy-making.
Second, industrialists' claims and suggestions were to some extent
used by planners as a professional resource in bargaining over
policy within the county council, with other local authorities and
agencies, with housebuilders and with central government. Then,
just as employers might have regarded their participation in
consultations as a reward for their rate-paying role, so too the
county council viewed participation as a potential lever for
subsequent influence. Thus, the incorporation of major industrialists
made it easier for the county to explain, insist upon and legitimate
interventive strategies, as well as using the power of big business
representation to stifle objections from small business and housebuilding interests. Finally, there were obvious public relations
benefits with ideological and political significance locally and
even nationally. Leading councillors and chief officers frequently
reminded county committees, district councils, Department of
Environment officials, members of the regional economic planning
council, and the general public, that their industrial liaison
groups were an important and valuable innovation. County press
releases on the occasion of the first meetings referred to them as
new initiatives which would promote better understanding between
industry and the county council. After a local meeting of the

regional economic planning council, the county Policy and Resources committee was minuted as noting with approval the 'new approach to industrial planning that was arising from the closer contacts now being developed ... (and) ... the good relations ... between local government and industry'. Through its liaison machinery the county could demonstrate its positive, forward-looking approach; it could show how local government and planning was geared into the needs of the local economy, and it could give the appearance of being a corporate, efficient and integrated organisation. In a Conservative-controlled authority, particularly at a time when the Labour government was requesting councils to assist industrial recovery, liaison with industry was good news.

Incorporation thus provided advantages to both industry and the local authority. The benefits were practical or substantive as well as symbolic or ideological. But generally there is a tension between these dimensions which leads to contradictions, because severe strains may be placed on a consensual relationship when either side wishes to convert or cash in the generalised assets of mutual understanding and goodwill. We cannot in this case be certain about the extent to which industrial firms would have acceded to inter-ventive planning policies or their willingness to support county restraint of private housebuilding and commercial development. We can reasonably infer that county influence over industrial capital was not dramatically enhanced by its attempts at co-optation or incorporation. However, the political and ideological implications of incorporation cannot be neglected. While the county structure plan's aims and corporate ambitions might not have been fulfilled and converted into real outputs, the explicit ideological commitment to wealth-creation and political incorporation of industrial capital were important in themselves.

CONCLUSIONS

This chapter has illustrated some aspects of the process by which a county council incorporated industrial groups into its structure plan, and has discussed some of the contradictions surrounding that process. Co-optation was directly linked with the local authority's political commitment to wealth-creation; it was a response to their perceived need to obtain industrial approval for the plan as well as their desire to acquire influence over economic and urban development. The incorporation of industrial interests in the formulation of planning policy was an outcome of a changed economic environment and changed political and professional attitudes within the council, but co-optation also provided further credibility for, and endorsement of, the strategy. It was also closely associated with the planners' strong professional interest in establishing liaison networks with the plan's major customers and other agencies. For the planners, co-optation enhanced prospects for successful implementation and at the same time strengthened their own position within the council bureaucracy and in relation to district council planning officials.

Collaboration through formal liaison arrangements did create some difficulties, however. Industrial consultation and participation in

policy discussions entailed some risk-taking by the local authority
in so far as demands were expressed which could not be easily or
directly met. It, therefore, exposed the county's limited powers
and their threshold of political commitment, and hence posed questions
about the council's (and structure plan's) usefulness to industry.
Senior councillors and officers seem to have regarded liaison as a
device for co-opting industrialists so that their interests would be
important guides but not overwhelmingly determinant elements in the
strategy. Evidence suggests that county planning policy was largely
congruent with industrial interests, but also that the county's
ability to implement the structure plan was restricted by various
factors. These limitations included statutory constraints on
structure planning, fragmentation of local government functions and
responsibilities, internal bureaucratic and professional factors,
the multiplicity and independence of other public agencies, central
government control, and political balances within the county council
itself and between it and the district councils. Even if the managers
of the local state had wanted or intended to exert direct influence
on industrial capital in an autonomous (or corporatist) manner, their
capacity to do so was severely limited.

Despite these constraints, council/industry liaison continued,
and was accorded great significance by officers and councillors
privately and publicly. Although the consequences of this process
can only be evaluated against specific decisions and/or inaction
by local authorities and capitalist groups, the incorporation of
industrial interests in structure planning had important ideological
and political functions. Without claiming that this interpretation
is generally applicable we can nevertheless argue that it illustrates
some of the most under-researched and problematic aspects of relations
between representatives of capital and the local state.

Evidently the bureaucratic and political mediation of capitalist
or anti-capitalist demands is theoretically complex and empirically
varied. At all levels of the state, political struggles, bureaucratic
and professional divisions, and financial and legal constraints set
limits on the state's ability to respond to demands and pressure,
and implement policies, whether they 'ultimately' serve capitalist
interests or not. Of course, these constraints and the very
institutional heterogeneity of the state raise fundamental questions
about its utility and effectiveness in relation to capital accumulation and legitimation. Hirsch has argued that the state is a
'heterogeneous conglomerate of only loosely-linked part apparatuses'
(Hirsch, 1978, p.100) and that diversification and fragmentation
are an inevitable reflection of class struggles. But he goes on to
claim that the state's institutional pluralism and heterogenous
structure allows it to relate to different classes more easily and
yet simultaneously protect and sustain conditions for capital
accumulation. Hirsch makes the unconvincing assertion that contradictions and complexity are inherent parts of state structure and
policy and are therefore the means of maintaining bourgeois
domination. It is, however, quite plausible to suggest that on
the contrary they may prevent or undermine such class dominance
and that the 'functionality' of state policy is contingent on many
factors. Pickvance, for example, has rejected the claim that state
intervention and state structure are directly functional for capital:

he favours a loose-link model of state-society relations precisely
because 'system-performance' is contingent - the state is not
independent, it is subject to different and often incompatible
demands, patron-client coalitions prevent the emergence of a coherent
state policy, and resources are limited (Pickvance, 1980). Thus,
the theoretical problem is to explain the conditions and circumstances
which account for different forms and effects of state intervention.

Several writers have suggested that there is a discernible pattern
in the organisational diversity of the state and that it is related
to types of political arrangements and the representation of
interests. Friedland et al. (1977) have argued that governmental
structures can be analysed as mechanisms for coping with contradictory
functions. They assert that basically the state undertakes economic
(accumulation) and political (integration) functions, and there is
a tendency to segregate these potentially contradictory functions at
different levels of government. Organisations and policies primarily
concerned with accumulation, they suggest, are often autonomous and
insulated from direct electoral or political influence, whereas
agencies concerned with legitimation are more accessible and local.
Dearlove has used this kind of argument to explain the re-organisation
of English local government and the historical transfer of
economically-relevant functions away from local to higher levels of
the state (Dearlove, 1979). And, as noted earlier, Cawson and
Saunders also suggest that policies concerned with 'state consumption'
functions tend to be performed locally and are the object of
'competitive' or pluralistic politics, whereas policies for 'social
investment' functions are located in semi-autonomous agencies which
are the object of 'corporate' politics (see also Saunders, 1981a,
1981b).

This dualistic model of state structure and politics is certainly
plausible, but its validity depends entirely upon the ideal-type
dichotomy between investment/consumption and productive/non-productive
functions. O'Connor (1973), Gough (1979) and Cawson and Saunders
all recognise that this dichotomy is not rigid, since most policies
can be regarded as having several dimensions and maintaining both
production and the reproduction of labour power. Indeed Cawson and
Saunders acknowledge that in operational terms it is difficult to
apply in local government because local authorities perform a
variety of functions containing elements affecting both investment
and consumption. This is particularly relevant to this case-study
because structure plans are oriented to several functions. As the
evidence above shows, what has been termed corporate interest
mediation occurred in parallel with conventional competitive
politics. This may, of course, have resulted from the indeterminacy
of structure plans as such, but it casts some doubt upon Cawson's
argument that structure planning will be correlated with corporatism
whereas development control will be associated with pluralist
politics (Cawson, 1977, 1978; see also Reade, 1980). Thus, the
thesis of the bifurcation of functions, interests and politics is
problematic because types of policy cannot be unambiguously assigned
to either production or consumption, and because at different
levels of the state the nature of political representation is mixed
and variable. Here we are thrown back upon empirical versus heuristic
uses of ideal-types, and the necessity for further research.

We cannot simply describe the co-optation process analysed above as the basis for a distinctive local corporatism, notwithstanding the conceptual ambiguities of corporatism. Certainly there were many close resemblances with Winkler's principles of corporatist administration and his emphasis upon permanent bargaining and continuous informal negotiations between the state and private economic groups (Winkler, 1977). But co-optation is not totally synonymous with corporatism even though it may be used as a corporatist technique. In so far as corporatism necessarily involves an asymmetrical power relation favouring the state over functionally representative interest groups, then the activities described here cannot be interpreted as evidence of corporatism. If, however, the concept is less restrictive, corporatism may be an appropriate descriptive term, but arguably it then loses its specificity since it merely connotes an organisational strategy on the part of the state and a variant of interest group politics. The distinction between intention and outcome is also very important in determining the existence or extent of corporatism, and clearly in this case we require much more empirical evidence about the actual consequences of strategic policies for different interests to decide whether quasi-corporatist arrangements and rhetoric had real effects in practice.

This returns us to the ideological and political significance of ambivalent state policies, organisational fragmentation, and varied and intricate linkages between capital and the state. Friedland and his colleagues have observed that in the USA: 'municipal activities at any given historical moment constitute an aggregation of functions, agencies and expenditures which may no longer be functional to the requirements of either accumulation or legitimation' (Friedland et al., 1977, p.466). Such a situation may seem paradoxical and puzzling initially, but can be explained by using the work of Offe. In his analysis of logics of policy production within the state (bureaucracy, rational planning, and participation) Offe stresses that none of these modes of decision-making and organisation can perform state functions without disturbing the accumulation process (Offe, 1975). There is accordingly a constant attempt to balance or reconcile contradictory demands or conflicting policies, and a corresponding ambivalence in the mode of organisation and internal state structure (ibid., p.144). But whereas Hirsch and others imply that it is because of fragmentation that the state can guarantee conditions for capital accumulation, Offe argues that, on the contrary, the state's role is necessarily impaired. Thus, he claims that there is no evidence to suppose that the state does reconcile legitimation and accumulation functions, and so there cannot be a balanced integration of the state and capital. For Offe the reality is one in which the state permanently searches for a structure and method of operation which attempts to balance those contradictions. This certainly seems to be a useful perspective on the process of incorporation in the case study described above.

Therefore, we can view this example of co-optation as illustrating in a small-scale way part of the local state's constant effort to reconcile divergent functions and manage contradictions. The structure planning exercise can be regarded as one of the many ways in which, through its totality of contacts, the local authority sought to filter and respond to competing demands. There are some obvious similarities here with Castells's account of industrial development in the Dunkirk region, where he showed that local government plans 'rationalise' interests and provide 'scenarios for compromise' between conflicting classes and strata (Castells, 1978, pp.84-7). He rejected the idea that such urban planning was merely a vast enterprise in ideological mystification but argued that it became an important political 'stake' over which different interests competed. According to Castells, urban planning effectively provides an arena for negotiations and therefore constitutes an urban political process. Thus, at one level, planning provides a rational-isation of, and legitimation for, specific policy objectives, and at another level it constitutes a mechanism for negotiation and conciliation between conflicting interests within the 'technical-neutral' framework of the plan and its procedures. This plausible view can be linked with Offe's analysis because it emphasises the importance of ideological and political factors and forces us to recognise their salience in policy formation. While it is vital to determine the concrete effectiveness of local state policies for capital, we must not disregard or neglect the ideological and political importance of systematic efforts by the state to incorporate major interest groups.

Clearly co-optation is merely one method by which the local state can attempt to deal with powerful agencies and interest groups. However, we need to know much more about the variety of inter-organisational relationships and the actors and mechanisms involved in networks for consultation and bargaining. This is necessary, first, because of the fragmentation of central and local government activities and the multiplicity of public and private sector organisations involved in state policy. Second, it is relevant because there is renewed interest in flexible, pragmatic and incremental decision-making, and contingency planning, due to the recession and fiscal crisis. Both factors reinforce the capacity of officials to wield considerable influence, since urban managers or state bureaucrats work as intermediaries between capital, the state and client populations (Pahl, 1977a). Senior local government officials are frequently crucial as front-line diplomats or negotiators with powerful interest groups and representatives of other state and public agencies. Indeed, professional planning ideology has encouraged planners to assume a more explicitly corporatist role and to develop reticulist skills (Royal Town Planning Institute, 1976). Further, technical expertise invoked by officials may apparently de-politicise issues and thereby extend bureaucratic and professional influence over policy formation and implementation. Thus, as Dunleavy (1980c, 1981a, 1981b) and Saunders (1981b) have argued, it remains necessary to examine the character and scope of professionals' power without exaggerating a priori their autonomy or discretion. It is therefore important to continue to analyse the roles and strategies of state bureaucrats in the mediation of interests and the management of networks if we wish to appreciate and explain the full complexity of relations between capital, politics and the state.

NOTES

1 This chapter is a revised version of a paper presented in 1981
   at the BSA/PSA Conference on Capital, Ideology and Politics,
   University of Sheffield, the Urban Studies Seminar, University
   of Kent, the Public Policy Seminar, University of Manchester,
   and the Sociology Seminar, University of Salford. I wish to
   thank participants for helpful discussions, and also Michael
   Harloe, Alan Hooper, Mike Goldsmith and Chris Pickvance for their
   comments.
2 The project was financed by the Social Science Research Council,
   whose support is gratefully acknowledged. The local authority
   and individuals involved must remain anonymous. No criticism
   of councillors or officers is intended or implied in the
   discussion which follows.

Chapter 6

THE POLITICAL PRACTICE OF THE LOCAL CAPITALIST ASSOCIATION
Roger King

INTRODUCTION

This chapter is based on a study of the Leeds Chamber of Commerce and Industry and takes up two main themes: the theoretical issues that inform work on capitalist organisations, and increased association between Chambers of Commerce and local authorities following local government reorganisation in 1974. The data base derives from examination of the minutes of the Leeds Chamber of Commerce's Council and associated committees, its year books, directories, bulletins and other of its public and semi-public documents for the period 1970-81. Additionally, local newspapers have been analysed for the same period and data are also drawn from interviews with leading members and staff of the Leeds Chamber, local authority councillors and officers, officials from government departments, and members and staff of other local organisations.

The system of business representation in Britain

A problem with a study such as this is that the efforts of business to advance or defend its interests collectively have attracted very little attention from social scientists. In comparison with that of trade unions the study of business associations is a relatively unchartered area, particularly analysis of local and regional groups. Possible reasons for this indifference are considered later but it does point to the need to present an initial account of the system of business representation in Britain. The Leeds Chamber of Commerce and Industry (LCCI) belongs to one of two systems of formal business organisation that operate 'somewhat disconnectedly' in Britain (Devlin, 1972, p.12). One is associated at national level with the Association of British Chambers of Commerce (ABCC) while the other is centred on the Confederation of British Industry (CBI).

Established in 1860, the ABCC is a weak and underfunded body in comparison with the CBI and the Chambers of Commerce movement exerts its main influence at local and regional level. However, considerable variation exists between the 87 incorporated Chambers belonging to the ABCC (a number of mainly small Chambers remain outside). Although around one half of Chambers' membership consists of manufacturers, by far the greater number of organisations known as Chambers of Commerce are little different from Chambers of Trade (ibid., p.54). In the smaller towns Chambers of Commerce mainly represent small retailers and shopkeepers but in the bigger towns and cities, such as Leeds, they operate more as a general business organisation reflecting the business composition of an area and including quite large manufacturers and public utilities as members. LCCI, for example, includes on its council the following: bankers, textile manufacturers, estate agents, a large departmental store owner, a major publisher, a big engineering company proprietor, a divisional manager of British Rail, the local Head Postmaster, and so on.

The ABCC is largely dominated by a 'first division' of the biggest Chambers (see Table 6.1). Many of these, including Leeds, also act as a regional Chamber, providing the regional co-ordinating body with its secretariat in return for a fee. Additionally, the directors of the six or seven largest Chambers meet informally to discuss issues prior to ABCC meetings. Although Chambers of Commerce offer a range of valued services not available from any other single source to their members and are the sole, government-approved body for issuing certificates of origin for exporters, acting as the Department of Trade's agents, they lack the public law status of their continental counterparts. The United Kingdom is one of the exceptional cases (along with the USA, Scandinavia and Switzerland) in which no form of obligatory, semi-public representation exists for capitalists. In the rest of Europe Chambers generally are recognised by law, often with a legal right to consultation by government, and are financed by some form of compulsory levy on business. In return they discharge certain functions which would otherwise be undertaken by a government body. For example, French Chambers administer the ports. ABCC policy is to seek a similar status for British Chambers although they have been rebuffed recently on this by the Conservative government. Staff in the Chambers particularly stress the financial and representational advantages of such a move although for many members the idea of a compulsory membership and levy, virtually an employers' closed shop, is anathema. Current lobbying for statutory status may reflect the development of closer and more formal consultative links between Chambers and local authorities.

Unlike the Chambers of Commerce movement the CBI's representational strength is at national level where it has established close ties with government. Funded and chiefly operated by big industrial companies the CBI has had difficulty in keeping small business members while its larger members baulk at closer relations with retailers, although they are less sensitive about big retailers who are often also manufacturers (Grant and Marsh, 1977, p.40). However, as was noted earlier (see Grant, chapter 4 in this volume), the CBI has sought recently to further strengthen its regional organisation, to become more involved in local politics, and to attain closer links with Chambers of Commerce at regional level. Many of the 800 or so trade associations and employers' organisations which draw membership from an individual industry or sub-industry and bargain over wages and working conditions, unlike Chambers of Commerce, belong to the CBI.

TABLE 6.1   Company membership, permanent staff and income of the
largest Chambers of Commerce (*)

Chambers	Members	Staff	Income (£)
London	8150	80	2,060,000
Birmingham	4105	89	597,600
Manchester	2964	75	465,000
Glasgow	2666	23	217,000
Merseyside	1919	30	264,000
Leeds	1616	21	248,460
Slough	1600	27	340,000
Coventry	1345	71	113,725
Sheffield	1341	24	202,515

Source: ABCC 1980
(*) At 1.10.1979

THEORISING BUSINESS-GOVERNMENT RELATIONS

One justification for the lack of academic attention given to
business organisations may be that they are relatively unimportant
for capitalists. That is, the real co-ordination and promotion of
capitalist interests lies in other forms such as the state, inter-
locking directorships, finance capital, or informal or social
networks. In this view, as Engels (1968) remarked:
> Capitalists are always organised. They need in most cases no
> formal union, no rules, officers, etc. Their small numbers, as
> compared with that of workmen, the fact of their forming a
> separate class, their constant social and commercial intercourse
> stand them in lieu of that.

Contemporarily it would appear that these other forms continue to be
important in co-ordinating business and some recent theories of
the role of the state in capitalist societies imply no real necessity
for business to formally organise to promote its interests.
Instrumentalist and structural Marxist perspectives on the state,
for example, suggest that capital is uniquely privileged by political
institutions. Instrumentalists, so-called because the state is
seen as representing an instrument by which the capitalist class
rules politically, claim that the economic influence of capital and
the common social backgrounds and milieux of state and business
leaders generally ensure even for Labour administrations that
political rule is exercised on behalf of capital (Lojkine, 1977;
Miliband, 1973). Structural Marxists explain the actions of
politicians and administrators more by reference to the structural
dependence of the state on capitalist accumulation (Holloway and
Picciotto, eds, 1978), but theorists from both perspectives suggest
that while the state unifies the different parts of capital it does
so primarily for large ('monopoly') capital which has distinct
interests.

A problem with these propositions is that capitalists do form
organisations. If business is inevitably privileged in the political
systems of advanced capitalist societies, why does it require

interest associations? Presumably it could be argued that business
associations form around small or 'non-monopoly' capital in reaction
to the state's concern for big business. But as some associations,
such as the CBI, cater predominantly for large capital this hardly
applies generally. Furthermore, rather than business not requiring
formal organisation to secure its concerns politically, it may be
that it is the effectiveness of such association which ensures that
governments, even socialist ones, maintain or advance capitalist
interests.

Two other perspectives on the political system regard the relation
between business and the state as more problematical. 'Managerialists'
see the goals and values of officials as a crucial element in
government decisions. The increasing rationalisation of administration
is viewed as providing state bureaucrats with the capacity to pursue
their own interests in determining policy, while at local level they
are regarded as performing an important mediating role between the
private and public sectors (Pahl, 1977a; Pickvance, 1977). This
perspective clearly allows theoretical space for the existence of
business organisations such as Chambers of Commerce; businessmen
organise to ensure that government officials take full account of
their claims in decision-making. In more 'conservative' variants
of this view the expansion of bureaucratic power constitutes a
source of economic danger to capitalist interests. The 'anti-
business' policies of 'collectivist' governments of both left and
right are pointed to as evidence that business does not automatically
benefit from state policies (Bacon and Eltis, 1978; Brittan, 1976).
The existence of business organisations may be regarded, in part at
least, as a response to the growth and perceived dangers of
government influence and intervention in the economy.

While managerialists emphasise the growing influence of the state
as a major constraint on the realisation of business interests,
pluralists point to the relative passivity of government as providing
that business interests are not necessarily more privileged than
others. The state acts as arbiter between contending class and
other interests and while businessmen organise to press their
demands, often with great effect, the political system is sufficiently
open to allow the successful mobilisation of countervailing power
(Dahl, 1961; Polsby, 1963). At American city level empirical
studies of key decisions by those operating with this perspective
found the political process to possess a high degree of autonomy
from the economic (Banfield and Wilson, 1966), although instrumentalist accounts indicate that businessmen and business groups have a
reputation for being politically dominant (Hunter, 1953; Miller,
1970). However, the relevance of American community power approaches
and findings for an understanding of organised business representation in British local politics is unclear for few such studies have
been undertaken in this country (Crewe, 1974, p.36; Dunleavy, 1980c,
p.26).

Despite difficulties with claims that capital is inevitably
privileged politically in capitalist societies it may be that in
comparison with labour there is less imperative for capital to form
interest associations. Offe and Wiesenthal (1979), for example,
argue that capital has at its command three different forms of
collective action to define and defend its interests: the firm

itself, in which many units of 'dead' labour are merged under a
unified command, informal co-operation, and the business association.
Workers, however, are dependent on formal association alone to achieve
bargaining power and the collective will to overcome individuality.
Historically, labour combines in response to the merging of the means
of production of small commodity producers into large industrial
firms. In turn this triggers business organisation as firms, in
addition to their continued merging of capital, recognise formal
association as a means of promoting their collective interests against
the challenge offered by labour organisation and political representation in an era of mass democracy. However, their preferred and most
efficient way of action is to respond individually to the constraints
and opportunities offered by the market. This is a less hazardous
method of control than offered by the political frame of action in
which agents perform, however nominally in actuality, on equal terms.

If it is accepted that organised political representation is a
less preferred source of influence for capital than individual action
in the market, this suggests that formal association occurs when
economic power is weakened and is no longer sufficient for controlling
the political process (Streeck, Schmitter and Martinelli, 1980, p.16).
It may be a response to the development of trade unions and socialist
parties, or to the increasingly systematic intervention of the state
in the economy and the decline of the market as a mechanism for
resource allocation. Collective capitalist organisations in such
circumstances may be better able than individual businessmen to both
resist attacks on entrepreneurial sovereignty and to calculate how
the long-run interests of members are best preserved (by political
concessions, for example).

None the less, in theorising the origins of at least some business
organisations we should beware too dominant an emphasis on the
'parallelism' thesis or factors associated with capital-labour
relations. A further reason why capitalists form associations may
lie in the need to overcome market 'irrationalities' or crises, such
as the inadequacies of communication or legal institutions. The
founding of the Leeds Chamber of Commerce in 1851, for example,
stemmed from the need for capitalist owners in Leeds to bring some
form of order to the local economic system. Its original members
were roughly the same group of people who had joined together since
1848 in the West Riding Trade Protection Association and whose
objects were to guard against the purchase of 'goods by fraudulent
and false pretence' (Beresford, 1951, p.25). The commercial world
for Leeds businessmen was expanding rapidly in the mid-nineteenth
century and increasingly involved more distant markets, unfamiliar
buyers, greater need for credit and the need for currency exchanges.
Furthermore, in the increasingly impersonal world of continental
markets and trans-oceanic contracts the loopholes for dishonesty
or sharp practice were becoming far greater.

Consequently a great deal of the Chamber's time in its first
decades was spent on trying to bring some form of increased
rationality to the local economy by seeking such reforms as the
codification of mercantile law, the provision of a district
registration of partnerships, heavier penalties against the fraudulent
use of trade marks, and longer sentences for jailed debtors. In part
this reflected the impatience of the commercial entrepreneur with the

practices and institutions of the landed gentry and the desire for
more 'businesslike' laws and procedures. Many local officials,
particularly in the law courts, often held appointment for life,
having purchased the office and with the work being done by underlings
paid a small fraction of the salary (ibid., p.47). The Leeds
Bankruptcy Commissioner appears to have been a major source of
criticism: for sitting irregularly, for being inefficient, and for
being expensive (ibid., p.42). The Chamber's demands for reforms
were generally accompanied by proposals for Tribunals of Commerce
composed of businessmen and commercially-minded lawyers to provide
cheaper and business-informed practices. Further signs of the
Chamber's pursuit of a more orderly market were seen in its demands
for cheaper and more efficient postal services, which reflected not
only widening markets but also the recognition that poor services in
Leeds gave commercial advantages to competitors in other towns.
There was also anxiety over the monopolisation of ownership of the
railway companies and fear that the result would be higher rates and
a more inefficient service.

Interest representation and corporatism

Recent discussions of the state have helped to raise the issue of
the modes by which different types of interests are represented in
the political systems of advanced capitalist societies. In one view
interest articulation through political parties and competing pressure
groups is increasingly accompanied by functional group representation
corresponding to the social organisation of economic production and
distribution. The representatives of capital and labour become drawn
directly and regularly into the governmental process with public
policy tending to be the outcome of bargained or concerted action
by state, capital and labour. Policy also may be implemented by ad
hoc or quasi-autonomous bodies reflecting a similar tripartite
composition. In exchange for such involvement the leaderships of
the economic groups are expected to successfully secure agreement
from members for state policy, and if necessary overcome internal
dissent (Cawson, 1978; Jessop, 1978; Pahl and Winkler, 1974; Panitch,
1980; Schmitter and Lehmbruch, eds, 1979). Explanations for these
developments tend to divide in the importance attached to changes
in society, particularly the increasing concentration and centralisation of economic activity, and that attached to regime encouragement
of corporatism as a response to 'ungovernability', the disorganisation
of political parties and their inability to build legitimacy, and
the ineffectiveness of market and bureaucratic forms of policy
making (Berger, 1981a). None the less there is agreement that
corporatist arrangements seek the depoliticisation of conflict and
may enable the state, among other goals, to support capital
accumulation more effectively by insulating economic policies from
popular struggles.
     The appositeness of corporatist models of interest intermediation
for analysis of business organisations such as Chambers of Commerce
is not immediately clear and we can identify one particular difficulty.
Corporatist arrangements, despite their formal symmetry, appear to
have different implications for capital as compared with labour

associations and this reflects a fundamental inequality in capital-labour relations (Panitch, 1980, p.180). While a central element of corporatist intermediation for many writers is that it emasculates labour and induces collaboration from its leaders, it is not really apparent what government gains from business by such arrangements. The apparently greater degree of influence exercised by business in public policy, in comparison with that exercised by unions, is achieved without capitalist organisations effectively controlling members in the manner of labour unions. As Offe (1981, p.150) notes:

> The traffic runs in one direction, because the viewpoint of
> organised capital can be transmitted to the political system but
> the spokesmen of these groups can make no binding commitments and
> seem to have no more than a highly informal and unreliable
> influence on the behaviour of their member units.

This suggests that the intermediary role played by trade unions is less likely to be performed by business associations. Do we assume, therefore, that business-government relations are not to be considered part of a system of corporatist intermediation? Or rather do we conclude that interest intermediation characterises only the relations between government and labour? For some, such as Crouch (1981), whose interest in corporatism has developed out of a concern with government-labour relations, the inclination is towards the former: organised business representation, it would appear, must be regarded at most as a form of underdeveloped corporatism. It lacks the crucial intermediary role of trade unions and it is this feature which distinguishes corporatism from other models of political representation such as traditional interest group theory. However, others operate with a less circumscribed view of corporatism. Offe (1981, p.135), for example, refers simply to the attribution of public status to a group, while Hernes and Selvik (1981, p.108), in describing trends toward corporatism at the local level, appear to mean no more than increased interaction between public and private bodies. These descriptions clearly allow not only business but a variety of groups to be regarded as part of corporatist arrangements irrespective of intermediation, although, of course, considerable theoretical specificity is forfeited by such wide-ranging definitions.

Offe (1981, p.136) points to two related but distinct processes that help focus analysis of the relations between organisations such as Chambers of Commerce and local authorities: (a) the extent to which groups are recognised and invited to assume a role in policy formulation and implementation by government, including the possible provision of resources, and implications for the regulation of internal relations between an organisation's leaders and ordinary members; and (b) the extent, level and consequences of concerted action with other economic actors, especially labour associations, including involvement in formal tripartite or similar bodies. We should recognise, however, that relations between economic interest groups and government are not necessarily stable, enduring or uniform but can be vitally affected by changes in regime type, levels of electoral competition, party ideology or market conditions (Berger, 1981b). Corporatist arrangements in Britain particularly lack the ideological and public justification found in some other countries and interest groups have proved resistant to such develop-ments. Nor need corporatist constellation in the consultative area

necessarily result in corporatist constellation at the level of final
resolution (Nedelmann and Meir, 1979, p.115).

Finally, the relevancy of the corporatist model for analysing
business organisation at the local level is especially unclear.
Neither local authorities nor Chambers of Commerce, for example, are
concerned with the development of formal incomes policies, a factor
that some see as an important stimulus to corporatist arrangements
at the national level (Panitch, 1980). Some regard local authorities
as primarily service delivery agencies whose concern with consumption
issues reduces the possibility of corporatist forms emerging at the
local level (see Cawson and Saunders, chapter 1 in this volume).
Furthermore, the admittedly sketchy material we possess on Chambers
of Commerce suggests that a predominant form of representation is
maintained through a network of informal rather than formal ties
(Saunders, 1979). However, whether we describe this as corporatist
or not, the creation in 1974 of local authorities sufficiently large
and autonomous to make their decisions of crucial concern to
businessmen may have helped to encourage the construction of more
regular and formalised relations between Chambers and, particularly,
the larger metropolitan authorities as a complement to well-
established informal contacts. Growing and shared perceptions of
an imperative to recapitalise declining local economies may reinforce
these developments in some areas. Similar changes are discernible
elsewhere. Hernes and Selvik (1981) refer to the increased organised
co-operation between municipalities and economic interest groups in
local Norwegian communities as 'municipal monopoly capital' and
suggest that this stems from both changes in economic conditions and
an expansion of local public authority. In Britain too there are
signs that while Chambers seek to influence economic development in
ways that enhance commercial opportunities for its members, local
authorities seek both legitimacy and entrepreneurial 'know how' from
the voice of local business for their economic policies. Chambers
of Commerce may also look for more regular liaison with local
government as part of an effort for greater influence over spending
decisions, although some Chambers appear wary of disrupting relations
with local politicians, especially in 'financially responsible'
authorities like Leeds.

THE ORGANISATIONAL STRUCTURE AND MEMBERSHIP OF THE LEEDS CHAMBER OF
COMMERCE AND INDUSTRY

Despite economic recessions the membership of the Leeds Chamber over
the last decade has stayed remarkably constant at around 1600
companies, of whom today approximately 800 are manufacturers, 600
are in the service sector and 200 in construction-related industries.
This composition largely mirrors that of the Leeds economy as does
the steady drift from manufacture to services in recent years.

Membership takes two quite different forms. The vast majority
of firms pay their fees (currently £50-£180, depending upon the size
of a company) to obtain the Chamber's business services, primarily
export documentation such as certificates of origin, and play no
active role. The 40-50 'activists' are those that serve on the
Chamber's Council and/or its committees or sub-committees. The

Chamber's Council is the main policy-making body and consists of 36
nominated members and a few ex-officio, mainly long-serving members.
Members are 'elected' for a three-year period (there are no contested
elections although nominated members are referred to as 'elected'
members), but they appear to continue for as long as they wish or are
able. Although there is a regular turnover of council members many
of the current membership have served for at least ten years.
    The absence of elections allows the officers of the Chamber to
meet two main aims for the Council's membership. First, to secure a
representative from each of the leading sectors of the Leeds economy.
Second, to secure the managing director or perhaps the deputy of a
company and normally someone who had displayed 'calibre' or 'soundness'
elsewhere, perhaps as president of a trade or employers' association,
or in the Junior Chamber of Commerce, or as a member of a Chamber
committee or sub-committee. Each Council member serves on one of
two main Chamber committees, either the Industrial and Commercial
Affairs Committee or the Law and Taxation Committee, which also have
sub-committees, although not all members of these committees are
Council members. Many 'active' companies appear to be those that
are either entirely administered locally (Yorkshire) or whose local
management appear to have a high degree of autonomy.
    The Chamber's management team (as it describes it) comprises the
following: (a) 'elected' officers, holding the positions of president,
vice president, immediate past president, honorary treasurer, and
chairmen of the Industrial and Commercial Affairs Committee, the Law
and Taxation Committee, Town Planning Sub-Committee, Rates Sub-
Committee, Overseas Trade Committee and the Local Government Co-
ordinating Committee; (b) permanent staff, namely the director,
assistant to the director, two assistant secretaries, the overseas
trade secretary and the membership manager.
    In practice, however, most influence lies with the group that
meets immediately prior to the monthly Chamber Council meetings to
discuss the agenda. These are the director, president, vice
president, immediate past president, honorary treasurer, and the
chairmen of the Industrial and Commercial Affairs Committee and the
Law and Taxation Committee. Their pre-Council meeting is a major
reason why Council meetings keep strictly to a one-hour schedule.
    Formal relationships between elected and permanent officers
resemble those in government. Elected officers are regarded as the
equivalent of ministers or leading councillors, initiating and
laying down policy through the Council which the director and his
staff then carry out. In formal bilateral meetings with the local
authorities, for example, it would be considered improper for the
director to meet an elected councillor without being accompanied
by an elected Chamber officer. However, most formal meetings consist
of elected and permanent officers from both sides. It is not unusual
for Chamber officers to refer to their 'counterparts' in the local
authorities, while the number of social functions at which the
president of the Chamber is expected to attend prompted one seriously
to remark that 'as President of the Leeds Chamber I frequently take
the place of the Lord Mayor'.
    None the less, the main representative link between the Chamber
and other bodies, particularly local government, is the director.
Nearly all the informal contact with the local authorities goes

through him and he is also involved in all formal representations.
He is described by one committee chairman as 'the spider at the
centre of the web', attending all committees and generally pulling
things together, often by submitting policy or position papers to
the Council. This nodal position derives in part from the permanency
of his position and everyday involvement in Chamber affairs. The
present director has been with the Leeds Chamber since 1959 as
assistant secretary, becoming director in 1974, while his predecessor was the Chamber's director from 1937. Presidents, however,
have limited 'careers', spending two years respectively as vice
president, president, and immediate past president. Furthermore,
many presidents leave a great deal to the director. Certainly the
overall impression confirms the claim by Offe and Wiesenthal (1979)
that business organisations are not confronted to the extent that
trade unions are by the dilemma of maintaining a precarious balance
between bureaucracy (which allows them to accumulate power) and
internal democracy (which allows them to exercise power). They
depend less on internal democracy, collective identity or willingness
to engage in solidary action, and their sanctioning potential (which
is comparatively low and involves withdrawing the functions of
advice and information that they may give to government) can be put
into effect by the leadership of the organisation alone.
    Finally, although the Chamber belongs to the Association of
Yorkshire and Humberside Chambers of Commerce, which is the regional
Chamber, and the West Yorkshire Group of Chambers, these are mainly
co-ordinating bodies, useful for reinforcing demands on particular
issues, and for representation at ABCC level. They offer few
constraints, if any, on the Leeds Chamber's representational activity
which in recent years has become predominantly associated with its
two main local authorities, the Leeds Metropolitan District Council
(LMDC) and the West Yorkshire Metropolitan County Council (WYMCC).

RELATIONSHIPS WITH THE LOCAL AUTHORITIES

Local government reorganisation in 1974 replaced Leeds County Borough
and West Riding County Council with the enlarged Leeds Metropolitan
District Council (LMDC) and West Yorkshire Metropolitan County
Council (WYMCC), with LMDC one of the five MDCs within the county
council's area. Both new authorities had Labour administrations,
although the Conservatives gained LMDC in May 1975 and WYMCC in
May 1977. The Leeds Chamber of Commerce and Industry enjoyed
friendly relationships with both former authorities, especially
Leeds County Borough. At the annual general meeting of the Chamber
in 1974 the president referred to 'the loss of old friends' and
expressed the hope for the same mutual co-operation with the new
local authorities. In fact the Chamber had already taken active
steps to secure this. The director had made contact with the chief
executives of LMDC and WYMCC the previous October and claimed to
have 'established with them the broad basis of co-operation'. Each
had been sent a short paper explaining what the Chamber hoped for
in the way of consultation and with a request for information on
the new people to contact. In January 1974 the new Lord Mayor of
Leeds had attended the Chamber's annual dinner 'so that the Chamber
could make its mark immediately'.

Yet a year after reorganisation it was clear that the Chamber's relationships with the two local authorities were not what it had hoped for. In May 1975 the president remarked in his annual address on the difficulty of maintaining good contacts and relations with the local authorities and he suggested that the Chamber needed more regular, formal and strategic meetings with them. The main problem lay with the county council and it centred on two major policy disputes. First, WYMCC's determination to control car traffic and promote bus priority and pedestrianisation within the inner towns and cities. This resulted in traffic regulation orders for Leeds which aimed at reducing car-parking provision, controlling traffic flow, and pedestrianising the Leeds central shopping area. The Leeds Chamber strongly objected to the scheme on the grounds that it hindered commercial business communication within the city and also harmed trade. However, despite hiring legal representation for the public enquiry (after initial misgivings about the cost) and with the tacit support of LMDC, the Chamber's opposition ended in failure and the scheme still operates.

The second objection to WYMCC arose over county council proposals to restrict office development in Leeds. Like other large cities Leeds' manufacturing base has been gradually declining, particularly engineering, while its service and office sectors have expanded. However, by the mid-1970s and following the property boom of the late 1960s, even office development in Leeds had become sluggish. The Leeds Chamber takes the view that the best hope for the Leeds economy lies in encouraging the development of Leeds as a regional administrative centre. This view is particularly advanced by an active group of leading estate agents within the Chamber, although some manufacturers would prefer more emphasis in Chamber policy to be given to the encouragement of manufacture (although not to large companies moving in from outside). In 1975, however, WYMCC proposed a policy which sought to limit the future siting of office blocks in Leeds on the grounds that further office development would over-burden central shops and car parks. The Leeds Chamber reacted adversely to this as running counter to both Leeds's interests and the 'natural flow of market forces'. These and other aggravations in relationships with the county council in the first year following reorganisation also followed from the Chamber's unfamiliarity with the personnel and expanded role for the new second-tier authorities, particularly their planning powers over the large town and city areas within their jurisdiction.

Relations with Leeds MDC were better. The district council itself was engaged in a bitter dispute with WYMCC over the latter's use of its planning powers, complaining that WYMCC was encroaching into district council responsibilities. At one point, the chief executive of LMDC publicly criticised WYMCC's 'power play' in trying to influence the details of planning policy. This feeling cut across party allegiances and in 1975 an all-party decision was taken calling for a public enquiry on the proposed pedestrianisation scheme in Leeds on the grounds that WYMCC had taken insufficient account of local commercial and trade interests. Consequently the Chamber and the MDC tended increasingly to regard themselves as allies against the depredations of the county council, particularly after May 1975 when Leeds MDC became Conservative-controlled and confronted a Labour

administration at County Hall. Nonetheless, LMDC's policy of
reserving key industrial sites for manufacture rather than allow
fuller reign for office development helped to prevent too close a
relationship emerging.

The experience of a year's reorganisation indicated that the
Chamber's established forms of representation were now inadequate.
Relations with Leeds County Borough had been good, but limited. For
example,

(a)   there were few meetings between 'teams' of Chamber and local
      authority elected and permanent personnel, and relations
      with leading councillors were particularly spasmodic. The
      director, for example, would never meet the leader of the
      council and reflects that local councillors 'were a law to
      themselves and would not have discussions with anyone'.
      Contact was maintained primarily at permanent officer level
      and with little involvement by the Chamber's elected officers.
      There was a marked reliance on more informal channels of
      communication, particularly through the director and his
      movement in the 'circuit' of local notables;

(b)   some local authority decisions could come as a surprise to
      the Chamber, especially if the leading councillors acted
      against the officers' advice. Much of the Chamber's
      representation was reactive to public policy and the director
      'would pick up things in the paper and say "the Chamber
      ought to have a view on this"'. Consequently involvement
      in the decision process tended to occur at a late stage;

(c)   Chamber representation was little concerned with the local
      authority's general policy or strategy and it often consisted
      of members' individual complaints;

(d)   the Chamber's committee structure had become moribund, diffuse
      and ill-attended and council meetings were largely stage-
      managed by the director with little participation by even
      the elected officers. Before meetings the director would
      'invent' an agenda, give the president notes and then write
      around to six or seven people to get them to talk at the
      meeting, 'otherwise they would just listen ... it was heavy
      going'. The result was that there were few worked-out
      policy documents or positions formulated in committees or
      working parties that could provide the basis for early,
      strategic involvement with the local authority. In part
      this may have reflected the predominance of private family
      business owners on the Chamber's Council who, according to
      the then director, lacked the concern of today's public
      company representatives with broader matters of economic and
      public policy. They 'simply would not play' with suggestions
      to revamp the committee structure and 'when we talked about
      members for Council it would be a case of "what about your
      nephew, Jack, or your son, Tom," and so on'.

The prospect of local government reorganisation raised anxiety
within the Chamber about its organisational structure and representational role. In 1972 the Chamber's officers put forward the case
for a revamped committee structure, better accommodation and improved
relations with Leeds local authority ('... relations are good, but
there is scope for much more work of this kind ... we should take the

initiative with them far more frequently and explore representation
on local authority committees ... the proposals to give new life to
the Chamber's committees may lead to this ...'). However, it was
only the experience of reorganisation, the appointment of a new
director and the election of a vigorous president that forced action
in 1975. In that year the number of major committees was reduced
from ten to three, to meet at regular, fixed times with secretarial
assistance, while the new Industrial and Commercial Affairs committee
was given the aim of producing a 'bank' or rolling stock of policy
and discussion papers to enable quick reaction to government
proposals. The new structure was regarded as the basis for an
expanded relationship with the new local authorities, for, in
addition, the Chamber's Council agreed that the Chamber would no
longer rely on contacts made at officer level but would seek regular
meetings with leading councillors and officials, preferably every
three months, and with a resolve for earlier and more strategic
involvement in the authorities' policy processes.

Leeds MDC

The number of organisational and personal links between the Chamber
and the two local authorities increased considerably from 1975. In
particular, a number of unminuted and unpublicised (by agreement)
meetings were started with Leeds MDC. At these meetings the local
authority were generally represented by the leader and the main
committee chairmen and their chief officers, while the president,
vice president, immediate past president, director and committee
and sub-committee chairmen usually represented the Chamber. Much
of the business at the first meetings was taken up with planning
issues, especially the preparation of WYMCC's structure plan and
LMDC's various local plans, particularly the central business area
plan, and centred upon the best way to encourage industrial and
commercial development in Leeds. One result was that the local
authority asked the Chamber to prepare papers on three particular
items: public relations for Leeds, including the provision of an
industrial development office, the provision of 'nursery' accommodation for new small businesses, and an interim office policy.
     From 1976, however, a great deal of formal discussion took place
in much smaller groups outside these full meetings. These tended
to take two particular forms: (i) meetings between a newly-formed
Town Planning Sub-Committee, composed entirely of estate agents and
chartered surveyors and including the director, and the chairman
and director of planning and his officials. The Town Planning Sub-
Committee developed much of the Chamber's planning policy and these
meetings were largely taken up with the broad outlines of the
structure and local plans; (ii) meetings to discuss specific local
area plans, particularly in run-down and inner-city areas, and at
which the director (or his assistant), occasionally the president
or vice president, the chairman of the Town Planning Sub-Committee,
and several local members would usually represent the Chamber. The
authority would tend to be represented by the chairman and director
of planning (or one of his officials), and perhaps one or two of
the area's local councillors.

These closer organisational links were increasingly reflected in closer policy positions. The Chamber was especially successful in influencing the district council's car-parking policy, notably the adoption of a considerably higher car-parking ratio to floor space in new office developments than the authority originally intended. Following the publication of the district council's car-parking document in May 1978 the Chamber's director was moved to claim that 'for the first time in ten years the district council and the Chamber are speaking the same sort of language'. Furthermore, the local authority also adopted more 'flexible' attitudes to warehousing development in Leeds and relaxed its intended provision on reserving key sites for manufacture. These planning discussions also generated further consultations and links, and by 1978 the Chamber and the district council jointly shared the chairmanship of a new Leeds Tourist Committee, were holding meetings at planning department level on staggered working hours, and, following the passing of the Inner Urban Areas Act in August, which designated programme authorities in receipt of inner-city funds (including Leeds), the local authority began to consult the Chamber about the draft of its inner-city programme. This last development stemmed in part at least from those local plan discussions between the Chamber and Leeds MDC that centred on a number of inner-city areas.

West Yorkshire MCC

These closer relationships between the Chamber and LMDC also reflected their common disenchantment with WYMCC. As with LMDC the Chamber established a much wider set of formal and personal links with WYMCC from 1975, including meetings between 'teams' of elected and permanent staff from both sides, and regular consultation had been set up with the departments of planning and transport to discuss drafts of the structure plan. Considerable co-operation was established with officials in WYMCC's industrial development office and the county council provided guidance for businessmen going on the Chamber's export promotion missions. However, these organisational links did not produce shared policy positions as they had done with the district council. The two major problems were a proposed West Yorkshire Bill, which would allow the county council to make direct grants and loans to individual companies, and the structure plan. The first, proposed in 1976, reflected WYMCC's desire to stimulate industrial development in the county, particularly to the west which contained the bulk of the declining textile industry. However, proposals to offer direct financial assistance by government to companies are generally anathema to the Chamber. It regards them as both unfair - taking ratepayers' money from successful companies and giving it to the less successful or to competitors from outside - and dangerous, as likely to be the start of a slippery slope in which financial assistance is given in return for government control of the company. Furthermore a general representative business body like the Chamber, unlike an employers' or trade association representing a particular industry, faces possible problems of internal unity if it supports special assistance to certain sectors or companies. It much prefers

government finance to be used for 'the general good' in the provision
of infrastructure, such as road building and the clearing of derelict
land. The successful campaign against the county council's provisions,
in which the Chamber mobilised the three other West Yorkshire Chambers,
threatened legal representation, and gained the support of a number
of local MPs, hardly diminished the Chamber's view that the second-
tier authorities were unnecessary.

The structure plan process, however, proved a longer-running
problem. It involved a state of almost continuous warfare between
the five district councils and WYMCC irrespective of the party
compositions of the different authorities. For example, although
both LMDC and WYMCC were Conservative-controlled in March 1978, this
did not prevent the former from severely criticising WYMCC's structure
plan proposals for ignoring the needs of Leeds. In November 1978
a well-publicised joint plea by the Conservative chairman of the
Leeds Planning Committee and his Labour shadow was made to WYMCC to
recognise the urgent requirement in Leeds for more land for industry
as Leeds was, it was claimed, facing an immediate exhaustion in the
supply of medium and large sites. The Leeds Chamber's objections
followed similar lines and was particularly concerned at proposed
restrictions on office and other service development in Leeds, plans
to direct industry to reserved sites, and the aim to limit car-
parking provision.

None the less, relations with WYMCC improved considerably in 1978.
Succeeding drafts of the structure plan more clearly recognised Leeds
as a regional and service employment centre and began to give
overriding priority to 'improving the local economy'. This did not
prevent the Chamber and Leeds MDC combining at the examination-in-
public of the structure plan to criticise restraints on development
and traffic in Leeds, but it did appear to remove some of the
difficulties in the relations between the Chamber and the county.
A more sympathetic Conservative administration from May 1977, and
the improved and more continuous consultations which had now become
established, may have been two factors behind better relationships.
Early in 1979 the Chamber attended the first meetings of a new WYMCC
Economic Advisory Board consisting of representatives at officer
level from the local authorities, the TUC, government departments
and employers' organisations. Furthermore, its well-prepared papers
on regional policy and transportation problems in manufacturing
areas were warmly welcomed by the county council as a basis for its
own policies. During the same period constructive meetings took
place between the Chamber's Town Planning Sub-Committee and WYMCC,
with LMDC representatives in attendance, to discuss the planning
application procedure, while small working parties with representatives from the Chamber, LMDC and WYMCC met to discuss the problems
of decline in the Leeds inner-city areas. Consequently it was with
some justification that the president was able to report at the
annual general meeting in May 1979 that 'I have been particularly
pleased at the close relations we have now built up with both LMDC
and WYMCC. They are a matter of routine, consulting us at an earlier
and earlier stage and we are firmly established as the one organisation which provides the measured views of the business community.'

By the beginning of 1980 the representational contacts between
the Chamber and the Leeds authority took the following forms:

(i)   two meetings a year between 'full teams' from both sides, including the leader of the council, chairman of major committees, and chief officers from the local authority, and the director, president, vice president, immediate past president, and chairmen or leading members of its committees and sub-committees for the Chamber;

(ii)   around 30-35 ad hoc meetings a year between small teams of Chamber representatives, such as the director, president and chairman of the Industrial and Commercial Affairs Committee, and elected and/or permanent representatives from particularly the planning, industry and administration departments. These usually take place around a 'rough agenda' on either the Chamber's or the local authority's premises and with the initiative for them coming from both sides. Although meetings between appointed officials generally take the form of a 'friendly chat', they tend to become 'more political' when councillors and elected Chamber officers are present, according to the Chamber's director;

(iii) 'everyday' or routine contact, usually by telephone and on first-name terms between the director of the Chamber or his assistant with top officials (mostly directors) and leading councillors (usually committee or sub-committee chairmen) in the authority;

(iv)   a range of informal or social contacts, not at Rotary or Round Table where few councillors or officials are members, but at functions and company openings where 'it is amazing what you can pick up over a gin and tonic' (Chamber director). As elsewhere business leaders and local authority officials and councillors are part of a local 'social circle', including common membership on a range of civic bodies such as hospital management committees and the local magistrates bench, and trek the same well-worn social pathways (Hampton, 1970; Saunders, 1979; Stacey, Batstone, Bell and Murcott, 1975);

(v)   multilateral meetings, such as the Leeds Group on Industry and Employment, at which representatives attend from other bodies such as the TUC, CBI or government. The Chamber tends to regard such meetings as having limited usefulness ('talking shops') and prefers bilateral, less public discussions with the local authority. However, it recognises their value in allowing the Chamber to disseminate its official policy papers to participants and also the opportunity they allow for making contacts which can be followed up more discreetly at a later time.

West Yorkshire MCC

Relations with the county council take a similar if less extended form. Full formal meetings are held twice a year, one in company with other West Yorkshire Chambers in January or February to discuss rates and expenditure, and one alone with the authority in mid-summer to discuss general matters. However, there are fewer ad hoc meetings with the county, around ten a year, partly because County Hall is ten miles away in Wakefield. Consequently contact 'is more

a question of telephone calls', usually between the director and top
officials in the planning and transport departments. Although the
Chamber is also represented on the authority's Economic Advisory
Board, it was 'late in the day finding out' about a new West Yorkshire
Small Firms Employment Fund and the impression is that the Chamber may
be kept less fully abreast with the county council's policy intentions
on some matters than it is with those of Leeds MDC.

FACTORS BEHIND THE DEVELOPMENT OF THE CHAMBER'S RELATIONSHIPS WITH
THE LOCAL AUTHORITIES

The improved relationships with WYMCC from around 1978 can be
attributed in part to the resolution of policy differences over the
West Yorkshire Bill and the partial resolution of difficulties over
the structure plan which allowed the gradually developing organisational contacts between the two to become reflected in closer policy
objectives. In turn, relations with both WYMCC and LMDC were
sustained by other factors.

   (i)   There was an increasing concern by the local authorities to
         develop the local economies in the face of declining
         industrial bases, deepening recession and rising unemployment.
         Initially this aim created difficulties in the relationship
         between the Chamber and WYMCC who, faced with declining
         textile and engineering industries that are predominantly
         clustered in areas to the west of Leeds, sought in their
         planning policies to encourage development in these parts
         of the county. However, even 'prosperous' areas have seen
         their levels of unemployment moving from just below to above
         the national average. In Leeds, largely as the result of
         restructuring and recession in the engineering industry,
         unemployment rates started to rise steeply after 1977 and
         job losses were no longer offset by an expanding service
         sector. The result has been to encourage recognition by
         both the Chamber and the county council of common economic
         problems. Nonetheless, the Chamber remains primarily
         concerned with the particular problems of the Leeds economy
         and its links are closer and better established with the
         district council. Both Leeds MDC and the Chamber have
         become increasingly conscious of steps taken elsewhere in
         the region by local authorities to attract new development,
         such as in Bradford and Sheffield, and of the need to entice
         investment to Leeds. This has encouraged the district
         council to turn even more to the 'voice of local business'
         for both commercial expertise and support for efforts to
         develop the local economy.
   (ii) The requirements on the reorganised authorities to construct
         structure and local plans have also played a major part in
         stimulating more regular contact between them and the
         Chamber, especially on planning matters. The Town and
         County Planning Acts of 1968 and 1971 gave a wider responsi-
         bility to planning departments and a more explicit require-
         ment to consider the economic implications of decisions.
         Johnson and Cochrane (1981, p.14), in their study of economic

policy-making by local authorities, discovered a broader and more constructive view of the planning legislation as local authorities reassessed priorities under the impact of more difficult economic conditions. The Chamber also recognised the impact that the larger authorities could have on a local economy that was becoming more reliant on office and service development, particularly if the authorities exercised the battery of negative as well as positive planning powers at their disposal. Much of the most important planning policy developed by the Chamber in recent years stems from the work of the Town Planning Sub-Committee which is composed entirely of estate agents and surveyors. (The Chamber justifies the composition on the grounds that these are 'neutral professionals', unlike builders and developers who are excluded because they could have a vested interest in a particular property or piece of land.) This group has been anxious that local authority policies do not hamper the economic development of Leeds, particularly as a regional office centre, and they have sought to ensure an influential voice for the Chamber, and thus their views, in local policy-making.

(iii)   Rivalry between Leeds MDC and the county council over planning responsibilities also engendered alliances between the district council and the Chamber. Feelings of local or civic pride that cut across party lines in a local authority tend to be strongest in cities such as Leeds which used to be county boroughs and have developed a historical view of their past strength and importance (ibid., p.88). Furthermore the local economy is a policy area which can justifiably be taken up at both county and district levels and metropolitan counties seem to have been particularly keen to become involved as they have few major spending responsibilities. At the same time larger metropolitan districts like Leeds have resented the loss of responsibilities to the second-tier authorities. As we have noted, when the metropolitan counties with responsibility for the county as a whole appear to neglect the particular concerns of the more 'prosperous' areas then there is a recipe for conflict. Out of such circumstances in Leeds the Chamber and the district council were able to forge a common 'localist' front against the county council.

(iv)   The Leeds Chamber of Commerce itself became a more 'business-like' body from the mid-1970s with a revamped and more efficient committee structure, bigger and better accommodation, and a growing stock of well-informed and well-researched policies that were nearly always put to the local authorities in a reasonable and constructive manner. This allows 'fair compromise' for both sides when it is required and helps, particularly with Labour politicians, to dispel notions that the Chamber consists simply of extreme Conservative right-wingers bent on securing a 'rate-payers' revolt'. Even the Chamber's successful opposition to the West Yorkshire Bill seems to have engendered a certain level of mutual respect as well as establishing useful contacts between the Chamber and the county council.

1980-

Since the election of a Labour administration in May 1980 relations
between the Chamber and Leeds MDC have become well-established. The
Labour leadership has shown itself to be even more business-oriented
and anxious to construct good relations with the Chamber than previous
Conservative administrations. The first meeting of the full teams
from both sides, which met in early July 1980, was described by the
Chamber's president as 'beneficial and amicable ... at which all the
representatives agreed that there was no reason why the Chamber
would not be able to develop a close working relationship with the
new administration'. (At this meeting the Chamber was represented
by the director, president, vice president, immediate past president
and the chairman of the Industrial and Commercial Affairs Committee,
while in attendance for Leeds MDC were the leader, deputy mayor,
deputy chairman of the Planning Committee, chairman of the Industry
Sub-Committee, chairman of the Education Committee, the director of
Industrial Development and the director of Administration.) There
is little doubt that this expectation has been fulfilled and on a
number of matters a high level of mutual co-operation has been
achieved.

Assistance to small companies

The district council has warmly supported the creation by the
Chamber in 1980 of the Leeds Business Venture, a trust set up in
partnership with local large companies to offer advice to intending
small entrepreneurs. The Leeds Business Venture is currently a
section of the Leeds Chamber of Commerce and during its first year
of operation it was supplied by the Chamber with secretarial back-
up, printing and general advice. Financial support was provided
mainly by twelve large 'sponsoring' firms each donating between
£250-£400, while Marks and Spencer Ltd also provided a young
management secondee to act as the Venture's first director. Although
the district council provided only moral encouragement to the Leeds
Business Venture in its first year – the Chamber claims that it
wanted to establish it as a private venture and would only consider
local authority assistance once the Venture's 'character' had been
set – Leeds MDC have since provided rent-free accommodation, funded
a secretary (who appears on the books of the Chamber of Commerce),
and helps with the Venture's running costs. The authority's
Industrial Development Unit liases closely with the Venture,
directing enquiries from small businessmen to its director and
sitting in on consultations by the Venture with applicants in case
it can offer advice on government loans. Two Chamber representatives –
an estate agent and a developer – also sit on a local authority
working party that explores plans for local authority provision of
low-rent accommodation for small companies.
     Finally, the Leeds Business Venture has also developed good
contacts with the county council. Its director is one of three
members of a panel of advisers that go through applications to the
county council's Small Firms Employment Fund before these are
considered by officials. The county's Industrial Promotions

Department also increasingly refer enquiries to the Leeds Business
Venture for advice. As in other places the local authorities in
West Yorkshire probably seek to encourage small firms because they
can do little to influence the location policies of large companies,
and also as they see small firms as more firmly rooted in the area
and feel that they can more easily cater for their needs (Johnson
and Cochrane, 1981, p.136).

Inner-City Programme Funds

Although the Chamber has commented to Leeds MDC since 1978 on the
balance of bids for inner-city money under the Urban Areas Programme
it has become increasingly involved in discussing individual schemes.
This results in part from ministerial guidelines issued to local
authorities (DOE, 1981, p.2) which state that
    Ministers see a role for the private sector not only as a source
    of investment but also as influencing the scope and content of
    inner-area programmes while they are still at draft stage.
    Indeed they will expect, before giving approval to programmes in
    future, to be satisfied that the voice of the private sector has
    been heard and that detailed consultation had taken place. This
    will normally be through members of the local Chamber of Commerce.
Although these guidelines provide a measure of discretion for local
authorities in determining the scale of consultation, Leeds MDC have
been keen to secure Chamber advice on inner-city matters. As a
result the Chamber has observer status at all meetings of the
Inner-City Sub-Committee, sitting with the local authority's officers
at the table, and being asked to contribute to discussions.
    The Chamber has four main tasks that have been agreed with the
local authority: to express its views on the balance between social
and economic projects and between revenue and capital spending; to
examine the viability of the economic job-creating projects being
put forward; to put forward views on priorities for inner-city
money; and to help some of the economic projects off the ground
if management expertise is required. Consequently the Chamber
receives from the local authority all the 'economic' and 'environ-
mental-economic' applications for inner-city funds. Preferring not
to veto applications ('we don't want to be Heseltine's spy or to be
part of the local authority and be bound by decisions we don't agree
with'), the director and assistant to the director grade applications
on the scale 1-5 in the light of general policy drawn up by the
Industrial and Commercial Affairs Committee. Occasionally the
director of the Leeds Business Venture will go and visit an applicant
on behalf of the Chamber to provide a better impression than is
conveyed by paperwork alone, although the local authority has
encouraged an application from the Chamber for funds from the inner-
city programme for a secondee to act as a catalyst for an improvement
in the individual schemes in the inner-city programme. The Chamber
has also applied for £60,000 from the inner-city programme to help
individuals start their own business in run-down central areas.
The scheme, which the Chamber 'cleared' first with officials and
councillors in the industry, planning and inner-city departments,
will provide individuals with cash up to £1500. This represents a

notable change of heart by the Chamber which has long set its face
against direct government assistance of this kind but which it
justifies by reference to the need for business regeneration in a
grim economic climate, to the small amounts involved, and to the
need to help small and start-up businesses, particularly in declining
urban areas.   Furthermore the Chamber claims to have set the conditions
and the criteria for distribution of the money and will be fully
represented on a panel that is to be set up to scrutinise applications.
    The extent to which this involvement may lead the Chamber to being
regarded by local businessmen as a branch of government is perhaps
indicated by requests for advice it receives from potential applicants
who may have been referred to the Chamber by a local councillor.   But
despite this concern with individual applications the Chamber regards
its influence as most importantly exercised in discussions determining
the overall balance of the inner-city programme.   Although it never
vetoes particular schemes, the Chamber argues consistently for a
switch from revenue and community service schemes to capital and
economic spending.   The Chamber still sets great store, however,
despite its incorporation into the local authority machinery, on the
more informal discussions with officials and politicians it continues
to have outside formal meetings.

The Land Register

The director of the Chamber is also a member of what is known as the
Group of Three, a team set up in Leeds and other major district
authorities by the DOE to consider recently-published registers of
unused or underused land owned by local authorities and statutory
undertakings (the other members being the director of planning and
a DOE official).   Its main task is to make recommendations for the
disposal of land even to the extent of recommending to the Secretary
of State for the Environment that he directs that the land be sold.
The Chamber is consequently strongly placed to influence the availability of such land, whether it be for housing or commercial
development.   The DOE specifically ruled out estate agents and
similar individuals from the Group's membership otherwise the Chamber
almost certainly would have nominated one of its leading Town Planning
Sub-Committee members.

The Leeds Group on Industry and Employment

The Leeds Group on Industry and Employment was inaugurated in
January 1981 by the district council to provide a forum that would
offer advice to the local authority on 'all matters relating to
industrial and commercial development, training and the creation of
job opportunities in the Leeds area'.   Meeting quarterly the Chamber
provides six employers' representatives to the Group, which also
includes CBI representatives, leading city councillors, trades
council and regional TUC members, and local MPs.   However, the CBI
and TUC members rarely attend and the infrequent attendances by the
trades council representatives are characterised by a certain level
of hostility to the employers' representatives.   As a result the

Group has worked less well than intended and lacks the influence expected for it, although the creation of working parties underneath the Group and containing a variety of local expertises rather than the 'big chiefs' at the main table appears to be producing good, detailed reports. However, the Chamber plays an active role in the Group's proceedings and after the chairman has introduced a topic he will invariably turn to the Chamber's president to continue the discussion.

Office and warehousing development

A series of discussions between the Town Planning Sub-Committee and the district council on reserving key sites for industry (and therefore prohibiting their use for office development or warehousing) removed a potential thorn in LMDC-Chamber relations and, according to the Chamber, resulted in 'a change of attitude by the local authority' and the construction of a policy which was 'now very sensible'.

Rates

Although the Chamber received a number of 'severe and vehement complaints' from members over a 7.2p supplementary rate levied by Leeds District Council in 1980 there was little sign that the Chamber's leadership would allow the issue to affect its relationship with the local authority. Instead it set up a special Rates Sub-Committee 'to ensure that the Chamber is fully briefed in discussions with the local authorities on the level of any future rate increase'. When this sub-committee was invited to spend a day inspecting the district council's books, with the promise of access to any official they wished, it concluded by pronouncing itself 'impressed by efforts being made to keep the rates to reasonable levels'.

As a result there appears some justification for recent Chamber claims that 'the Leeds MDC recognises the Chamber almost as a partner' with constant consultation between the two bodies. For its part, the Chamber has been forced to set up a special Local Government Co-ordinating Committee to handle the Chamber's increased involvement in local authority matters, and to appoint an assistant to the director whose sole responsibility is local authority representation. There is little sign that these developments are temporary, at least while economic recession helps push the Chamber and local authorities together. The loss of intermediate assisted area status for Leeds in August 1982, which importantly also cuts Leeds off from EEC money for improvements to the industrial infrastructure, such as access roads to industrial estates, and the increased recognition that local authorities might be the only bodies with a sufficiently localist orientation to help local economies, are major factors that are likely to sustain the levels of co-operation recently reached between the Chamber and the local authorities.

PARTY POLITICS, REPRESENTATION AND CORPORATISM

The Chamber publicly regards itself as a 'non-party political' body
and scrupulously avoids identification with any of the major parties.
For example, a request from a local Conservative Club to share
premises with the Junior Chamber of Commerce was turned down as
endangering this position. However, the Chamber regularly has in
active membership a sprinkling of ex-Conservative councillors and
undoubtedly most members vote Conservative. Chamber officers are
also more likely to be involved in the same social networks as
Conservative rather than Labour politicians and consequently it takes
a little longer to construct personal links with the leaders of an
incoming Labour administration. Yet the Chamber also maintains
extremely good relationships with several local Labour MPs, such as
Denis Healey, Mervyn Rees, Ken Woolmer and Stan Cohen, providing
them with information that can be used in the House of Commons and
mobilising their support when necessary against Conservative legislation (the Chamber makes the greatest use of opposition MPs, whatever
the party). Furthermore, the development of formal organisational
links with the local authorities in recent years appears to have been
little affected by party composition. Nor does the presence of
Conservative councillors and ex-councillors in the membership bestow
representational advantage on the Chamber as they possess fewer
'pathways' to local leaders and officials than the director and
other Chamber officers.
    This is not to deny that particularly in the first few years
after reorganisation the Chamber's policy positions were closer to
those of the Conservative party than the Labour party, and that the
change of control from Labour to Conservative in both authorities
(LMDC in 1975, WYMCC in 1977) eased the Chamber's relationship with
them. It especially diminished the dual threat of an 'anti-private
motorist' and 'anti-office' county council. Yet it is important
not to exaggerate these differences. Many of the Chamber's grouses
with the county council sprang from an unfamiliarity and irritation
with a new second-tier level and the feeling that Leeds's interests
were being ignored in favour of other parts of the county. Moreover,
Chamber and district council criticism of WYMCC were only partly
abated by the change in control in 1977 and on several occasions
both Conservative and Labour leaders on LMDC publicly combined
against the county council. The Chamber has also achieved its
closest links with LMDC during the present Labour administration
and good relations are being established with the recently-elected
(May 1981) Labour WYMCC, helped no doubt by the Chamber's public
letter to the Secretary of State for the Environment criticising
proposed penalties on the authority for 'over-spending'. WYMCC and
LMDC remain amongst the lowest-rated metropolitan authorities in
the country and even with supplementary rates from the county and
district there has been little sign of a 'ratepayers' revolt' by the
Chamber against the local authorities.
    In both local authorities a 'pro-business' and 'pro-Chamber'
outlook characterises the leadership, reflecting a shared concern
to attract new investment to the locality. If anything, Labour
leaders appear more concerned than their Conservative counterparts
to seek 'technical expertise' and legitimacy from the Chamber. Some

Chamber activists suggest that Conservative councillors feel that
they already 'know about business' and consequently do not approach
the Chamber as much as Labour administrations. Furthermore, some
Chamber officers are unhappy at the steady replacement of businessmen
by professionals such as solicitors and accountants in the ranks of
Conservative politicians at national and local level, and feel that
the Conservative party no longer fully understands the view of
business. Some Conservative councillors for their part feel that the
Chamber may co-operate too closely with Labour administrations and
achieve a consultative status on schemes such as the inner-city
programme denied the official opposition.
    The Chamber therefore is concerned less with electoral than
administrative politics. As one of its leading officers remarks,
    Many businessmen take the feeling that having voted for their
    local Conservative councillor and he has just lost, they have
    finished and have to put up with what LMDC do to him. We try
    and make people understand that they don't have to give in ...
    that even without a vote you have some sort of say ... and it is
    really worth their while subscribing.
The overriding aim is to construct good relationships with local
authority leaders irrespective of their political colours and the
Chamber's primary concerns with planning and the need to attract
development to combat rising unemployment have helped legitimate
its claim to 'non-partisanship' in the eyes of local leaders, for
these are the kinds of issues that are often regarded as 'technical'
and out of the ambit of 'party politics' (Kirk, 1980; McKay and Cox,
1979). This emphasis on administrative politics is perhaps also
revealed in the Chamber's rejection of government and others'
proposals purportedly aimed at giving businessmen a stronger
electoral position in local politics, such as a business vote, local
referendums before supplementary rates, and statutory co-option
onto local authorities or their committees of business representatives nominated by Chambers of Commerce. These are regarded as
ineffective, incapable of political achievement and fraught with
technical difficulties (who should cast the vote for a company and
should all companies have the same vote irrespective of size?).
It much prefers that a statutory right be given to Chambers to be
consulted by local authorities on policy decisions affecting industry
and commerce in its area, and constantly reiterates that the most
practical advantage accrues to members in the maintenance and
expansion of its current consultative links with local government.
    However, this increasing involvement with the local authorities
presents problems for the Chamber, particularly for its permanent
staff. One is a strategic dilemma: the extent to which the Chamber
may become identified with unpopular local government decisions.
More pressing, however, is pressure on the Chamber's resources. The
Chamber's leadership is acutely sensitive to the size of its membership subscriptions and fears that too sharp an increase will lose
it members, particularly as only a tiny proportion of members are
active and therefore aware of the Chamber's representational efforts
and their efficacy.
    This suggests that businessmen may be as resistant as some trade
unionists to the incorporation of their organisations into a branch
of government. In addition to membership opposition to proposals to

give Chambers statutory public status there are few signs that the
possible corporatist ad hoc agencies with which the Chamber is
involved, WYMCC's Economic Advisory Board and LMDC's Leeds Group on
Industry and Employment, are as yet little more than advisory forums.
They have no real powers of decision nor do they indicate the
development of forms of concerted action between capital, labour and
the state.   The regional TUC rarely turn up to meetings of the Leeds
Group while the local trades council displays a marked hostility to
the employers' representatives when its delegates infrequently attend.

However, despite the absence of systematic intermediation and
concertation, the Chamber is attributed with an increasingly higher
public status by government.   This is characterised by more extended
and formal consultation between the Chamber and the public authorities
and provision of resources to assist the Chamber in its 'governmental'
activities.   It marks a shared recognition of the importance of
providing roads, land, accommodation and other forms of infrastructural
social investment for regenerating the local economy.   Yet while the
advantages to the Chamber of such co-operation are reasonably apparent -
it enables the Chamber to press more effectively for policies that
aid local business - it is less clear what is gained by the local
authorities.   They may obtain a certain legitimation for policies,
particularly for resource claims made to central government and EEC
vote-holders, feel that they avoid possible obstructive activity from
local businessmen on such matters as rate precepts, and perhaps gain
a certain technical or commercial expertise.   But these hardly seem
compelling factors.   Local authority departments are organised around
the provision of specialised services to identified client groups,
and perhaps they respond to newly perceived issues or responsibilities
by seeking a new group of clients (Johnson and Cochrane, 1981, p.132).
In this case recognition of the role local authorities can play in
developing the local economy is accompanied by a reorganisation of
the committee and departmental structure to take up the challenge
and, in turn, this leads to the development of the appropriate
'client' relationship with the Chamber of Commerce and other economic
actors.

Finally, the 'corporatisation' of Chambers of Commerce may develop
through the actions of a Conservative government opposed to the
corporate state.   This may happen if the government, following the
work that the Chamber already undertakes for the Department of Trade
on export documentation and for the Department of the Environment
on inner-city programmes and local registers of land, transfers
responsibilities from government agencies to Chambers in line with
'privatisation' policies.   This is being mooted for government export
promotion work, small firm advisory services and some forms of
industrial training provision.   If corporatism is regarded by
business and social market governments as a more acceptable structure
than more direct and bureaucratic forms of state intervention and
provision, then seeking the privatisation of some public agencies
may be a likely strategy for Chambers of Commerce to employ in
extending their range of 'licensed' activity.   Such developments
would indicate that corporatism may involve not only the politicisa-
tion of private power but also the privatisation of public power.

Chapter 7

STATE FARE: TRADE ASSOCIATIONS, TRADE UNIONS AND GOVERNMENT

Neil Killingback

This study is concerned with the political action and attitudes of a group of small businessmen engaged in the London taxicab service during the 1930s particularly those who joined a trade association. Traditionally, small businessmen have been portrayed as the victims of change within modern capitalist society. In particular, large-scale enterprises, created by amalgamation and concentration, are seen as holding intrinsic economic advantages over them. Moreover, the development of organisations of working people extend their political influence and economic power to the detriment of small business. In other words, small businessmen are threatened by the dual nature of socialisation within capitalist societies.

One strand of conventional thought within political science suggests that the source of the marginalisation and powerlessness of small businessmen rests with the contradictory elements of their world v iew (Killingback, 1980). On the one hand, as owners of small-scale enterprises, small businessmen have a lifelong investment in the survival of private property in a very individual and unsocialised form. The ownership and control of the business represents both individual identity and self-determination. This individualism, so the argument runs, permeates their whole social outlook. They think, in other words, like capitalists, believing that competition between enterprises leads to social progress. Consequently, for small businessmen, society must protect private property because it makes manifest individual freedom, choice, and liberty. As a corollary to this type of liberalism, they articulate a belief in a free market economy which is anti-monopolistic.

On the other hand, however, small businessmen oppose collectivism and abhor united action. Their individualistic beliefs, moreover, prevent them organising effectively. King (1980) characterises them as notorious 'non-joiners', unable to defend and express their interests in a social order dominated by organisations. Their failure to organise has dire consequences: they become isolated from the changing political mechanisms of capitalist democracies and alienated from the political system. Furthermore, their anti-collectivist beliefs intensify their feelings that government has become too interventionist.

Small businessmen, then, are conventionally seen as unorganised

with the result that they are isolated and powerless, both
politically and economically. They are caught, it is argued, between
working people, whom they despise, and the more economically secure
middle class and bourgeoisie, to whom they aspire. This theme has
been taken up in recent debates on British small businessmen.
Bechhofer et al. (1974, 1978a, 1978b) maintain that small businessmen,
especially individual owners, exist outside the class structure of
advanced capitalist societies. In particular, their studies claim
that small shops have been marginal economic enterprises for over
two centuries. Second, Gellately (1974), in a comparison of small
businesses in Britain and Germany, states that they have been
politically ignored in Britain, and they have had to satisfy
themselves with the meagre rewards of self-help. However, a biography
of Oswald Mosley (Skidelsky, 1975) and a recent study of British
Fascism (Lunn and Thurlow, 1980) have prompted a revision of the
image of small businessmen in the 1930s by drawing attention to their
call for social protectionism and attempts to achieve it.

This study is not concerned to undermine the general validity of
those theories of the politics of small businessmen which suggest a
causal relationship between economic insecurity and political
insignificance. Instead, it seeks to demonstrate that British
small businessmen in the 1930s organised to protect their interests,
sought regulation of the price mechanism in the market, and looked
favourably upon state intervention and monopoly. Attention is
focused on taxi-drivers because of the diverse economic structure
of that service, its system of state control, and the new forms of
competition emerging during this period.

THE EXTENT OF GOVERNMENT INTERVENTION IN THE MARKET-PLACE

The London taxicab service came under governmental control in the
seventeenth century, and this has continued, in part, to ensure
public safety and also to regulate the market. The state, by the
1930s, controlled the fare structure of the service, the design and
roadworthiness of the vehicle, and the supply of cabs and drivers
through a system of licensing strictly administered by the
Metropolitan Police Commissioner's Office (Georgano, 1972; 'New
Survey of London Life and Labour', 1934, vol.8). In return for
these regulations, the licensed taxicab operator received the
monopoly right to 'ply for hire' along the streets of London in
a circle of six-miles' radius from Charing Cross. Its execution,
however, was also tightly supervised by the police force in the
course of its duty.

Monopoly was exercised publicly and not by an individual, or
group of taxicab owners. The rights of the passenger were protected
by the operation of a scaled taximeter. Under these circumstances,
every driver and company was at the same level in business.

There is no competition in the usual sense of the word between
cab proprietors. Cab ranks can be used by any London cab, and
if a member of the public hires a cab from a rank he does in
practice take the first one.... If he hires a cab in the street
he normally stops the first one he sees. In any case, he has no
means of telling who is the owner of a particular cab. (Runciman
Report, 1953, p.9.)

The Home Secretary was ultimately responsible for the regulations, and
representations had to be made to the Home Office for any change in
control or fare structure. This system was an inducement to the
formation of occupational interest groups, and the associations of
the trade were both the suppliers of information and consultative
bodies (Beesley, 1973). Thus, public authority controlled and
regulated the London taxicab service and free and perfect competition
did not operate.

BUSINESS FORMS

The taxicab service was structured in a complex manner. There were
a few large private companies that employed 'journeymen' taxidrivers.
In addition, there were a great many small companies which controlled
less than 50 cabs. Private companies owned around 60 per cent of
all the licensed London taxis (Fox, 1935). A common feature of
these types of business was the capitalist social relation. The
drivers, however, did not relate to the owners as wage-labourers.
A driver was free to choose for whom he worked as he pleased, which
meant that quite often the 'journeyman' driver was baillee paying
a hire-charge for the cab ('New Survey ...', 1934, pp.95-7). Some
drivers were on a flat-rate system - paying for the hire of the cab
limited by hours and mileage - while others, particularly those
organised by the TGWU, worked on commission. Members of the TGWU
bitterly resented the flat-rate system because it induced individual
competition at the expense of solidarity. (The largest private
company operated this system because it fostered 'hard work' ('New
Survey ...', ibid.)) The commission system, on the other hand,
gave the drivers much more freedom and influence because they could
reject an unsuitable cab or terms. 'The proprietor must offer
such terms to the journeyman as will induce him to take out his
cabs, the journeyman being at full liberty to pick and choose the
proprietor to whom he goes for his cab' ('New Survey ...', 1934,
p.94). As well as these companies, there was a third important
group: the owner-drivers, owning on average between two and four
cabs. (Ownership in excess of four led to the individual being
classified as a proprietor.) During the 1930s about one-third of
London taxis were operated by owner-drivers, some 2,500 in all.
    It was emotionally and physically taxing being an owner-driver.
He had to work, on average, a longer day than the journeyman driver
with no bonus for Sunday or night work. In 1932, the gross earnings
of an owner-driver were calculated as having to be in excess of £1
per day if hire purchase debts were payable, and 12s 6d if they had
been paid ('New Survey ...', 1934, p.98). Once those debts had
been cleared, owner-driving brought favourable rewards. Like the
journeyman drivers, however, owner-drivers relied upon 'tipping'
to make good their earnings. The close contact between journeymen
and owner-drivers made individual ownership the aspiration of many
journeymen (Runciman Report, 1953, p.8).
    At all times in this period licensed drivers exceeded the number
of licensed cabs. The excess of licensed drivers favoured the
larger companies which offered better terms and conditions and,
in return, helped to guarantee them a supply of drivers. Consequently,

the less skilful drivers were available for 'doubling' with the
owner-drivers. These conditions necessitated organisation among
the owner-drivers, which held common cause with the organised
journeymen, as both desired to reduce individual competition between
journeymen, i.e. to institute uniform terms and conditions so as
to regularise the supply of labour. They claimed that there were
too many drivers and too few cabs, leading to intensified competition
for fares, a situation exacerbated by the flat-rate system. Overall,
however, the state regulation of the fare structure and the subsequent
suppression of price competition benefited small proprietors and
owner-drivers. As a result, competition centred upon the expertise
and appearance of the driver, knowing the best location for fares,
being at the right place at the right time. These were factors
which did not disadvantage the owner-drivers.

ECONOMIC SITUATION AND CIRCUMSTANCES

The licence system limited the number of cabs and drivers: there
was no absolute freedom of entry. Hence, the government by its
regulations and orders, albeit outwardly for public safety, intervened
in the economic affairs of the service. No fixed limit operated in
respect of numbers of cabs or drivers to be licensed. Once all the
stringent requirements had been fulfilled, then a licence was
granted as a right, for either the cab or driver.
    State regulations benefited, to some measure, the smaller-scale
enterprises. The strict conditions for roadworthiness, involving
maintenance costs and garaging expenses, served to attenuate the
expansion of the larger-scale concerns. Economies of scale,
therefore, were limited, with the result that the large proprietors
supported a stable price system (Georgano, 1972; Turvey, 1961,
pp.84-6; Hindley Report, 1939).
    Just as important as the licensing system of vehicles, the state
controlled the supply of labour. Before a fully competent driver
became a 'cabbie', he had to pass a difficult examination system,
based on knowledge of London, expertise and psychological character,
to the satisfaction of the Office of the Metropolitan Police
Commissioner:
    The Commissioner - against whose decision there is no right of
    appeal - must be satisfied in the first place that the applicant
    is of good character and business repute, and that having regard
    to his general financial position he is a fit and proper person
    to hold a cab licence (Hindley Report, 1939, p.10).
The stringency of these regulations is illustrated by the fact that
an applicant would be refused a licence if it was discovered that
he had held a licence during the previous three years but had
failed to act as a cabbie, except under extenuating circumstances
of illness or reasonable cause. Moreover, any candidate who failed
any part of the examination three times was highly unlikely to
receive a licence.
    The long and rigorous examination system regulated the number of
entrants, with an estimated success rate of only 25 per cent
(Georgano, 1972, p.80). The examination itself was open and
meritocratic, while no financial barriers operated to reduce the

supply of labour. There could be no arbitrary refusal of a licence
as long as all the conditions were fulfilled. All in all, the effect
of state control produced a sense of professionalism, civic service,
and good character among taxi-drivers, irrespective of their economic
relations.

Small-scale cabdrivers viewed state regulation and control
favourably because it constrained competition. It limited the
expansion of the large companies and kept the number of licensed cabs
and drivers under control. In return, the 'cabbies' received a
monopoly to 'ply for hire'. Thus, owner-drivers supported state
regulation as providing 'fair competition', rather than the freedom
of the market. In 1938, for example, they made representation to
the Home Office for the need for extended government intervention
into the sphere of public transport:

> They made no complaint of the general system of control, or,
> save in a minor respect ... of the methods of administration;
> on the contrary the need for control, particularly of the
> construction and fitness of the vehicle was accepted as essential
> for the protection of passengers and in the interests of
> traffic (Hindley Report, 1939, p.26).

Fundamentally, the acquisition of a licence to ply for hire depended
upon individual characteristics, a fact that served to legitimate
individual ownership and make individual - rather than collective -
labour important. Any other limitation on the number of cabs and/or
cab licences would have conflicted with the interests of the owner-
driver and small proprietor. A restriction on the number of cabs
fit to ply for hire would have only benefited the large-scale
capitalists who would have been able to exploit their economies of
scale. Moreover, limitation on the number of cabs would also have
intensified the competition between the journeymen and both owner-
drivers and journeymen rejected any unilateral limitation on the
number of cabs, whilst ODA rejected this proposal unanimously
('ODA Gazette', July 1939, p.7). Under the existing conditions
the small owners and owner-drivers, who 'doubled' their cabs on a
shift system with a journeyman, acquired a supply of labour at
acceptable wage rates. Any restriction would have given the large
companies more power to attract labour and so force small enterprises
out of existence. To all intents and purposes, the status quo
caused no hardship to the owner-driver and it also encouraged a
positive association between the individually-based capitalist and
wage labourer. On the contrary, any restriction on the number of
drivers' licences conflicted with all sections of business interest.
Proprietors and owner-drivers objected to any such restriction
because it would encourage a monopoly condition solely among labour,
which then would increase its negotiating power at the expense of
the owner-driver and proprietor.

The owner-drivers also benefited from the commission system;
more so, when it was regulated by a collective agreement. They
disliked the flat-rate hiring system because it increased
competition between all drivers, particularly with no limitation on
the number of hours worked. On the other hand, the payment of a
daily wage to all journeymen drivers, irrespective of takings,
conflicted with all capitalists' interests for such a condition of
employment would not exert discipline on the journeymen. The

commission system, however, ensured that the journeymen had a stake
in the optimum use of the cab.

Government regulation established the parameters for largely
uniform economic conditions and within that context, market forces
were assumed to operate. Thus, the government never deliberately
refused licences as a measure to control the service. At the very
most, the Hackney Carriage Office could tighten the conditions of
fitness for a vehicle, and in this manner remove the redundant
capacity. It would have been politically unacceptable for individuals
to have been prevented from earning a living by the requirements of
monopoly, as a government report indicated:

> It is less easy to bring about a reduction in the number of
> licensed vehicles by the exercise of a power of limitation.
> It would not be reasonable or just to deprive existing licence
> holders of their licences on grounds relating neither to the
> fitness of the licence holder nor the suitability of his vehicle.
> (Hindley Report, 1939, p.57)

State regulation, therefore, assumed that monopoly rights were
inviolate as long as the service submitted to the conditions of
control, while free price competition was excluded. Limitation of
entry coexisted with the necessity of control for public safety
with the understanding that the government should not use its power
of limitation as direct power to limit numbers. State control, then,
included an obligation that the inherent political power would not
be directly used against any sector of the service, or make the
economic situation any worse, thus safeguarding small enterprises.
State intervention, in other words, would not promote any restructuring of capital in the taxicab service. Such a change would
have needed to alter the conditions of the trade, laid down by
statute and ministerial order, and would marginalise small-scale
capital.

On one occasion, ministerial orders ensured the continuation of
capital investment in the taxicab service. In 1933, the Home
Secretary acted (politically) to protect private capital, particularly that invested in larger-scale enterprises. He announced an
increase in the initial hiring fee so as to make the larger operators
more profitable, despite opposition from owner-drivers and journeymen. This decision to increase the scale of charges indicated that
state intervention included another guarantee, that government
action could be used to improve the status quo. Moreover, organised
interests would be consulted in decision-making. Consequently,
state regulation did not appear to contradict the fundamental
interests of any section of the taxicab service.

The normal day-to-day business of the taxicab service, therefore,
operated under government control. Those conditions suited small-
scale private enterprises. On some issues, owner-drivers could
ally with organised labour, on others they had a common interest
with big business. Three major issues occupied the politics of
small-scale owner-drivers: the fares structure, police control,
and the privileges and rights of monopoly. All interests preferred
monopoly because it secured their livelihoods. A threat to
monopoly was viewed as a threat to their economic existence.

ORGANISING AGAINST MARGINALITY

This section focuses on the successful activity of the owner-drivers
to prevent their economic marginality. Concerted political action
demands organisation, and we start with that association among the
owner-drivers and proprietors.

   Although each section of the service had its own organisation,
there was some overlapping. In the main, the LMCPA represented small
and medium sized companies, the majority possessing between four to
ten cabs. It entered into a negotiated agreement with the TGWU
(Cab Section) over terms and conditions, particularly the commission
rate, which became the norm for the service, although the largest
companies offered a different contract excluding trade union
recognition. The Owner-Drivers' Association (ODA), as its name
suggests, drew its membership from owner-drivers. To be eligible
for membership, a small owner had to spend time 'cabbing' and own
cabs to a maximum of four. In 1932, it had around 1,000 members.
Some owner-drivers chose, however, to join the LMCDCTU, known as
the 'Green Badge' after the licence-badge to drive a taxi. The
LMCDCTU was a registered trade union, exhibiting the features of a
friendly society. Unlike the TGWU, however, it was not involved
in any negotiations about conditions or terms of work. The 'Green
Badge' union was, to a large extent, excluded from the triumvirate
of LMCPA, ODA and TGWU that set the general conditions of work.
In response, the LMCDCTU made much of its claim to independence as
a cover for its lack of political influence.

ORGANISATIONAL CONCERNS

(i) Owner-Drivers' Association (ODA)

The ODA organised about 50 per cent of the very small owners and
owner-drivers. Individual ownership was reflected in the worldview
of this group, but they also recognised that organisation was all-
important to their economic standing:
   The ODA is the keystone in the whole structure of our industry.
   It was founded by men of an independent nature who wished to
   advance by their own endeavours, at the same time maintaining
   that high standard of efficiency that commands the respect and
   prestige by which we are known. That is the tradition we must
   follow. ('ODA Gazette', July 1939, p.7)
Organisation, then, facilitated the regulation or consolidation of
existing relations and protected small business interests. The
individual who remained outside the association was out-of-touch
with modern business requirements. Monopoly rights and regulations,
as they existed, were accepted and defined as 'fair competition'.
   There were also overt political tendencies within the ODA. Some
individuals were active Communist party members, a fact noticed by
Scotland Yard and some employers, but these members made no secret
of their beliefs or actions, nor did anyone try to remove them,
despite allegations from the ODA of Communist infiltration within
the TGWU. For his part, the chairman of the ODA admitted that some
of his members were Communists, but argued that they were a non-

political body in the Owner-Drivers' Association, and there is no
evidence that members of the ODA held any antipathy to Communists.
On the contrary, the 'Daily Worker', on some occasions, held a more
privileged status than other newspapers.

(ii)   London Motor Cab Drivers' Co-operative Trade Union (LMCDCTU)

This organisation, as its name suggests, placed a great deal of
emphasis on its self-help activities, in particular the protection
offered against alleged police persecution. In its literature, the
LMCDCTU described itself as an organisation for journeymen. However,
it essentially adopted a worldview unifying the objectives of
journeymen and owner-drivers in opposition to the large proprietors.
> There are some 'mushes', who, being lucky enough to get a night
> man to follow them, put themselves in the same category as being
> proprietors and really think that it is with the proprietors
> that their allegiance lies. ('Green Badge Journal', 15 January,
> 1938, p.3)

The LMCDCTU attempted to recruit journeymen in order to discipline
them to the interests of the small enterprises of owner-drivers.
Thus, the LMCDCTU opposed a TGWU proposal for an increase in the
commission rate from $33\frac{1}{3}$ per cent to 40 per cent, or the introduction
of a daily wage system. Like the ODA, the LMCDCTU supported 'fair
competition', and this formed the basis for their proposed unity
of small capitalist enterprises and labour. Fair competition for
them meant that price competition was excluded from the market,
and in its place they believed that competition rested solely on
efficiency, individual service and the character of the driver.
A free market, on the other hand, would destroy small-scale
enterprises. Consequently, the LMCDCTU moralistically renounced it:
> What sort of comradeship will ever exist among a body of men
> whom the police demand shall be 'fit and proper persons' if they
> are to continue to follow the example of the 'old sweats', in a
> battle of 'slashing', 'cutting', and the lowering of their own
> character and decency in the eyes of the public and their co-
> workers for the satisfaction of the demon 'greed' ... I, like a
> good many other drivers, confine myself to the rules of comrade-
> ship. ('Green Badge Journal', 31 July, 1937, p.8)

In the existing economic conditions there was no substitute for
organisation even among individual labour-based capitalists. Thus,
an editorial of the 'Green Badge Journal' extolled the virtues and
necessity of organisation; there was a 'need for organisation, vital
to their livelihood' ('Green Badge Journal', 14 August, 1937, p.11).
   The LMCDCTU mistrusted the TGWU - in part, because it was a
general union recruiting all public transport workers including
competitors of the taxicab service, and, second, because they
thought Communist-inspired agitation within it promoted industrial
conflict. However, the LMCDCTU distinguished responsible trade
union organisation from political agitation. In short, the LMCDCTU
resented the intrusion of politics - of any kind - into economic
affairs. In their world, politics and economics were mutually
exclusive.

(iii)   Transport and General Workers Union (Cab Section)

At first glance, it would appear that the TGWU was the least likely
organisation to be supported or joined by owner-drivers. Yet some
did join and the ODA was committed to common action with them in
the defence of fair competition. Fair competition facilitated the
alliance of organised labour and small-scale capital and to members
of the TGWU it represented a fair day's wage for a fair day's work,
while regulating the conditions of work, including control of the
labour market. The state of fair competition corresponded with
some degree of monopoly penetration into the market on the part of
capital and labour. In the taxicab trade it was represented in
the monopoly right to ply for hire and a challenge to this
prerogative brought about a concerted defence from all sections of
the service.

THE IDEOLOGY OF FAIR COMPETITION

The cornerstone of the worldview of the owner-driver was fair
competition, because under its conditions the small-scale enterprise
was reproduced. The whole notion of fairness rested upon the
exclusion of the price mechanism from the market; hence the price
charged for any journey was uniform irrespective of the business
concerned and it followed that any form of price reduction
represented 'unfair' competition. Through fair competition, the
economic relation between each driver-journeyman focussed on the
individual and his cab. To act fairly in business was to act
professionally, but this was also a commitment not to act
rationally and pursue profit. Fair competition, therefore,
represented the moral rejection of the idea of a free unfettered
market by owner-drivers, organised labour and large proprietors.
   These 'principles' of fair competition formed the basis of state
regulation. Consequently, they became accepted as the natural
state of affairs without any requirement for conscious articulation.
Moreover, regulated competition influenced racialist attitudes.
Jewish proprietors and drivers featured in the service, but fair
competition attenuated anti-semitism. Without market forces and
free competition there was no economic insecurity, or process of
social declassing, on which racial prejudice could grow or political
mobilisation take root.
   Overall, free competition within the taxicab service was
excluded by state regulation. Small-scale businessmen looked
favourably upon public control, for they recognised that it gave
them economic security. Moreover, fair competition produced
stability in economic affairs and alleviated the economic pressures
on the larger companies, while protecting the small-scale owners.
   In the next section, I shall focus upon a direct challenge to
fair - regulated - competition in the form of private-hire companies.
There are three objectives in the discussion: to explain the nature
of the challenge, to illustrate fair competition and the commitment
of small businessmen to monopoly, and to analyse the politics of
the response.

THE CHALLENGE OF THE PRIVATE-HIRE COMPANIES

Private-hire vehicles offered an alternative means of transport in
the same manner as a taxicab, with one important distinction: they
were cheaper. The cars of the private-hire companies were not
covered by the statutory regulations governing taxicabs and there
were no tests or inspections on the vehicles. Ordinary production-
line cars were used at lower fixed-capital costs to the proprietors.
As maintenance and operative costs were also low, the companies
lowered the cost of a 'fare'. The charge for a journey was set by
the economic calculations of the company and not by the Home
Secretary. Finally, the driver for a private-hire firm did not
have to gain a special public transport licence. On all counts,
therefore, the private-hire vehicles were, during the 1930s, exempt
from any form of regulation or control.
    The economic challenge of private-hire companies increased with
their ability to attract qualified and expert taxi-drivers by an
offer of better wages and conditions. Competition, from the stand-
point of the nascent private-hire companies, did not rest upon
individual enterprise, but upon effective, rational, business
organisation. Hence, these companies offered a wage-rate system
with guaranteed earnings, in addition to a bonus system, because
each driver was not locked into competition with every other driver
on the street.
    Private-hire companies were more sophisticated enterprises and
required a higher level of capital investment. They did not operate
on the streets like cabs, because legally they could not ply for
hire, but rather a customer contacted the firm in advance to
arrange a contract. An enterprise needed access to a telephone,
garage, a system of business communication. All these factors made
the private-hire form of business inaccessible to individually-
based capital. Private hire satisfied a consumer demand similar
to the taxi service. In some areas, they were the only viable
service available, particularly as the taxicab system was concentrated
in inner London. The private-hire service, in effect, introduced
price competition into the regulated taxi service, while it escaped
the costs and regimentation of regulation.
    The competitive effectiveness of private hire increased during
the 1930s, partly as consumer expenditure on taxis declined, and
in part through its penetration\into the periphery of inner London.
In these circumstances, the cheaper private-hire fare was seen as
'cutting' the price of a taxi-fare by the taxi operators, and as
nothing less than unfair competition. Towards the close of the
decade, the organisations of the taxi service began to vigorously
campaign against private hire. They started to mobilise politically
to achieve redress, which under the circumstances meant some form
of government intervention.
    At the annual general meeting of the ODA in November 1937, the
chairman laid stress on the menace of private hire:
    We cannot over-emphasize the importance of the wasteful and
    unfair competition, and the great danger to the public who are
    thus left unprotected. They, by having a cheap vehicle, are
    undercutting us because if the conditions of fitness which apply
    to your cab were applied to them, they could not undercut you.
    ('ODA Gazette', December 1937, p.12)

Every organisation of the taxicab service complained that private-
hire companies were unregulated, and not subject to state control.
A member of the ODA and the TGWU (Cab Section) recommended that their
efforts should concentrate upon the extension of public control to
private hire:

> Private Hire is the most serious menace the Cab Trade has ever
> been faced with.... Either the Cab Trade must win the fight, or
> the conditions for cabmen, in the way of long hours, lower income
> and general precariousness, will be such that present-day
> conditions, bad as they are, will be prosperity in comparison.
> ('ODA Gazette', October 1938, p.23)

The ODA exhorted all owner-drivers to demonstrate against private
hire. They were joined in this call by both the TGWU and the large
cab proprietors; the former because they were afraid of the imminent
loss of skilled jobs, and the latter because they feared a decline
in their business.

The LMCDCTU joined the general protest, but they carefully refused
to ally with the other organisations. Their condemnation of private
hire rested on the same grounds, particularly that competition based
on cheaper prices would marginalise small-scale capitalist enterprises. They too saw the spectre of unfair competition: 'It is a
cut-price taxi service masquerading under a private hire disguise'
('Green Badge Journal', 15 January 1938, p.3). Private hire, in
their view, was morally wrong. It was unacceptable because it
encouraged competition and the 'survival of the fittest', and if
it continued owner-drivers would be at the mercy of free competition
in an unregulated market. An editorial in the 'Green Badge Journal'
succinctly defined the future of owner-drivers in a free market:
'economics is against us' ('Green Badge Journal', ibid.).

In response to the economic challenge of private hire, the
three predominant organisations - the ODA, TGWU and cab proprietors'
association - formed a joint committee dividing the costs between
them. 'Green Badge', however, remained aloof. The essential
element of the joint committee's platform contended that private-
hire companies enjoyed commercial success because they were exempt
from state control. As the regulations sought to ensure public
safety, there was no reason, they argued, for private hire to be
free from control. Their campaign, therefore, sought to pressurise
the government into extending state regulation. To achieve this
end several methods were used. Drivers were encouraged to write
to their MPs, an advocate was enlisted to present their case to
the Home Secretary, and the joint committee proposed a series of
meetings to educate their respective members and to maintain support.
One such meeting in June 1938 witnessed some 3,000 drivers and
owners present, and the following resolution was readily accepted.

(1) That this meeting of the London Cab Trade protests at the
long delay on the part of the Home Secretary in answering their
representations on the question of Private Hire, this delay
having seriously prejudiced the livelihood of those engaged in
the Cab Trade;
(2) That this meeting demands that all Private Hire vehicles
shall be made subject to the same stringent control as exercised
by the Commissioner of Police over the Cab Trade;
(3) That this meeting declares its solidarity of purpose and

calls upon the Joint Committee to mobilise the Trade further to
combat this menace in every possible way. ('ODA Gazette', June
1938, p.3)

Neither prorogation by the government, nor economic decline turned
the trade associations away from pluralist-democratic political
action and they resolved to exert more pressure within the institutional framework. Several MPs raised the issue in favour of the
'Cab Trade'. All these efforts were rewarded in a Home Office
inquiry under Sir Clement Hindley (Hindley Report, 1939). This
inter-departmental committee publicly stated that it had been
constituted because of joint representations of trade associations
and trade unions in the London taxi service (Hindley Report, 1939,
p.25).

The Hindley Committee thoroughly examined the private hire
companies. It had no reservations about their business methods, but
it recognised that imprecision as to the legal meaning of plying
for hire aggravated the situation by fostering discontent among the
taxi service. The committee reported in favour of incorporating
private-hire companies under some form of statutory control,
especially as the leading private-hire companies had asked for it.
These companies accepted the argument for public safety, but they
also wished to exclude the 'irresponsible', i.e., small-scale
operators. In other words, these successful companies were asking
to be brought under the protective umbrella of the state, so that
free competition could be regulated within their own sphere:

> The witnesses were strongly in favour of the private-hire trade
> being brought under public control. They viewed with alarm the
> rapid increase in the number of concerns and individuals in the
> trade, many offering vehicles for hire at rates below those
> which they regarded as possible for a well-organised and
> reliable service. They pointed out that there was nothing to
> prevent a person from purchasing a cheap second-hand car and
> using it for carrying passengers for hire. Those firms which
> had endeavoured to organise an efficient and well-regulated
> public service regarded the lack of any control or check as a
> menace both to the trade and to the public generally. (Ibid.,
> p.30)

The established private hire companies advocated a licensing
system which sought to determine the type of vehicle, institute a
system of inspection and supervision, examine the condition of the
car and competence of the drivers, and set conditions of service
(including a minimum wage), and regulate the price structure by a
scale of minimum mileage rates. As for the taxicab organisations,
they sought to defend their monopoly right to ply for hire. To
them, the exemption from control 'privileged' private hire, and made
it more profitable. The Hindley Committee recognised the validity
of the taxi service claim to monopoly:

> The position was that the cab trade had lost the monopoly it had
> hitherto enjoyed, and, restricted as it was by the system of
> control, could do nothing to meet the competition except to press
> for similar restrictions to be placed on private-hire vehicles
> which were in fact doing cab work. (Ibid., p.27)

In order to secure that monopoly right the Hindley Committee
suggested a measure of control without the full stringency of the

taxi regulations and which did not condone private hire with a right
to ply for hire. Members of the Hindley Committee recorded that they
had received no communication from the very small private-hire firms;
there was no evidence that they objected to governmental control and
none came to speak in favour of the economic liberalist view.

The Hindley Report decided for control of private hire companies,
despite its curtailment of free competition and the consequent
consolidation of monopoly. The interests of public safety and social
well-being necessitated some form of state control, whatever the
particular interests involved:

> While these trade interests both lay stress on the need for
> control in the public interest, it is not unfair to say that
> their primary motive is to obtain protection for their own
> respective trades from the effects of competition.... In an issue
> of this nature, however, sectional interests cannot be allowed
> to outweigh the interests of the general public, and if the two
> interests are not the same the latter should prevail. The
> protection of vested interests is not, moreover, a matter for
> legislation unless it is in the general public interest that such
> protection should be afforded. (Ibid., p.31)

The complex transport requirements of an urban conurbation thus
necessitated regulation for business, commercial and social life.
A completely free and open transport system created chaos and the
public had no safeguards for the competence, reliability and
character of the private-hire driver, because the service was 'open
to all and sundry'. The whole history of public transport, it was
argued, had shown the correctness of government control:

> The private hire services now cater for much wider sections of
> the community and are rapidly becoming an important and wide-
> spread form of transport, competing for custom with the older
> services.... The history of these services has taught the lesson
> that unregulated profit-seeking and competition in the field of
> public transport leads to unfortunate results and eventually
> compels the Government to intervene. (Ibid., p.34)

Private business interests - the established private-hire
companies - and aims for public safety converged on the need for
the restraint of competition. Here was an acceptable face of
capitalism, with safeguards and standards that protected the interests
of private companies. In addition, an intensification of competition
between private-hire companies could encourage unacceptable methods
and activities: the spiral of a free market 'may lead to a reduction
of charges to an uneconomic level at the expense of the safety of
the vehicle and the wages and conditions of service of drivers,
(that) cannot be viewed without anxiety' (ibid., p.35).

The inter-departmental government report emphasised the damaging
social consequences of the free market. Government intervention
would prevent economic marginalisation of inefficient enterprises
and forestall social unrest. It was in the public interest,
economically and politically, to constitute fair - regulated -
competition. Furthermore, it provided for the protection of the
monopoly of the taxicab service.

Private hire served to unite the major trade organisations. The
LMCDCTU had remained outside the Joint Committee, but they, too,
had roundly condemned private hire and free competition. Their

independence isolated them from both the ODA and the TGWU and
proprietors' association. However, like the other organisations, the
LMCDCTU defended monopoly privileges against the challenge of free
competition, and to this end they retained their commitment to
pluralist democracy. Self-help and pressure group activities
effectively countered the emergence of free competition. In this
manner, too, the Joint Committee effectively exerted political
influence. As a result, private hire remained a trade dispute, an
internal problem of economic relationships, that was solved by internal
political organisation and lobbying. The resolution of this issue
proved the political viability of the trade associations. Moreover,
the commitment to affirmative action by the National Government in
favour of the regulation of market forces protected small businesses
and individual enterprises in the taxicab service.

CONCLUSIONS

It is now possible to assess the degree to which these British small
businessmen corresponded to conventional conceptions of their
ideology and actions; viz., that they are anti-monopolistic and
proponents of the free market, that they are 'anti-joiners', and
that they oppose the organisations of working people on the one
hand and big business on the other. It must be added that the
prevalent economic goal of the time was stability; in fact, this
reflected the extent to which monopoly and price control dominated
the market. Fair competition guaranteed a high level of economic
stability by excluding free and unfettered competition and sustained
small businesses against the effects of market forces. In the case
of the London taxi service, the government was seen as responsible
for fair competition and its associated monopoly privilege to ply
for hire. Moreover, these conditions formed the basis for an
alliance between labour, small capital and larger proprietors in
which 'fairness' meant stability.
      The monopoly privilege to ply for hire was jealously guarded and
defended by all sections of the service. An attack upon it by free
competition, in the economic form of private hire, brought about a
unified defence. The small businessmen of this sector identified
their survival with the continuation of monopoly, or, to put it
another way, monopoly and control of the market reproduced small-
scale capital (Killingback, 1980). The extent to which established
businessmen sought to introduce monopoly conditions is indicated by
the fact that the small private-hire companies, a fairly recent
fledging form of capitalist enterprise, specifically asked the
government to intervene and control their interests and ensure a
safe and reliable public service.
      This case study provides evidence which suggests that the most
important feature of the worldview of these small businessmen was
the ideology of fair competition and its associated rejection of
the principles of the free market. Price control safeguarded small
businessmen from competition and they campaigned determinedly for
the modulation of economic relations. In these circumstances the
London taxicab service manifested a high degree of organisation among
its small business sector. The basis for association lay in a

conscious attempt to exercise some measure of control over economic conditions and relationships. The trade association functioned to discipline its members in their acceptance of a business code of conduct corresponding to a professional ethic. In effect, trade associations fulfilled the functions of a pre-capitalist guild; its members showed little commitment to the maximisation of profit and unbounded accumulation of capital. The small-scale owners of private property wanted to be relieved of the burdens and necessities of the private ownership of capital; instead they satisfied themselves with a secure and stable share of consumption. The membership of the ODA and LMCDCTU continuously articulated a worldview rooted in a guild mentality.

However, this indicates that small business's trade associations not only achieved success in the economy, they also held political power and influence. The process of pluralist democracy legitimated and encouraged association, because it was accepted as the means of representation of business interest. Moreover, monopoly and price control were never challenged by the law. This suggests that the attitudes and actions of British small businessmen corresponded to the concept of 'social protectionism' (Winkler, 1976). In fact, protection permeated the dominant ideology of British society in the 1930s such that small businessmen formed an integral part of economic operations and its social formation. They did not exist in the interstices of society, nor did they feel the need to have to legitimate their social position because it never came under economic attack. They did not experience social declassing because the trade association, supported and encouraged by government, prevented their economic marginalisation and political powerlessness. Social protectionism retained its legitimacy while price maintenance continued to be effective. It was the abolition of the latter that was to undermine the position of small business.

GLOSSARY

ODA	Owner Drivers' Association
LMCDCTU	London Motor Cab Drivers' Co-operative Trade Union
TGWU	Transport and General Workers' Union
'mush'	owner-driver
'journeyman'	cab driver employed by some form of enterprise

Chapter 8

BOURGEOIS SOCIAL MOVEMENTS IN BRITAIN: REPERTOIRES AND RESPONSES (1)

Brian Elliott, Frank Bechhofer, David McCrone and Stewart Black

REPERTOIRES OF PROTEST

On Monday 12 July 1976 some 200 people gathered outside the Customs and Excise Office in London. The crowd consisted of relatively well dressed middle-class individuals marching to and fro carrying placards and shouting. Most of them had never been on a demonstration before, but this morning they had gathered to make a visible protest about a matter that concerned them: taxation. Some of the workers in the offices looked out and gestured to the crowd with two fingers. Two youngsters carrying a black-edged photograph were thrust to the front of the demonstration and the assembly set up a chant 'VAT kills: kill VAT'.

What was going on? What were the youngsters doing there? Some days earlier the VAT inspectors had called on a Mr Constantinescu, an elderly small businessman, and demanded to see his business records and accounts. For six hours they searched the house room by room and left at 2.00 a.m. taking with them a number of files. A few hours later Mr Constantinescu was dead. He had committed suicide.

The demonstration was the response of a number of small business groups - the Association of Self Employed People and the National Federation of the Self Employed and others. They had gathered to register their sense of outrage at what they considered to be the unwarranted power of the Customs and Excise officers and the iniquities of an unpopular tax. The adolescents were there to lend effect, to add a touch of pathos, for they were the grandchildren of the late Mr Constantinescu.

From the Customs and Excise office the demonstration set off and marched to Westminster where the leaders were received by David Mitchell (chairman of the Tory Party Small Business Bureau) and two other Conservative MPs who listened sympathetically to their grievances. (2)

A few months earlier, in January 1976, newspapers carried the story of another form of protest. Members of the National Federation of the Self Employed had embarked on a campaign of civil disobedience, refusing to pay over their national insurance contributions, refusing to fill in questionnaires, demanding that tax collectors come and

gather their monies directly and sending in cheques signed on
improbable items - like pairs of knickers. (3)

In the two years prior to that, a couple of military figures,
General Walker and Colonel Stirling, had established a pair of
vigilante groups, Civil Assistance and GB '75, both predicated on
the supposed imminence of a general strike and the collapse of law
and order in the UK. Their intention was to establish cells of
local worthies - 'apprehensive patriots' was one description - who
could be mobilised in order to defend 'freedom' and maintain
essential services. (4)

In August 1976, a dispute at a small photographic processing
laboratory led to one of the most publicised confrontations between
unions and a small employer. George Ward's sacking of some of his
workers led to mass picketing, to Labour MPs joining the picket
lines and the emergence of one Major Gouriet as the constant support
and adviser of the embattled employer. Major Gouriet was the
director of another recently founded group - NAFF (the National
Association for Freedom) and when post office workers refused to
handle the Grunwick laboratory's mail, this organisation set up a
strike-breaking, alternative delivery system. Pony Express, they
called it. (5)

These four instances serve to convey, we hope, something of the
flavour of that period from the mid- to late 1970s in Britain.   In
February 1974 the Heath government was defeated. According to the
popular press, the responsibility for its downfall rested principally
with the miners and with other trades unionists whose opposition to
the Tory Industrial Relations Act had been a marked feature of the
latter part of Heath's administration. During the election campaign,
there was much scare-mongering about the power of the unions and
the prospect of industrial anarchy. It was a time rich in apocalyp-
tic pronouncements in the media and a time of fear and discontent
among many of the middle class in Britain. The latter were responding
not just to the electoral defeat of the Tories but to many of the
policies adopted by Heath and his so-called 'Right Progressives'
during the latter years of his government. Inside the Tory party
there was much dissatisfaction with a leadership which had apparently
moved away from the free-market philosophy and anti-statism of
'Selsdon Man' to embrace an incomes policy and widespread state
intervention in attempts to modernise or at least manage the decline
of the British economy. (6) In the country at large, the period
following the elections of 1974 was marked by the flourishing of new
organisations and diverse forms of social protest by middle-class
groups. Demonstrations, lobbies, 'Open Door' TV programmes outlining
the discontents of small businessmen, legal action against the
Attorney General, the publication of innumerable newsheets, attempts
at strike-breaking and efforts to create a so-called 'third force'
to represent the collective interests of the allegedly unorganised
self-employed and petit-bourgeois groups - all these and more can be
found in the latter half of the 1970s.

Such mobilisations of middle-class groups have not, up to this
point, attracted a great deal of attention in sociology. A few
researchers, like King and Nugent, have reported the results of their
own studies and brought together the work of a handful of others
intrigued by the most recent 'middle-class revolt', and there are

some accounts of earlier forms of bourgeois discontent, but for the
most part, the attempt to study collective action and more particularly
forms of protest, has dwelt on the actions of the obviously oppressed.
(7)   Examining middle-class unrest seems to us worthwhile. It
reminds us that some of those who are not manifestly poor or subjugated
may yet from time to time set themselves against the state, against
established authorities, and utilise a wide range of tactics to
influence politicians and bureaucrats. It leads us to explore the
changing modes whereby their interests are represented and defended.

Our introductory remarks indicate something of the variety of
forms of social protest which are available to those who wish to
register their grievances in our kind of society. It is plain that
there exists a wide but not infinite 'repertoire' of contestatory
behaviour. There are demonstrations, strikes, parliamentary petitions,
rock concerts for or against particular causes, formal associations
and lobbies, mass marches and the systematic violence of urban
guerillas. In earlier periods, we can point to rick-burning, machine-
smashing, food riots, charivari and many forms of street theatre and
tableaux. The repertoire of protest is not something fixed; it is
conditioned by historical circumstances. Different forms of protest
emerge at different historical periods reflecting the changing shape
of the social structure, the changing resources, skills and needs
of groups of actors and the nature of the economies and politics in
which they are set. So, if each historical period produces extensions
and restriction of the protest repertoire - throwing up innovatory
forms here, casting others as archaic and ineffectual there - what
factors inform the choice of disgruntled citizens when they try to
mobilise and register their indignation? Charles Tilly (1978, p.156)
suggests five things:
  (a)   the standards of rights and justice prevailing in the
        population;
  (b)   the daily routines of the population;
  (c)   the population's internal organisation;
  (d)   its accumulated experience with prior collective action;
  (e)   the pattern of repression in the world to which the
        population belongs. (8)
Contestatory action is never allowed an open course - always it
is moulded to some degree by institutions and individuals who have
the capacity to shape the means and resources available to those
seeking change. Whether we are dealing with revolutionary movements
or more limited protests, the point is essentially the same: those
in authority contrive by diverse means to channel, to manipulate, to
manage protest - cajoling or coercing the agitators and their
organisations into approved pathways of protest. In some recent
accounts, like those of Piven, Fox and Cloward (1977), dealing with
labour unrest or the civil rights movement in the USA, we have good
illustrations of precisely these processes.

But these efforts as it were 'from the top' are not the only
constraints on the choice of protest forms. Selections from the
'repertoire' are conditioned too by the history of protest accumulated
by particular groups, strata or classes. Thus, in seeking to
understand why a particular group opts for any given set of defiant
actions, we have to bear in mind the ways that it has tried before
to exert influence upon events. As we shall see, there are legacies

of collective action embedded in the cultural histories of social
groups.

And that is hardly surprising if we choose to notice the
continuities as well as the novelties in the organisation of the
day-to-day lives of occupational groups or social strata. Persisten-
cies in the social and economic locations of particular groups,
similarities from generation to generation in the daily routines
enjoined by a trade or profession will reproduce some of the
constraints which have bounded their patterns of prior action.
Forms of protest are, of course, related to the skills, resources
and general organisation of occupational and community life.

And all of this is set in a context. Each society and each period
is marked by distinctive kinds of permissiveness and limitation on
the rights of groups and individuals to register their grievances
in more or less direct ways. In Britain the rights to form a union,
to strike, to picket, the rights to organise a march or hold a
public assembly - all these are established. But the rights to
strike or to picket have been won only in the comparatively recent
past and, as recent debate concerning picketing shows, they are
subject to change: to extension, perhaps, or to curtailment. In
some other societies at the present time, rights to unionise or to
hold mass meetings are by no means clearly established. Quite apart
from formal rights and restrictions there are, in every social
system and every economic order, generalised notions of justice and
morality and these too play a part both in the genesis and the
expression of protest. As writers like Hobsbawm (1959) and Rudé
(1964) and Thompson (1971, 1975) have shown, crowds and mobs in the
eighteenth century were frequently reacting to what they saw as
attacks on the moral basis of an economy, not just to material
discomfort, and their action was seldom mindless or random. Their
targets - whether persons or property - were selected because they
had symbolic significance within a moral system. And so it is today.
Large-scale, durable or effective forms of protest involve notions
of moral hurt as well as economic duress.

In this chapter we shall try to explore the shaping of recent
bourgeois protest by looking at the collective actions that have
occurred under the auspices of two contrasting associations - the
National Federation of the Self Employed (NFSE) and a body which
originally called itself the National Association for Freedom
(NAFF) - latterly the Freedom Association. In doing so, we shall
pay particular attention to the ways in which protest is shaped by
the structure of power and by the constraints which flow from the
everyday lives and social relations of the associations' members.
As we develop the argument, we can make some reference to those
other issues - the accumulated experience of protest each draws
upon and say a little about their conceptions of justice and
morality.

THE ORGANISATIONS

The National Federation of the Self-Employed began in August 1974.
It grew up in an unexpected way from the efforts of a former officer
of the National Union of Small Shopkeepers in Lytham St Anne's in

Lancashire. No one, least of all the founder, expected it to
develop in the dramatic way that it did. Norman Small had an
unpromising track record as the initiator of several other schemes
to establish small business groups all of which had failed - at
least in their ostensible purposes - though all had yielded money
in the form of subscriptions. The new body caught the peak of that
wave of petit-bourgeois indignation following the increase in the
self-employed national insurance levy and was sustained by deep
discontent over the collection of value-added tax. The speed with
which membership grew and funds rolled in completely outstripped
the capacity of the original organisers to cope. Within ten months
the association was claiming a membership of 40,000 and it looked as
though they would have something like half a million pounds in
subscriptions. NFSE, as its title indicates, emerged as a federal
body linking together a series of local groups which grew up in
response to Norman Small's original letter calling for mobilisation
of what he depicted as a numerous but unrepresented constituency.

NFSE was, and it remains, an association made up chiefly of small
businessmen - shopkeepers, small builders, garage proprietors,
hoteliers, the owners of small manufacturing establishments and
various other self-employed individuals, working together in some
37 regional groups. (9) Its attention has been devoted chiefly to
specific government policies which impinge in obvious, and it is
felt, unjust ways upon its small business members. Thus, it has
sought to win for the self-employed better rights to social security
benefits to match the increased levy they were paying; it has fought
long and hard to prevent the raising and complication of the rates
of value-added tax, and has joined forces with other organisations
to challenge the powers given to Customs and Excise inspectors
responsible for overseeing the collection of that tax. It has also
opposed the Employment Protection Act and the system of small
business licencing which requires those in the building industry who
wish to be taxed as self-employed persons, to obtain a certificate -
the 714 certificate - bearing a photograph and issued only after
the Inland Revenue has been presented with satisfactory accounts
covering three prior years' business.

NFSE began and has continued to derive much of its support in
regions outside the south-east of England. Its headquarters have
remained in Lytham St Anne's in Lancashire and it is from there that
the activities of its numerous and widely scattered branches are
co-ordinated. If we think about the geography of protest, it appears
as a body growing up in the regions and slowly moving towards devices
that can be effectively employed to win influence as it were 'at
the centre'.

NAFF on the other hand is a very different organisation: one
which developed and has maintained most of its following in London
and the Home Counties. Although it has established branches across
the country, its general appearance is of a body which was created
close to the centres of political and economic power and one which
has not sought to create and sustain anything like as complex a
structure of regional organisations as the main small business and
self-employed association. NAFF was formed in the wake of the
publicity that surrounded the death of one of the McWhirter twins
(Ross McWhirter was shot shortly after the publication of his

pamphlet 'How to Stop the Bombers' in November 1974) but it had been conceived before that event. It grew out of that same atmosphere of apprehension that gave rise to the vigilante groups and the renewed efforts of old campaigners for right-wing causes - like Edward Martell, Lady Birdwood, Air Vice-Marshal Donald 'Pathfinder' Bennett and others who set up a 'patriotic' press - the Current Affairs Press - at that time. NAFF's purpose was altogether broader than that of NFSE. It sought to change values and political commitments, to defend 'rights' and 'freedoms' from attack, as it saw it, from Labour governments and the power of the unions. The rights which it seeks to defend are specified in its Charter of Rights and Liberties (10) and many of them - 'freedom to live under the Queen's peace', 'freedom of religion and worship', 'freedom of speech and publication' - are, as Neill Nugent (1979, p.84) observes, unexception- al and can hardly be said to be under serious threat.   But a number of 'freedoms' which occur lower down the list are the ones to which NAFF has addressed itself most assiduously and these, on inspection, are 'rights' which are much more obviously related to 'bourgeois' interests. Thus, item 8 in the Charter refers to the 'freedom to belong or not to belong to a trade union or employers association' and has been the starting point for a long and continuing campaign against the 'closed shop'. The rights of property are identified in points 9, 10 and 11: 'the right to private ownership', 'the right to dispose or convey property by deed or will', the 'freedom to exercise choice or personal priority in spending, and from oppressive, unnecessary or confiscatory taxation' - these broad formulations encompass an array of discontents concerning state power over the use and transmission of property and, of course, taxation. NAFF's campaigns have been directed chiefly at what it sees as the unwarranted extension of state power and at the part played in the formulation of government policy and in day-to-day industrial practice by organised labour.

NAFF seeks to do two things: to shake the middle class out of its alleged complacency by pursuing various direct actions against selected aspects of state and union power, and to mount a broad campaign of moral re-education of the British middle class.

NAFF began and has largely remained, a highly centralised organisation run, not by petit-bourgeois but by much bigger business- men and their allies in the worlds of politics, journalism, the universities and the military. The National Council of the organisa- tion reflects very clearly the attempt to establish links with parties, with big business, with other 'freedom' associations, with journalists and a variety of 'opinion makers'. Thus, there are six Tory MPs on the council; Lady Morrison of Lambeth as a token of supposed Labour support; there are figures associated with large commercial and industrial enterprises like Sir Frank Taylor of Taylor Woodrow or Hugh Astor, a director of Hambros Bank and the Phoenix Assurance Association; Lord de L'Isle, also a director of Phoenix Assurance and formerly Governnor General of Australia; there are journalists like Robert Moss, Brian Crozier and Peregrine Worsthorne; a writer - John Braine - and three academics. Teresa Gorman the leader of the Association of Self-Employed People, represents a link to the petit-bourgeois protest organisations and Ralph Harris, the director of the Institute of Economic Affairs,

provides a tie to an organisation responsible for much of the
economic theorising used by the so-called radical right. Apart
from these members, sundry public figures, like the late Douglas
Bader, and Alex Bedser, have sat on the council. The composition
of the council suggests that it has been assembled with an eye to
the symbolic value of the well-known names and to the maintenance
of a broad network of influence. It has little real power.

NAFF has sought to articulate the despair of many traditional
right-wing elements who looked upon the actions of the moderate or
progressive group in the Tory party and those of the Labour administration under Wilson and Callaghan as a real threat to values and
interests they hold dear.

CHANGING FORMS OF PROTEST

If the repertoires of protest are subject to the constraining
processes suggested by Tilly and others, it ought to be possible to
find evidence of this in our study of these middle-class mobilisations of the last few years. And indeed, the many interviews we
conducted with the leaders of the associations, with politicians,
journalists and others, do provide us with such evidence, but it
seemed to us sensible to supplement these with a simple content
analysis of the kinds of agitation and protest recorded in the
'house journals' of the two associations which most interest us.
Since our collection of these journals, despite our best efforts,
were incomplete for earlier years, our analysis covered 'First
Voice', the journal of NFSE, from October 1976 to October 1980 and
'Free Nation' from January 1978 to October 1980. Any 'evidence'
produced on this basis must be treated in a circumspect way, but
the exercise does serve to corroborate and in some ways amplify our
impressions gained from interviews and other data.

The material in 'First Voice' suggests that NFSE throughout this
period began to change from what we might regard as an 'outsider'
organisation to an 'insider' one (Grant, 1977). The early issues,
covering October 1976 to mid-1977, contain frequent references to
direct and obvious forms of defiant action. There were demonstrations and meetings, campaigns of non-co-operation with the tax
authorities, attempts to co-ordinate the efforts of NFSE with a
wide variety of other middle-class associations in what was talked
of as a 'Third Force' to represent the self-employed. There was
some campaigning against the proposed Employment Protection Act
along with advice to members to 'get rid of surplus labour now'.
Of 134 items recorded, only 5 refer to meetings of NFSE representatives with members of parliament or civil servants.

The period from mid-1977 to mid-1979 as portrayed in 'First
Voice' seems to be one with much lower levels of collective action
(only 57 collective actions recorded). Attempts at direct action
still occur - for instance the scheme to refuse services to striking
power workers, and following the failure of an expensive recruitment
campaign, there was, as McHugh observes, a good deal of belligerent
posturing but no marches or demonstrations are recorded. (11) Only
one instance of direct contact with central government is reported.

A third period, from mid-1979 to October 1980 reveals higher

levels of activity once more but this time there is a striking
increase in the number and proportion of actions involving either
contact with government or the work of newly-created specialist
committees. By the end of our series, there are no fewer than
eleven committees busy holding meetings, calling for cases, talking
to ministers and generally acting like 'insider' pressure groups
who have established their legitimacy and now have relatively easy
channels of communication with the centres of power. And at the
same time there is reported only one example of 'direct action' in
the 110 events identified as 'collective actions'.

Crude though such analysis is, it seems to confirm our impression
of NFSE as an organisation that has shifted away from the kinds of
direct action which gained it much publicity in its earliest phase
to more conventional and, from the point of view of ministers and
civil servants, more acceptable forms of representation. The game
has changed from protest to persuasion.

An examination of 'Free Nation', the monthly newssheet put out
by NAFF, also reveals interesting changes in the patterns of action
sponsored by the organisation. Far more of 'Free Nation''s pages
are taken up with articles of a general, often hortatory nature
than one finds in 'First Voice'. There is much invective directed
against well-known Tories representing the progressive wing of the
party, like James Prior or Ian Gilmour, much criticism of the
unwarranted power of the state or the need for 'libertarianism',
numerous articles about the threat of communism at home and abroad,
often written by emigrés from Eastern Europe, and a regular piece
on religious affairs.

The issues sampled do not yield such distinct periods as 'First
Voice' suggested, but somewhat surprisingly the more recent issues
of 'Free Nation' report more collective actions in the last year
than in the two previous years. Behind this lies a probable shift,
modifying what has hitherto been a very centrally directed organisation to one which is encouraging the branches to do more for
themselves. (12) Throughout most of its life NAFF has depended
very heavily on the energy and commitment of a handful of people,
chiefly those who make up its executive committee, as the number of
meetings, demonstrations, and dinners addressed by McWhirter or
Gouriet or, to a lesser extent, Moss and De L'Isle make plain.
With the departure of Gouriet and the much reduced activity of Moss,
the loosening of central control and the attempt to stimulate
grass-roots, local actions have become necessities.

The analysis of 'Free Nation' reveals that while there is a great
deal of rhetoric directed against government (and the Thatcher
government as well as the previous Labour administration come under
attack) most of the real action is aimed at what NAFF's leaders
clearly regard as the pernicious power of the trade unions and at
legislation entrenching union rights. NAFF portrays British unions
as bodies which have gained enormous and illegitimate power, thanks
largely to governments, Tory as well as Labour, which have incorporated them in the processes of administration, thereby legitimating
union actions which, in NAFF's view, curtail basic liberties of
individual workers and erode traditional rights of property holders.
Thus, NAFF continues to engage in or to encourage strike-breaking –
this after all constituted some of its earliest and most widely

publicised activity - from the 'liberating' of cars and drivers on
a strike-bound channel ferry, through the Pony Express operation
at Grunwick and the injunctions against the Attorney General and
the Union of Post Office Workers, to recent offers of help to
picketed hospitals. In its attacks on unions and union legislation
NAFF has employed a wide array of devices. It has explored the
repertoire of protest very fully. Its resort to 'public good' legal
actions to attack the law-makers represents an interesting method
of registering protest and one which requires both sizeable funds
and a good deal of legal expertise, but it has also organised marches
and rallies, handed in petitions at the House of Commons, held Free
Enterprise Days, fêted the Californian Senator responsible for
Proposition 13, taken 'closed shop' cases to the European Court at
Strasbourg, celebrated the opening of a libertarian bookshop and
even organised three rock concerts (Rock Against the Reds) whose
proceeds were sent to the free trade union in Poland. The evidence
from the recent issue of 'Free Nation' suggests that the use of
legal actions, at least on the grand scale of Gouriet vs The Attorney
General, are now less favoured (hardly surprising when that resort
to the law cost NAFF £90,000) and that petitions and lobbies have
increased somewhat. However, there is nothing to indicate that
NAFF's contacts with the legislature is of the kind which NFSE has
evolved. NAFF does not present research documents to ministers
and their civil servants. The broad nature of its objectives, the
structure of the organisation and the predilections of its leaders
preclude that kind of conventional pressure group activity.
    The changes in NAFF's repertoire of action seem, by comparison
with NFSE, rather minor. NAFF continues to use the law as a means
of registering and publicising its indignation but in place of those
dramatic and expensive cases initiated by Gouriet, there are now a
whole series of modest legal battles up and down the country, mainly
cases where NAFF is involved in supporting workers dismissed because
they refuse to join a closed shop. More of the action now seems to
be taking place at the local level and on the initiative not of the
central executive but of local branches. NAFF is an association
which is trying to sustain protest activity. It seeks to express
the continuing indignation felt by established bourgeois elements
who resent the ways in which the state has taken organised labour
into the processes of government, (13) who see union power undermining
the authority of employers and who identify union leaders as Marxist
subversives. It goes on trying to express this discontent and to
continue its 'education' of the middle class.

THE STRUCTURE OF POWER

If these then are the major changes that have occurred, how, precisely,
can we account for them? We can take first the influence of what
Tilly calls the structure of power. In what ways were the 'pathways'
of protest shaped by the structures of power? How was the protest
mediated by central political processes? It is easiest to see this
in the case of NFSE.
    The most obvious political response to the unaccustomed agitation
among the minor entrepreneurs and self-employed workers has come

from the Tory party. When it was in opposition between 1974 and 1979 it saw small business as a relatively distinct and partially organised constituency which it wanted to incorporate into its own organisation. Nothing makes this plainer than the activities of the Small Business Bureau set up in the Spring of 1976 by David Mitchell. Its purposes are set out in a pamphlet issued to party organisers. The Bureau's aims are summarised as follows (Conservative Party Small Business Bureau, 1977):

(a) To keep in touch with a large cross section of small business-men, centrally and locally; to collect, collate and analyse their views and problems and brief the parliamentary party;

(b) Through its newspaper to report back to subscribers on the work being done on their behalf in parliament. In this way businessmen can be sure that their pressure on the party is up to date and constant;

(c) To forge effective links with other small business organisa-tions in the UK and Europe;

(d) When the Conservative party is in government, to provide an ongoing small business voice as an alternative to the civil service;

(e) To research through local and central study groups into all aspects of small businesses – to publish a series of working papers on small business topics, designed to highlight problems and suggest solutions.

The SBB runs a regular newssheet, organises conferences and has developed a network of local branches. It initially aimed to have branches in all 623 constituencies (in practice it has branches in about 80) and it claimed that it gave what no other small business or self-employed pressure group could give, 'a direct say in Conservative policy planning'.

The disaffection of the small business groups from conventional party politics was, as Margaret Thatcher acknowledged, in part a condemnation of the Tories. Under Heath the Tories had neglected what Gamble (1974) calls the politics of support. Given that this is the party which has traditionally, if not always very sincerely, portrayed itself as the 'natural home' of the small businessman, it is not surprising that a new leader seeking to secure electoral support should urge the closest possible contact between the Tory party and the new small business groups; they must be captured. And the way in which constituency workers can help in this process is nicely spelled out in the official pamphlet.

In a little article entitled Through the Eyes of an Agent, there is a description of how an agent, finding it hard to get small business people to join the Conservative association, used the Bureau as a method of recruitment (Conservative Party Small Business Bureau, 1977, pp.16-17):

The main problem seemed to be that most of these people ran their own small businesses. There was no question of their joining the Conservative association - they were convinced that their businesses would suffer as a result.

Determined not to be beaten, and with nothing to lose, I resorted to the 'slowly, slowly' method. My first step was to hunt out the literature from the Small Business Bureau. 'Come to a meeting', I entreated, 'no, not a political meeting, a

business meeting. Anyone can come - it's free! Bring your
friends'. They did, and still do, and two weeks after the first
such meeting the Branch began to thrive. My first proof of one
of the advantages to be gained by using the Small Business
Bureau....Many of those who join the Bureau would not otherwise
come near the Tory organisation.... Once they have been to a
meeting ... their attitude to our organisation changes completely
and they are then on the fringe of the association net.

There is no doubt that it served the party's electoral interests
to sympathise with, to encourage, small business organisations and
to attempt to incorporate them. Our interviews, though, indicate
clearly enough that among the small business leaders there was a
good deal of suspicion about the sincerity of this new enthusiasm
for their concerns. There was a widespread apprehension that once
returned to power the Tories might well be much less solicitous
towards them. There was awareness too that much of the attention
directed to them was a reflection of the ambitions of one man,
David Mitchell, who acted as a political entrepreneur - seeking to
amplify and channel petit-bourgeois discontent in order to build
for himself a political career. (14)

If the efforts of the Bureau were designed to link small business
discontent to the electoral programme of the party, the efforts
of the Tory backbench Committee on Small Business served to guide
the representation of interest into conventional lobbying channels.
Paul Dean, as chairman of that committee, encouraged the raising
of small business grievances on the floor of the House and his
counselling of the NFSE leaders encouraged them away from their
campaigns of harassment of the bureaucracy towards more 'professional'
lobbying at Westminster. Our interview with him (20 June 1978)
confirmed what some small business leaders had told us - that he
had acted as their mentor - directing what he referred to as their
initial 'evangelical fervour' into the provision of detailed,
factual and reliable briefs for himself and his colleagues.

The pressure to direct protest along familiar lines - to contain
and cope with it, also came out clearly in our discussion with
Robert Cryer, the minister with responsibility for small business
in the Callaghan government. Though generally scathing about the
new small business organisations (he compared NFSE very unfavourably
with some much older bodies with well-established links to Whitehall
departments, like the Small Firms Council of the CBI), he acknowledged
that they were becoming more unified and capable. 'But', he observed,
'none of them present information like the NFU. Anything happens -
next morning there's a paper from them on your desk' (Interview,
21 June 1978). The inference to be drawn from his remarks was
plainly that if it wanted to have any political clout, NFSE would
have to conform to the conventional pattern of the best-run,
professionally-staffed lobbies.

By 1976 there were some indications that the Labour government
was beginning to take notice of the vociferous protests from the
self-employed and small business organisations. As Roger King
(1979, pp.123-4) remarks

the important appointment of Harold Lever with special responsibility for small firms, tax concessions, promises to alleviate
the administrative burden, general praise for the efforts of

the small sector and the enquiry by the Wilson Committee into
Financial Institutions, which was particularly concerned with
the problems faced by small and medium-sized firms in raising
capital, mark the more favourable attitude of the Callaghan-led
Labour Government.

Even on the left wing of the party there was some support, for a
number of MPs, including Eric Heffer, saw small enterprises as one
of the means of revitalising the economies of inner-city areas.

But the effect of this new attentiveness to the claims of small
business tended to work in one direction. It encouraged the
routinisation of representation, discouraged small business leaders
from taking any forms of direct action, and enjoined them to model
themselves on conventional lobbies. Politicians would accept
representations and listen to arguments provided they were delivered
by small delegations armed with well-rehearsed, well-researched
briefs. The issues addressed had to be narrow, specific matters
on which legislators might hope to act. In the process, alternative
forms of expression - the marches and demonstrations, the threats
to utilise the strike weapon or the concern with broad matters of
general economic philosophy or values - these almost sank from view.

NFSE then has moved progressively nearer to a trade lobby in
its style of operation as the growth of its narrowly-focussed
committees makes plain. Unlike the Association of Self Employed
People, it has rejected any attempt to provide what Teresa Gorman,
leader of ASP, refers to as a 'coherent philosophy' for small
business. NFSE spends little time on the discussion of 'libertarian'
principles or debates about the 'social market economy'.

The route that it has taken then has been shaped in important
ways by the responses of those in positions of power. The apparent
disdain with which it was treated in Westminster and Whitehall in
its early years and the advice and encouragement provided latterly
by sympathisers in all parties have persuaded it to proceed in the
manner of the established lobbies. To that end, it now has a London
office and a well respected research officer to service its various
specialist groups. The decisions to move in this direction have
often been the subject of fierce debate inside the organisation and
the establishment of a much more formalised, bureaucratic structure
has dismayed some of its activists.

In the case of NAFF, it is difficult to point so explicitly to
the effects of the structure of power largely because, although it
tried from time to time to confront governments (over the '714'
legislation and the closed-shop principle) its main thrust has always
been towards much less specific changes. NAFF seeks first and
foremost to alter the climate of opinion and to do this in large
part through hoped-for shifts in policy by the party of the right.
Moreover, NAFF addresses much of its effort to confrontations with
those who are still themselves contending for power- the trades
unions. It seeks to undermine the position of the TUC by extensive
propaganda, by litigation and by rallies outside Transport House or
at the annual congress. It rarely lobbies MPs and has made no effort
to win influence inside the civil service. (15) Consequently, it
has been subject to little of the steering, little of the unsolicited
advice on tactics that NFSE encountered.

Our interviews with MPs revealed something of the attitudes

towards NAFF in the House of Commons. Labour MPs were generally
disparaging or downright hostile. Far from seeking in any way to
channel NAFF's protests, they dismissed them as nothing more than
the expression of the more extreme fringes of the Tory party. Apart
from the memories of NAFF's role in the Grunwick dispute or its
actions against Attorney General Silkin, Labour MPs also suspected
NAFF of sponsoring subversion within the Labour party. Alex Lyon,
for instance, received and published information that NAFF provided
funds for the supporters of Reg Prentice when his constituency
party in Newham North East sought to prevent his re-selection. NAFF
never denied the allegations. Having conducted some inquiry into
the association, Alex Lyon depicted NAFF as a body representing the
opinions of an elderly, somewhat blimpish element in the Tory
constituency who were, he suggested, chiefly concerned about the loss
of social power they had experienced in post-war Britain. (16) This
certainly gybes with our own view of the organisation as one which
orchestrates the nervous response of sections of the old middle
class who lament their loss of political 'voice', the infringements
on their rights as property owners and the limitations placed upon
them as employers.

Among the Conservative MPs we interviewed, the reactions were
varied. There was plainly a good deal of distaste for what were
regarded as its extreme views but some of those who were part of
the Thatcherite clique saw advantages in having such a ginger group
to sway opinion in the party. Several times we were told that NAFF
was more like an alternative party than a pressure group and from
one MP who was a member of NAFF's council there was speculation
that the association might well put up its own candidates. The
leaders of NAFF certainly had considered such a possibility but they
had deliberately rejected this - as they saw it - unpromising route
for the development of their protest. One Tory MP, stressing the
extent to which NAFF was like a political party, described it as
having the potential to become 'a sort of respectable National
Front'. (17)

NAFF does not need to lobby Tory MPs, for when it wants to exert
influence at Westminster it does so principally through the networks
of social contacts its executive and council enjoy. After all, there
are six Tory MPs on the council and four of them, Mitchell, Boyson,
Ridley and Knight, were close to Margaret Thatcher in opposition
and two are now in important posts. The fact that Margaret Thatcher
has given some endorsement to the association by attending one of
its annual dinners is further indication of the friendly personal
relations that bind the 'radical right' of the party and NAFF.

Looking at NAFF one is reminded of Hobsbawm's (1975, p.244)
remarks about the social resources of Europe's nineteenth-century
bourgeoisie:

the classical recourse of the bourgeois in trouble or with cause
for complaint was to exercise or to ask for personal influence,
to have a word with the mayor, the deputy, the minister, the
old school or college comrade, the kinsman or business contact.

Such contacts are an important part of NAFF's weaponry and help to
explain why the association has not developed an elaborate organisational structure as NFSE has done.

Thus, while NFSE has clearly changed, in its organisation, in its

leadership and in its means of voicing its constituents' grievances,
NAFF has remained largely unaltered. Though it has lost its chief
executive, whose taste for action proved a little too expensive for
the association, (18) the renamed Freedom Association presses on with
essentially the same structure, broadly the same selection of tactics,
and with the central figure - McWhirter - continuing to provide much
of the energy for its campaigns. With the Tories now in power and
with policies addressed to at least some of the 'ills' identified
by NAFF it is likely that the association will find it harder and
harder to sustain its activities. The encouragement of greater
autonomy in the branches, the slimming down of the central staff and
the suggestion that they relinquish their Grape Street office,
probably signal some real decline in the fortunes of the best
established 'freedom' association of the late 1970s. The breadth
of its concerns and the cultural styles and preferences of its
leaders have prevented the kind of channelling and moulding, the
processes of institutionalisation that have given to NFSE a good
chance of survival.

THE CONSTRAINTS OF EVERYDAY LIFE

We said at the beginning that social protest is shaped in part by
the commonplace experience of groups and strata, that the repertoires
of collective action available to different sets of actors are
constrained by their positions within society. How might we argue
this with respect to the two associations we have been examining?
     NFSE developed out of the immediate experience of a diverse
stratum of small businessmen and self-employed people. Specific
impositions, like the 8 per cent National Insurance levy and the
problems entailed in the collection of value-added tax were the
triggers which released a more diffuse sense of injustice and
material and social insecurity. The new association orchestrated
the discontents of many different occupational groups into something
much nearer a class interest and held the promise of more effective
representation than that provided by traditional trade associations.
(19)
     NFSE 'captured' the discontent on a local basis. Most of its
members were entrepreneurs or traders or small employers who operated
in small-scale markets. For the most part, they lacked connections
with centres and organisations of national power, a fact which was
underlined by the retention of the headquarters in a small town in
Lancashire. The skills, resources, and horizons of NFSE were
initially very limited. It had large numbers and a lot of money,
but a very restricted, not to say parochial, conception of its real
capacities. It reflected the social characteristics of its members,
their 'local' commitments, their limitations of expertise, their
lack of connection to elite networks - in short, a whole array of
constraints stemming from social background and the cultural, economic
and temporal limitations imposed by the kinds of work in which they
were engaged. (20)
     The great resentment of bureaucracy and the suspicion of political
process - common accompaniments of petit-bourgeois enterprise -
helped shape the early collective action and contributed much to the

internal wrangling which was a feature of NFSE's first two years.
The fear of 'bureaucracy' lay behind the resistance to the idea that
NFSE should employ a full-time staff, should try to produce research
papers, set up specialist committees and handle its finances (21) in
a regular way. It inhibited moves to make the Federation more like
a pressure group and kept alive a penchant for more direct and
flamboyant action.

The hostility to bureaucracy stems from the way in which aspects
of small-business life are regulated; the way forms have to be
filled in, taxes calculated and returns made to impersonal agencies
whose rules, demands for information and purpose are often only
vaguely comprehended. It reflects immediate personal experience of
the frustrations of negotiating bureaucratic procedures and the kind
of critique of state power to which it gives rise falls a long way
short of the thorough-going and more intellectualised arguments
made by an association like NAFF.

Within NFSE there is a good deal of ambivalence about the role
of the state and its involvement in market relations, for while
there are many criticisms of government interference, this co-exists
with a belief that only governments can limit the powers of giant
corporations and establish the conditions of 'fair trading' in
which the independent businesses can survive. Moreover, while there
is much rhetoric about the evils of 'corporatism' among NFSE
officials, there are at the same time several influential officers
who rigorously support the functional representation which a 'third
force' implies.

For the small bourgeois, cultural history conspires with present
experience to close off certain avenues of political expression. In
France and Belgium shopkeepers, garage proprietors and others of
this stratum have, from time to time, gone on strike, but in
Britain, although the suggestion that NFSE organise a strike has
been made, it has never really been accepted. Unlike bureaucratised
middle-class groups, small businessmen in Britain seem reluctant
to include the strike as part of their repertoire of protest. From
time to time it has been proposed that NFSE should attempt to
involve itself more directly in politics and maybe put up candidates
at elections, but this too has generally been opposed. There is
recognition that its members' political opinions are by no means
homogeneous and that there is (certainly by comparison with NAFF)
little direct experience of political campaigning among its leaders,
while there is also some awareness of the poor prospects for third
parties in Britain.

NAFF is an organisation recruiting from a rather different
stratum. It has a more haute-bourgeois character. NAFF is rooted
firmly in the Home Counties, and as far as one can tell, draws its
support from a relatively elderly section of the established middle
class. (22) The themes which it articulates appeal to an older
generation in part because they so frequently invite reflection
and comparison of the present with some idealised past. 'Free
Nation' contains much that appeals to a generation raised in
comparative comfort in the 1920s and 1930s, who fought for king and
country and now lament the passing of institutions, mores and
attitudes which gave structure and security to their lives.

The methods whereby NAFF tries to register and disseminate its

views reflect the similarities of educational and social experience
of its leaders and no doubt a good many of its members. The public
school and Oxbridge education, the membership of clubs, the overlapping of military service careers, the contacts made in business,
all these provide the infrastructure for that network of social
contacts that can be utilised to spread NAFF's message in the
corridors of power. The branches of NAFF, the local organisations,
appear much less important than its central organisation - the
executive committee, the staff at Grape Street producing 'Free
Nation'. NAFF is an association which first and foremost speaks
to and draws upon the skills of those who are already well-placed
in the structures of wealth and power in Britain, which is not to
deny that it makes some effort to address a wider audience. In its
campaign to re-educate a broadly defined middle class it invokes
the doctrines of Hayek and Friedman, but since these are accessible
to only a small section of that population, it uses 'Free Nation'
for the production of popularised, simplified versions of these
messages. The writings of some of the professional journalists
like Moss and Crozier and those too of the academics contributing
to this newssheet have been designed to interpret the mysteries of
Hayek and Friedman for a broader readership.

From time to time NAFF has attempted to incorporate the discontent
of the small business constituency and there was a point where one
of the Federation leaders appeared to be trying to link the two
bodies, but inside the Federation these moves were quickly spotted
and resisted. (23) NAFF saw NFSE's regional structure as providing
cells (rather like those of the vigilante patriots) which could be
called upon if the need arose to fight union actions, (24) but most
of the leaders of the small-business group were fearful of the loss
of independence which might come from any close association with
NAFF. And they knew too that many of their members did not share
NAFF's passionate anti-Communism nor its unremitting antipathy to
organised labour. (25)

Though NAFF may be undergoing some important changes now, throughout
most of its life it has been a highly centralised, elitist association
run by those whose extensive business, social and political commitments
facilitated the exercise of 'old boy' influence but largely precluded
the possibilities of running a complex bureaucratised structure of
country-wide groups on the NFSE pattern. The style of the National
Association for Freedom - its structure and its tactics - reflect
the skills and resources, but also the constraints of its 'establishment' leadership.

CONCLUSION

In the latter half of the 1970s, Britain's relative economic decline
became more acute and more obvious. In their attempts to manage
this decline both major parties had evolved what many regarded as
'corporatist' strategies bringing the employers' organisations and
the unions into fragile partnerships with government. Both the
economic decline and the political programmes to cope with it posed
threats to traditional bourgeois elements for not only did they
confront in their business activities the financial problems which

beset the country but as other groups - especially organised labour -
acquired more 'voice' in the political system, some among them felt
their political and indeed their social influence to be declining.

The formation of the large number of new organisations articulating
aspects of their discontent took on, more and more, the character of
a class response. Class interests were identified, opposition to
other classes was specified and efforts were made to mobilise both
'grande' and 'petite' elements of the bourgeoisie. (26)   Their
efforts were directed against Labour governments, against the
'progressive' elements of the Tory party, against organised labour,
against parts of the state apparatus which meant many of the
'untrustworthy' members of the 'new', the bureaucratised middle
class. (27)

Between 1964 and 1979 the Tory party was in office for only four
years and consequently was unable to defend or promote the interests
of many of its traditional supporters. Even when it was in power
under Heath it seemed to many that their concerns were largely
ignored. Thus, by 1974 there was among many small businessmen and
some larger ones too a sense that the party which historically had
carried their banners was now unable to represent them. Whereas
the Tory party had previously been able to claim that it was
responsive to the needs of small as well as large business interests,
and that consequently there was little need for the formation of
aggressive non-parliamentary groupings or alternative parties, by
the mid-1970s that boast rang hollow. (28)

In this chapter we have focussed on two of the largest and
arguably most important of these new associations which sprang up
to articulate the fear and indignation of what was perceived as
the economic, political and social decline of bourgeois elements in
British society. One represents petit-bourgeois elements, the other
members of the established, often the haute bourgeoisie. Each has
experimented with a wide variety of devices for expressing their
senses of grievance, but as they have developed, so the range of
their repertoires seems to have contracted. One, NFSE, appears
largely to have relinquished its noisy, defiant public displays
and to have evolved as a relatively sophisticated but quite
conventional pressure group. Incorporation is the price it has paid
for a prospect of durability. NAFF's trajectory seems rather
different. It still finds much to object to in the policies of the
Thatcher government whose election it so ardently supported, but
there are several indications that it is now in decline.

The brief histories of these collective bodies and their
repertoires of protest have been shaped by a variety of factors,
by the prior experience of protest - which has led NFSE back towards
the model of a trade association and sustained NAFF's reliance on
'old boy' networks - by the constraints imposed by daily routines
and mundane experiences of their constituent populations and by the
responses of those in positions of power. Just as there are
repertoires of protest, so too there are 'repertoires of repression' -
ranging from outright coercion through all kinds of manipulation
to blithe disregard.

In their different ways each organisation has contributed to
the growth of sentiments and actions favourable to the 'new right'
in Britain. Both played a part in the election of the Thatcher

government and the promulgation and defence of ideas central to
that government's philosophy. In different ways each is urging a
reshaping of the modern state in ways which will restore to bourgeois
elements those prerogatives purloined or usurped (as they see it) by
the 'service' class or the force of organised labour. (29) Thus,
studying the formation and careers of the new 'middle-class' associations allows us to catch a glimpse of those political processes
whereby economic and social structures are continuously reshaped.

NOTES

1 This paper originally appeared in the 'Sociological Review',
   vol.30, no.1, February 1982, pp.71-96. The material reported
   here was gathered in the course of a project, 'Mobilising the
   middle class', financed by the SSRC under grant number HR 5319.
2 Our information about the demonstration and the events surrounding
   it comes partly from the newspapers, see, for instance, the
   'Guardian', 13 July 1976, partly from interviews with a number of
   those who led the march, and partly from the account provided in
   'Counterattack', no.3, 1976, the house journal of the Association
   of Self Employed People.
3 Newspapers carried descriptions of these events (see 'The Times',
   29 December 1975 and 1 and 2 January 1976) and the strategies of
   defiant action are discussed in 'First Voice', the monthly
   journal of NFSE.
4 We are grateful to Roy Wallis (1977) for information on these
   groups.
5 For the most extensive discussion of the Grunwick affair, see
   Rogaly (1977).
6 It is interesting to note that the first of the recent wave of
   middle-class protest organisations, the Middle Class Association,
   was formed in November 1974 as a means of expressing opposition
   to Heath and contributing to his downfall. We have this from
   the founder of MCA, the Tory MP John Gorst. Interview, June 1978.
7 See King and Nugent (1979), Nugent and King (1977) and the
   discussions about the rise of the 'radical right' in 'Marxism
   Today' (Jacques, 1979; Hall, 1980). For the slightly earlier
   period Thayer (1965) is worth consulting as is the well known
   work by Parkin (1968), and for the turn-of-the-century unrest
   see Brown (1974).
8 One can trace the development of his interest in these themes
   through earlier published work such as Tilly (1973, 1975) and in
   some of his unpublished papers available from the Center for
   Research on Social Organisation, University of Michigan. See for
   instance Repertoires of Contention in America and Britain.
9 The Federation kindly made available to us analyses of their
   membership in June 1979 and October 1978. They make plain the
   importance of retailers, small builders and those in other service
   businesses and serve to correct the emphasis John McHugh gives to
   small farmers in his analysis of the Federation's membership.

Compare the table below with that in J. McHugh (1979).

Sector	1979 (June)		1978 (October)
		N	%	%
Primary		2668	8.3	8.0
Manufacturing & Engineering		2051	6.4	5.6
Construction		6141	19.1	18.6
Services & Distribution		9908	30.9	31.1
– Transport	1250 (3.9%)			(4.0%)
– Wholesale	788 (2.4%)			(2.5%)
– Retail	7539 (23.5%)			(23.6%)
– Dealers	331 (1.0%)			(1.0%)
Commercial & Financial Services		2335	7.3	8.0
Professional & Scientific Services		2852	8.9	9.5
Miscellaneous Services including:		6112	19.1	16.3
– Hotels	741 (2.3%)			(2.2%)
– Restaurants	403 (1.2%)			(1.2%)
– Pubs	556 (1.7%)			(1.9%)
– Garages	2263 (7.1%)			(6.7%)
		32.067	100	100

10 The NAFF Charter consists of fifteen points:
    1 The right to be defended against the country's enemies.
    2 The right to live under the Queen's peace.
    3 Freedom of movement within the country and in leaving or re-entering it.
    4 Freedom of religion and worship.
    5 Freedom of speech and publication.
    6 Freedom of assembly and association for a lawful purpose.
    7 Freedom to withdraw one's labour, other than contrary to public safety.
    8 Freedom to belong or not to belong to a trade union or employer's association.
    9 The right to private ownership.
    10 The right to dispose or convey property by deed or will.
    11 Freedom to exercise choice or personal priority in spending, and from oppressive, unnecessary or confiscatory taxation.
    12 Freedom from all coercive monopolies.
    13 Freedom to engage in private enterprise and pursue the trade or profession of one's choice without harassmen.

14   Freedom of choice in the use of state and private services
     (including education and medicine).

15   The right to protection from invasion of privacy.

11   We cannot agree with John McHugh's assessment (1975, p.69) that
     by mid-1978 'NFSE had gone back to the initial phase of the
     clarion call when it sought influence through a capacity to
     disrupt the administrative process and undermine Government
     policy'. It may have shought to attract new members through a
     revival of aggressive rhetoric but with the appointment of its
     new research office, John Blundell, it soon embarked on the
     preparation of well-researched documents specifying grievances
     and the cultivation of regular contacts at Westminster and in
     Whitehall through which these could be presented.

12   This would be in line with what Norris McWhirter told us of his
     hopes for change in the character of NAFF when we interviewed
     him in January 1978.

13   As Parkin (1971, p.135) pointed out several years ago, in Britain
     'trade union leaders have been absorbed into the apparatus of
     the state ... union leaders were represented on only twelve
     government committees in 1939; by 1948 they were on sixty and
     by the early 1950s they were on more than eighty'. In the
     years of Wilson, Heath and Callaghan through policies of
     'tripartism' and 'social contracts' their involvement in the
     day-to-day management of the economy increased. It is to the
     kind of state that encourages this that NAFF objects.

14   The opportunistic manner in which Mitchell had seized on the
     discontent of small business was made very evident in an
     interview with him in June 1978 when he said how he cast his
     eyes around for an issue and 'small business seemed obvious'.
     He took his idea of having special representation for this
     sector of the economy to Lord Thorneycroft who told him he could
     develop the idea as long as it did not cost the party any money.

15   Our interview with Norris McWhirter (January 1978) indicated
     that he regarded the civil service as indifferent or even
     hostile to NAFF.

16   Interview with Alex Lyon, April 1979.

17   Interview with John Biffen, April 1979.

18   It is interesting to note that at the time of writing John
     Gouriet had just announced, in a letter to the 'Daily Telegraph',
     the formation of a new freedom group, appropriately called
     Freedom in Action, 'Daily Telegraph', 23 December 1980.

19   We have tried to provide a detailed explanation for the rise of
     these and many other 'middle-class' associations in the 1974-9
     period. That task we started in a tentative way in an earlier
     piece (Bechhofer et al., 1978b).

20   Some of these constraints are well-illustrated in research on
     small businessmen conducted by R. Scase and R. Goffee (1980),
     and by our own earlier work on shopkeepers (Bechhofer et al.,
     1974).

21   Indications of the very casual way in which finances were handled
     in the early period of its development are found in the amusing
     stories told of a treasurer who paid expenses to NFSE officials
     from a fat roll of banknotes he carried in his hip pocket.

22   We have not been able to obtain any comprehensive and reliable

data on branch membership. Our observations are made on the basis of interviews with leaders, attendance at a small number of NAFF meetings, reading of 'Free Nation' plus other media coverage of the Association.

23 David Kelly was a member of NAFF and although it is not clear whether he joined in his own right or as a representative of NFSE the fact is that by mid-1976 it had become customary inside NAFF to talk of 'NFSE's place' on the Council. After Kelly resigned from NFSE, Owen Dyer was delegated to take up this place but after attending one meeting he wrote a report highly critical of NAFF and the link was severed. For some newspaper coverage of this, see the 'Guardian', 23 December 1976.

24 Interview with David Kelly, 24 July 1978.

25 Scase and Goffee (1980) illustrate the diverse and inconsistent views of unions among their sample of small business owners. Since a good many small entrepreneurs come from working-class backgrounds we should not be surprised to find some degree of sympathy and support for trades unions in this stratum.

26 See for instance Hutber (1976; 1978).

27 The suspicion and disdain with which the bureaucratised middle class, especially those employed in state agencies, is viewed by NAFF came out very clearly in our interview with Jackson, the ex-major, who replaced John Gouriet in 1979.

28 Comparison with the political histories of societies like France, Germany, Belgium, Canada and even the USA reveals how, at least until recently, the UK Tory party has been relatively successful in keeping petit-bourgeois interests largely contained within its boundaries, and thus preventing the growth of third parties or very vigorous grass-roots movements of this stratum.

29 Scase and Goffee (1980) discuss the attempts by the present government to restore the power of employers and restrict the rights of employees in their study of small businesses.

BIBLIOGRAPHY

ABERCROMBIE, N. and URRY, J. (1983), 'Capital, Labour and the Middle Classes', London, Allen & Unwin.

ABROMEIT, H. (1980), The nationalised industries in the context of the British political system, 'Arbeitspapiere des Fachbereichs Wirtschaftswissenschaft der Gesamthochschule Wuppertal', Wuppertal.

AMBROSE, R. (1976), The British land-use non-planning system, 'Antipode', vol.8, no.1.

BACON, R. and ELTIS, W. (1978), 'Britain's Economic Problem: Too Few Producers', London, Macmillan (2nd edn).

BANFIELD, E. (1958), 'The Moral Basis of a Backward Society', Chicago, Free Press.

BANFIELD, E. and WILSON, J. (1966), 'City Politics', New York, Harvard University Press.

BARRATT BROWN, M. (1981), 'Britain in Crisis', Nottingham, Spokesman.

BECHHOFER, F. et al. (1974), The petits bourgeois in the class structure: the case of the small shopkeepers, in Parkin, F. (ed), 'The Social Analysis of Class Structure', London, Tavistock.

BECHHOFER, F. and ELLIOTT, B. (1978a), The voice of small business and the politics of survival, 'Sociological Review', vol.26.

BECHHOFER, F. et al. (1978b), Structure, consciousness and action: a sociological profile of the British middle class, 'British Journal of Sociology', vol.29, no.4.

BEESLEY, M. (1973), Regulation of taxis, 'Economic Journal', vol.83.

BELL, D. (1974), 'The Coming of Post-Industrial Society', London, Heinemann.

BENSON, J.K. (1978), The interorganisational network as a political economy, in Karpik, L. (ed.), 'Organisation and Environment', London, Sage.

BERESFORD, M.W. (1951), 'The Leeds Chamber of Commerce', Leeds, Leeds Incorporated Chamber of Commerce.

BERGER, S.D. (1981a), Introduction, in Berger, S.D. (ed.), 'Organising Interests in Western Europe: Pluralism, Corporatism and the Transformation of Politics', London, Cambridge University Press.

BERGER, S.D. (1981b), Regime and interest representation: the French traditional middle classes, in Berger, S.D. (ed.), op.cit.

BLANKE, B. et al. (1978), On the current marxist discussion of the analysis of form and function, in Holloway, J. and Picciotto, S. (eds) (1979), 'State and Capital', London, Arnold.

168

BLUNDEN, G. (1975), The supervision of the UK banking system, 'Bank of England Quarterly Bulletin', no.2, pp.188-94.
BOADEN, N., GOLDSMITH, M., HAMPTON, W., and STRINGER, P. (1979), Public participation in planning within a representative local democracy, 'Policy and Politics', vol.7, pp.55-67.
BODDY, M. and FUDGE, C. (1980), The local state: theory and practice, paper given at a conference on the local state at the School for Advanced Urban Studies, University of Bristol, 6 December.
BRAVERMAN, H. (1974), 'Labour and Monopoly Capital', New York, Monthly Review Press.
BRITTAN, S. (1971), 'Steering the Economy', Harmondsworth, Penguin.
BRITTAN, S. (1975), The economic contradictions of democracy, 'British Journal of Political Science', vol.5.
BRITTAN, S. (1977), 'The Economic Consequences of Democracy', London, Maurice Temple Smith.
BROADBENT, T.A. (1977), 'Planning and Profit in the Urban Economy', London, Methuen.
BROWN, A.J. (1972), 'The Framework of Regional Economics in the UK', London, Cambridge University Press.
BROWN, K. (ed.), (1974), 'Essays in Anti-Labour History', London, Macmillan.
BUCK, T. and ATKINS, M. (1978), Social class and spatial problems, 'Town Planning Review', vol.49, pp.209-21.
BUCK, T. (1979), Regional class differences, 'International Journal of Urban and Regional Research', vol.3, pp.516-26.
BULLOCK, P. and YAFFE, D. (1975), Inflation, the crisis and the post-war boom, 'Revolutionary Communist', vol.3, pp.5-45.
BURNS, S. (1977), 'The Household Economy', Boston, Beacon Press.
BUSWELL, R. and LEWIS, E.W. (1970), The geographical distribution of industrial research activity in the UK, 'Regional Studies', vol.4, pp.297-306.
CARNEY, J., HUDSON, R. and LEWIS, J. (eds), (1980), 'Regions in Crisis', London, Croom Helm.
CASTELLS, M. (1978), 'City, Class and Power', London, Macmillan.
CASTELLS, M. (1980), 'The Economic Crisis and American Society', Oxford, Blackwell.
CAWSON, A. (1977), Environmental planning and the politics of corporatism, University of Sussex, Urban and Regional Studies, working paper, no.7.
CAWSON, A. (1978), Pluralism, corporatism and the role of the state, 'Government and Opposition', vol.13, no.2, pp.178-98.
CAWSON, A. (1979), Representational crises and corporatism in capitalist societies, paper given to a conference of the European Consortium for Political Research, Brussels, April.
CAWSON, A. (1982), 'Political Structure and Social Policy', London, Heinemann.
CBI, (1965), 'Annual Report', London.
CBI, (1976a), 'The Road to Recovery', London.
CBI, (1976b), 'Industrial Policy in the European Community', London.
CBI, (1977), 'Annual Report', London.
CBI, (1978a), 'Britain Means Business', London.
CBI, (1978b), 'Annual Report', London.
CBI, (1979), 'Annual Report', London.
CHANNON, D.F. (1977), 'British Banking Strategy and the International Challenge', London, Macmillan.

CLARKE, M. (1981), 'Fallen Idols: Elites and the Search for the
Acceptable Face of Capitalism', London, Junction Books.
CLARKE, S. (1977), Marxism, sociology and Poulantzas's theory of
the state, 'Capital and Class', vol.2, pp.1-31.
COCKBURN, C. (1977), 'The Local State', London, Pluto Press.
COCKBURN, C. (1981), The material of male power, British Sociological
Association Conference Paper, Aberystwyth.
COHEN, R.B. (1981), The new international division of labour,
multinational corporations and urban hierarchy, in Dear, M. and
Scott, A.J. (eds), 'Urbanisation and Urban Planning in Capitalist
Society', London, Methuen, pp.287-315.
COMMITTEE OF LONDON CLEARING BANKERS (1978), 'The London Clearing
Banks: Evidence by Committee of London Clearing Bankers to the
Committee to Review the Functioning of Financial Institutions',
London, CLCB/Longman.
CONSERVATIVE PARTY SMALL BUSINESS BUREAU (1977), 'Branching Out:
Constituency Organisation and the Bureau', London, Conservative
Party.
COOKE, P. (1980), Dependency formation and modes of integration in
the historical and contemporary case of Wales, UWIST, Department
of Town Planning, Papers in Planning Research.
COOKE, P. (1983), 'Theories of Planning and Spatial Development',
London, Hutchinson.
CREWE, I. (1974), Introduction: Studying elites in Britain, in
Crewe, I. (ed.), 'British Political Sociological Yearbook', vol.1:
'Elites in Britain', London, Croom Helm.
CRICK, B. (1981), 'Unemployment', London, Methuen.
CROSSMAN, R. (1976), 'The Diaries of a Cabinet Minister', vol.2,
London, Hamish Hamilton/Jonathan Cape.
CROUCH, C. (1981), Research on corporatism in Britain: an interim
report, paper to SSRC Workshop on Corporatism, Oxford, July.
DAHL, R. (1961), 'Who Governs?', New Haven, Yale University Press.
DARKE, R. (1979), Public participation and state power, 'Policy
and Politics', vol.7, no.4, pp.337-55.
DARKE, R. (1981), Attitudes towards public participation, 'Local
Government Studies', vol.7, May/June, pp.61-6.
DEARLOVE, J. (1973), 'The Politics of Policy in Local Government',
London, Cambridge University Press.
DEARLOVE, J. (1979), 'The Reorganisation of British Local Government',
London, Cambridge University Press.
DEVLIN, (1972), 'Report of the Committee of Inquiry into Industrial
and Commercial Representation', London, Association of British
Chambers of Commerce/Confederation of British Industry.
DOE (1981), 'Ministerial Guidelines on Inner Area Programmes',
London, Department of the Environment.
DUNLEAVY, P. (1979), The urban basis of political alignment,
'British Journal of Political Science', vol.9, pp.409-43.
DUNLEAVY, P. (1980a), The political implications of sectoral changes
and the growth of state employment, part 1: the analysis of
production cleavages, 'Political Studies', vol.28, pp.270-83.
DUNLEAVY, P. (1980b), Part 2: Cleavage structures and political
alignment, 'Political Studies', vol.28, pp.527-49.
DUNLEAVY, P. (1980c), 'Urban Political Analysis', London, Macmillan.
DUNLEAVY, P. (1981a), 'The Politics of Mass Housing in Britain,
1945-1975', London, Oxford University Press.

DUNLEAVY, P. (1981b), Professions and policy change, 'Public Administration Bulletin', no.36, pp.3-16.

DUNNING, J.H. and MORGAN, E.V. (1971), 'An Economic Study of the City of London', London, Allen & Unwin.

ECKSTEIN, H. (1960), 'Pressure Group Politics: the Case of the British Medical Association', London, Allen & Unwin.

ELKIN, S.L. (1975), Comparative urban politics and interorganisational behaviour, in Young, K. (ed.), 'Essays on Urban Politics', London, Macmillan.

ENGELS, F. (1968), quoted in Streeck, W. et al. (1980), The organisation of business interests, International Institute of Management paper, Berlin, March.

ESPING-ANDERSEN, G., FRIEDLAND, R. and WRIGHT, E. (1976), Modes of class struggle and the capitalist state, 'Kapitalistate', vol.4, pp.186-220.

FIDLER, J. (1981), 'The British Business Elite', London, Routledge & Kegan Paul.

FINE, B. and HARRIS, L. (1976), State expenditure in advanced capitalism: a critique, 'New Left Review', no.98, pp.97-112.

FLYNN, R. (1979), Urban managers in local government planning, 'Sociological Review', vol.27, no.4, pp.743-53.

FLYNN, R. (1981), Managing consensus: strategies and rationales in policy making, in Harloe, M. (ed.), 'New Perspectives in Urban Change and Conflict', London, Heinemann.

FOTHERGILL, S. and GUDGIN, G. (1979), Regional employment change: a sub-regional explanation, 'Progress and Planning', vol.2, pp.155-220.

FOX, W. (1935), 'Taximen and Taxiowners', London, Labour Research Department.

FRASER, D. (1973), 'The Evolution of the British Welfare State', London, Macmillan.

FRIEDLAND, R., PIVEN, F. and ALFORD, R. (1977), Political conflict, urban structure and the fiscal crisis, 'International Journal of Urban and Regional Research', vol.1, no.3, pp.447-71.

FRIEDMAN, M. (1962), 'Capitalism and Freedom', Chicago, Chicago University Press.

FRÖBEL, F., HEINRICHS, J. and KREYE, O. (1980), 'The New International Division of Labour', London, Cambridge University Press.

FUCHS, V.R. (1968), 'The Service Economy', New York, National Bureau of Economic Research.

GALBRAITH, J.K. (1972), 'The New Industrial State', London, André Deutsch.

GALBRAITH, J.K. (1974), 'Economics and the Public Purpose', London, André Deutsch.

GAMBLE, A. (1974), 'The Conservative Nation', London, Routledge & Kegan Paul.

GARTNER, A. and RIESMAN, F. (1974), 'The Service Society and the Consumer Vanguard', New York, Harper & Row.

GELLATELY, R. (1974), 'The Politics of Economic Despair: Shopkeepers and German Politics, 1890-1914', London, Sage.

'GENERAL HOUSEHOLD SURVEY 1977', London, OPCS.

GEORGANO, G.N. (1972), 'A History of the London Taxicab Service', Newton Abbot, David & Charles.

GERSHUNY, J. (1978), 'After Industrial Society', London, Macmillan.

GERSHUNY, J. and PAHL, R. (1980), Britain in the decade of the three economies, 'New Society', 3 January.

GIDDENS, A. (1973), 'The Class Structure of the Advanced Societies', London, Hutchinson.

GIDDENS, A. (1981), 'A Contemporary Critique of Historical Materialism', London, Macmillan.

GLYNN, D. (1978), The last 14 years of incomes policy – a CBI perspective, 'National Westminster Bank Review', November, pp.23–34.

GOUGH, I. (1979), 'The Political Economy of the Welfare State', London, Macmillan.

GOWER, L.C.B. (1982), 'Review of Investor Protection', London, HMSO.

GRANT, W. (1977), Insider groups and outsider groups, paper given at the European Consortium for Political Research workshop on 'Political attitudes and behaviour of the middle classes in Europe', Berlin.

GRANT, W. (1981), The development of the government relations function in UK firms, discussion paper, International Institute of Management, Berlin.

GRANT, W. and MARSH, D. (1977), 'The Confederation of British Industry', London, Hodder & Stoughton.

'GREEN BADGE JOURNAL' (1931–9), London.

GREENFIELD, H.I. (1966), 'Manpower and the Growth of Producer Services', New York, Columbia University Press.

HABERMAS, J. (1976), 'Legitimation Crisis', London, Heinemann.

HALL, P. et al., (1973), 'The Containment of Urban England', 2 vols, London, PEP and Allen & Unwin.

HALL, S. (1980), Thatcherism – a new stage?, 'Marxism Today', February.

HAMILTON, F.E.I. (1978), Multinational enterprise and the EEC, in Hamilton, F.E.I. (ed.), 'Industrial Change', London, Longman.

HAMPTON, W. (1970), 'Democracy and Community', London, Oxford University Press.

HECLO, H. and WILDAVSKY, A. (1981), 'The Private Government of Public Money', London, Macmillan.

HERNES, G. and SELVIK, A. (1981), Local corporatism, in Berger, S. (ed.), 1981a.

HINDLEY REPORT (1939), 'Interim Report on the Inter-Departmental Committee on Cabs and Private Hire Vehicles', London, Cmnd 5938.

HIRSCH, J. (1978), The state apparatus and social reproduction, in Holloway, J. and Picciotto, S. (eds) (1979), 'State and Capital', London, Edward Arnold.

HIRST, P. (1977), Economic classes and politics, in Hunt, A. (ed.), 'Class and Class Structure', London, Lawrence & Wishart.

HOBSBAWM, E. (1959), 'Primitive Rebels', London, Manchester University Press.

HOBSBAWM, E. (1975), 'The Age of Capital, 1848–1875', London, Weidenfeld & Nicolson.

HOLLAND, S. (1975), 'The Socialist Challenge', London, Quartet.

HOLLOWAY, J. and PICCIOTTO, S. (eds) (1979), 'State and Capital', London, Edward Arnold.

HUNTER, F. (1953), 'Community Power Structure', New York, University of North Carolina Press.

HUTBER, P. (1976), 'The Decline and Fall of the Middle Class', London, Associated Business Programmes.

HUTBER, P. (ed.) (1978), 'What's Wrong with Britain?', London.

INCOME DATA SERVICES (1980), 'Report', London.
JACOBSON, D., WICKHAM, A. and WICKHAM, J. (1979), Review Article,
'Capital and Class', vol.7, pp.125-30.
JACQUES, M. (1979), Thatcherism - the impasse broken, 'Marxism Today',
October.
JENSON, J. and SIMONSEN, K. (1981), The local state, planning and
social movements, 'Acta Sociologica', vol.24, pp.279-91.
JESSOP, B. (1978), Capitalism and democracy: the best possible
political shell?, in Littlejohn, G. et al., (eds), 'Power and the
State', Croom Helm.
JESSOP, B. (1979), Corporatism, parliamentarism and social democracy,
in Schmitter, P. and Lehmbruch, G. (eds), 'Trends Towards Corporatist
Intermediation', London and Beverly Hills, Sage.
JOHNSON, N. and COCHRANE, A. (1981), 'Economic Policy-making by
Local Authorities in Britain and Western Germany', London, Allen &
Unwin.
KILLINGBACK, N. (1980), 'The Politics of Small Business in Britain
during the 1930s', unpublished D.Phil. thesis, University of Sussex.
KING, R. (1979), The middle class revolt and the established parties,
in King, R. and Nugent, N. (eds) (1979).
KING, R. (1980), Small business, economic liberalism and the
Conservative Party, paper to the PSA/BSA Political Sociology Study
Group, Manchester Polytechnic.
KING, R. and NUGENT, N. (eds), (1979), 'Respectable Rebels', London,
Hodder & Stoughton.
KIRK, G. (1980), 'Urban Planning in a Capitalist Society', London,
Croom Helm.
KRECKEL, R. (1980), Unequal opportunity structure and labour market
segmentation, 'Sociology', vol.14, pp.525-50.
LEIGH, R. and NORTH, D.J. (1978), Regional aspects of acquisition
activity in British manufacturing industry, 'Regional Studies',
vol.12, pp.227-45.
LOJKINE, J. (1977), Big firms' strategies, urban policy and urban
social movements, in Harloe, M. (ed.) 'Captive Cities', London,
John Wiley.
LUNN, K.J. and THURLOW, R.C. (1980), 'British Fascism', London,
Croom Helm.
MACAFEE, K. (1980), A glimpse of the hidden economy in the national
accounts, 'CSO Economic Trends', February, pp.81-7.
McHUGH, J. (1979), The self-employed and small independent entre-
preneurs, in King, R. and Nugent, N. (eds), 1979.
McKAY, D. and COX, A. (1979), 'The Politics of Urban Change', London,
Croom Helm.
McENERY, J.H. (1981), 'Manufacturing Two Nations', London, Institute
of Economic Affairs, research monographs, no.36.
MACPHERSON, C. (1962), 'The Political Theory of Possessive
Individualism', Oxford, Clarendon Press.
MACPHERSON, C. (1966), 'The Real World of Democracy', Oxford,
Clarendon Press.
MACPHERSON, C. (1977), Do we need a theory of the state?, 'Archives
Européen de Sociologie', vol.18, pp.223-44.
MANDEL, E. (1975), 'Late Capitalism', London, New Left Books.
MARQUAND, J. (1980), The role of the tertiary sector in regional
policy, Brussels, Commission of the European Communities, regional
policy series paper, no.19.

MARX, K. (1973 edn), 'Grundrisse', Harmondsworth, Penguin.
MARX, K. (1976 edn), 'Capital', vol.1, Harmondsworth, Penguin.
MASSEY, D. (1978), Regionalism: some current issues, 'Capital and Class', no.6, pp.106-25.
MASSEY, D. (1980), Industrial restructuring as class restructuring, CSE Working paper, no.604.
MASSEY, D. (1981), The UK electrical engineering and electronics industries: the implications of the crisis for the restructuring of capital and locational change, in Dear, M. and Scott, A.J. (eds), 'Urbanisation and Urban Planning in Capitalist Society', London, Methuen.
MAY, T.C. (1975), 'Trade Unions and Pressure Group Politics', Farnborough, Saxon House.
MERSEYSIDE SOCIALIST RESEARCH GROUP (1980), 'Merseyside in Crisis', Birkenhead.
METCALFE, D. (1980), Unemployment: history, incidence and prospects, 'Policy and Politics', vol.8, pp.21-37.
METCALFE, L. and McQUILLAN, W. (1979), Corporatism or industrial democracy?, 'Political Studies', vol.27, no.2, pp.266-82.
MIDDLEMAS, K. (1979), 'Politics in Industrial Society', London, André Deutsch.
MILIBAND, R. (1973), 'The State in Capitalist Society', Quartet.
MILIBAND, R. (1977), 'Marxism and Politics', London, Oxford University Press.
MILLER, D. (1970), 'International Community Power Structures', Indiana, Indiana University Press.
MILLER, S. (1975), Notes on neo-capitalism, 'Theory and Society', vol.2, pp.1-35.
MINNS, R. and THORNLEY, J. (1978), 'State Shareholding and the Role of Local and Regional Authorities', London, Macmillan.
MONOPOLIES COMMISSION (1968), 'Barclays Bank Ltd, Lloyds Bank Ltd, and Martins Bank Ltd: a Report on Proposed Mergers', London, HC319.
MORAN, M. (1981a), Monetary policy and the machinery of government, 'Public Administration', no.59, pp.47-61.
MORAN, M. (1981b), Finance capital and pressure group politics in Britain, 'British Journal of Political Science', vol.11, pp.381-404.
MURGATROYD, L. and URRY, J. (1982), The restructuring of a local economy: the case of Lancaster, in Anderson, J. et al. (eds), 'Social Geography and Industrial Change', London, Academic Press.
NATIONAL BOARD FOR PRICES AND INCOMES (1967), 'Bank Charges', London, Cmnd 3292.
NATIONAL ECONOMIC DEVELOPMENT OFFICE (1980), 'British Industrial Performance', London.
NEDELMANN, B. and MEIER, K. (1979), Theories of contemporary corporatism: static or dynamic?, in Schmitter, P. and Lehmbruch, G. (eds), op.cit.
'New Survey of London Life and Labour' (1934), vol.8, London, King.
NEWTON, K. (1976), 'Second City Politics', Oxford, Clarendon Press.
NUGENT, N. (1979), The National Association for Freedom, in King, R. and Nugent, N. (eds), 1979.
NUGENT, N. and KING, R. (1977), 'The British Right', Farnborough, Saxon House.
O'CONNOR, J. (1973), 'The Fiscal Crisis of the State', New York, St Martin's Press.

'ODA GAZETTE', (1931-9), London.

OFFE, C. (1975), The theory of the capitalist state and the problem of policy formation, in Lindberg, L. et al. (eds), 'Stress and Contradiction in Modern Capitalism', London, Lexington Books.

OFFE, C. (1981), The attribution of public status to interest groups, in Berger, S. (ed.), 1981.

OFFE, C. and WIESENTHAL, H. (1979), Two logics of collective action, 'Political Power and Social Theory', vol.1.

PAHL, R. (1977a), Managers, technical experts and the state, in Harloe, M. , op.cit.

PAHL, R. (1977b), Stratification: the relations between states and urban and regional development, 'International Journal of Urban and Regional Research', vol.1, pp.6-18.

PAHL, R. and WINKLER, J. (1975), The coming corporatism, 'Challenge', March/April, pp.28-5.

PANEL ON TAKE-OVERS AND MERGERS (1979), Written evidence, in Committee to Review the Functioning of Financial Institutions, 'Second Stage Evidence', vol.1, London.

PANITCH, L. (1980), Recent theorisations of corporatism, 'British Journal of Sociology', vol.31, no.2, pp.159-87.

PARKIN, F. (1968), 'Middle Class Radicals', Manchester, Manchester University Press.

PARKIN, F. (1971), 'Class Inequality and Political Order', London, Paladin.

PARKIN, F. (1979a), 'Class, Inequality and Political Order', London, Paladin.

PARKIN, F. (1979b), 'Marxism and Class Theory: a Bourgeois Critique', London, Tavistock.

PEREZ-DIAZ, V.M. (1978), 'State, Bureaucracy and Civil Society', London, Macmillan.

PFEFFER, J. (1981), 'Power in Organisations', London, Pitman.

PICKVANCE, C. (1977), From social base to social force, in Harloe, M., op.cit.

PICKVANCE, C. (1980), Theories of the state and theories of urban crisis, 'Current Perspectives in Social Theory', vol.1, pp.31-54.

PIVEN, F., FOX, E. and CLOWARD, R. (1977), 'Poor People's Movements', New York, Pantheon Books.

POLSBY, N. (1963), 'Community Power and Political Theory', New York, Yale University Press.

PRAIS, S.J. (1976), 'The Evolution of Giant Firms in Britain', London, Cambridge University Press.

PRED, A. (1977), The choreography of existence: comments on Hagerstrand's time-geography and its usefulness, 'Economic Geography', vol.53, pp.207-21.

PRED, A. (1981), Social reproduction and the time-geography of everyday life, 'Geografiska Annaler', vol.63, pp.5-22.

PRETECEILLE, E. (1974), 'L'Appareil juridique de la planification urbaine', Paris, SCU.

PRETECEILLE, E. (1976), Urban planning, 'Antipode', vol.8, no.1., pp.69-76.

PRETECEILLE, E. and REGAZZOLA, T. (1974), 'L'Appareil juridique de la planification urbaine', Paris, SCU.

RADCLIFFE, L. (1959), 'Report of the Committee on the Working of the Monetary System', London, Cmnd 827.

RADCLIFFE, L. (1960a), 'Minutes of Evidence of the Committee on the Working of the Monetary System', London.

RADCLIFFE, L. (1960b), 'Principal Memoranda of Evidence of the Committee on the Working of the Monetary System', London.

READE, E.J. (1980), Town planning and the corporatism thesis, Sociologists in Polytechnics, paper no.10.

ROGALY, J. (1977), 'Grunwick', Harmondsworth, Penguin.

ROLL, L. (1978), Memorandum, in Committee to Review the Functioning of Financial Institutions, 'Evidence, First Stage', vol.8, London, pp.71-97.

ROTHWELL, R. and ZEGWELD, W. (1979), 'Technical Change and Unemployment', London, Pinter.

ROYAL TOWN PLANNING INSTITUTE (1976), 'Planning the Future', London, RTPI.

RUDE, G. (1964), 'The Crowd in History', New York, Wiley.

RUNCIMAN, W. (1953), 'Report of the Committee on the Taxicab Service', London, Cmnd 8804.

SABOLO, Y. (1975), 'The Service Industries', Geneva, International Labour Organisation.

SAUNDERS, P. (1979), 'Urban Politics', Hutchinson, London.

SAUNDERS, P. (1980), Local government and the state, 'New Society', 13 March.

SAUNDERS, P. (1981a), 'Social Theory and the Urban Question', London, Hutchinson.

SAUNDERS, P. (1981b), Community power, urban managerialism and the local state, in Harloe, M. (ed.), op.cit.

SAYER, A. (1979), Theory and empirical research in urban and regional political economy, University of Sussex, Urban and Regional Studies, working paper, no.14.

SAYERS, R.S. (1976), 'The Bank of England 1891-1944', 3 vols, London, Cambridge University Press.

SCASE, R. and GOFFEE, R. (1980), 'The Real World of the Small Business Owner', London, Croom Helm.

SCHMITTER, P. (1974), Still the century of corporatism?, 'Review of Politics', vol.36, pp.85-131.

SCHMITTER, P. and BRAND, D. (1979), Organising capitalists in the USA: the advantages and disadvantages of exceptionalism, paper presented to the International Institute of Management conference on employers' associations, Berlin, November.

SCHMITTER, P. and LEHMBRUCH, G. (eds) (1979), 'Towards a Theory of Corporatist Intermediation', London, Sage.

SCHONFIELD, A. (1965), 'Modern Capitalism', London, Oxford University Press.

SELECT COMMITTEE ON NATIONALISED INDUSTRIES (1970), 'First Report: The Bank of England', London, HC258.

SELECT COMMITTEE ON NATIONALISED INDUSTRIES (1976), 'Seventh Report: The Bank of England', HC 672.

SELZNICK, P. (1949), 'TVA and the Grassroots', Berkeley, University of California Press.

SHOWLER, B. and SINFIELD, A. (1981), 'The Workless State', Oxford, Martin Robertson.

SIMMIE, J. (1981), 'Power, Property and Corporatism', London, Macmillan.

SINGH, A. (1977), UK industry and the world economy: a case of
de-industrialisation, 'Cambridge Journal of Economics', vol.1,
pp.113-36.
SKIDELSKY, R. (1975), 'Oswald Mosley', London, Macmillan.
SOCIAL SCIENCE RESEARCH COUNCIL (1979), 'Central-Local Government
Relationships: A Report', London, SSRC.
STACEY, M. et al. (1975), 'Power Persistence and Change', London,
Routledge & Kegan Paul.
STREECK, W. et al. (1980), The organisation of business interests,
International Institute of Management paper, Berlin, March.
THAYER, G. (1965), 'The British Political Fringe', London, Blond.
THOMPSON, E.P. (1971), The moral economy of the English 18th century
crowd, 'Past and Present', 50.
THOMPSON, E.P. (1975), 'Whigs and Hunters', London, Allen Lane.
TILLY, C. (1973), Does modernisation breed revolution?. 'Comparative
Politics', vol.5, no.3.
TILLY, C. (1975), Revolutions and collective violence, in Greenstein,
F. and Polsby, N. (eds), 'Macropolitical Theory Handbook of
Political Science', vol.3, Reading, Mass., Addison-Wesley.
TILLY, C. (1978), 'From Mobilization to Revolution', Reading, Mass.,
Addison-Wesley.
TITMUSS, R. (1963), 'Essays on the Welfare State', London, Allen &
Unwin.
TOURAINE, A. (1974), 'The Post-Industrial Society', London, Wildwood
House.
TRADE, DEPARTMENT OF (1979), 'Ferguson and General Investments
Ltd: Investigations under Section 165 (b) of the Companies Act
1948: Inspectors' Report', London.
TROTSKY, L. (1934 edn), 'History of the Russian Revolution', London,
Gollancz.
TURVEY, R. (1961), Some economic features of the London cab trade,
'Economic Journal', vol.71.
URRY, J. (1981a), 'The Anatomy of Capitalist Societies', London,
Macmillan.
URRY, J. (1981b), De-industrialisation, households, and forms of
social conflict and struggle, Lancaster Regionalism Group Working
Paper, no.3.
URRY, J. (1981c), Localities, regions and social class, 'International
Journal of Urban and Regional Research', vol.5, pp.455-74.
WALLIS, R. (1977), Movement, context, and decline: a study of two
incipient social movements, unpublished mimeo, University of
Stirling.
WATKINSON, V. (1976), 'Blueprint for Industrial Survival', London,
Allen & Unwin.
WESTAWAY, J. (1974), The spatial hierarchy of business organisations
and its implications for the British urban system, 'Regional Studies',
vol.8, pp.145-55.
WESTERGAARD, J. and RESLER, H. (1976), 'Class in a Capitalist
Society', Harmondsworth, Penguin.
WILLIAMS, M. (1972), 'Inside Number 10', London, Weidenfeld &
Nicolson.
WILSON, SIR H. (1971), 'The Labour Government 1964-70: a Personal
Record', London, Weidenfeld & Nicolson/Michael Joseph.
WILSON, SIR H. (1980), Committee to Review the Functioning of
Financial Institutions, 'Report', London, Cmnd 7937.

WINKLER, H.A. (1976), From social protectionism to national socialism, 'Journal of Modern History', vol.48, no.1.
WINKLER, J.T. (1976), Corporatism, 'Archives Européens de Sociologie', vol.17, pp.100-36.
WINKLER, J.T. (1977), The corporatist economy: theory and administration. in Scase, R. (ed.), 'Industrial Society', London, Allen & Unwin.
YOUNG, K., MASON, C. and MILLS, L. (1980), 'Urban Governments and Economic Change', London, Social Science Research Council.
ZAWADZKI, K.K. (1981), 'Competition and Credit Control', Oxford, Blackwell.

INDEX